Note to the reader

We want express our sincere hope that this book will enrich your spiritual journey. In these turbulent times, developing a personal connection with Christ is more important than ever.

We also want to let you know that we've designed this book to make it easier for you to find references within each paragraph. The two-column layout was specifically chosen to make the book more compact and easier to read.

We genuinely appreciate your decision to acquire this book and we hope that it exceeds your expectations. Thank you so much for choosing us!

Design by SaintilWay Productions

Table of Contents

Section 1

Heaven's Law of Benevolence and Its Purpose

Chapter 1
Coworkers With God

"Honor the Lord with thy substance, and with the first fruits of all thine increase: so shall thy barns be filled with plenty, and thy presses shall burst out with new wine." *Proverbs 3:9, 10.* (CS 13.1)

"There is that scattereth, and yet increaseth; and there is that withholdeth more than is meet, but it tendeth to poverty. The liberal soul shall be made fat: and he that watereth shall be watered also himself." *Proverbs 11:24, 25.* (CS 13.2)

"The liberal deviseth liberal things; and by liberal things shall he stand." *Isaiah 32:8.* (CS 13.3)

Divine wisdom has appointed, in the plan of salvation, the law of action and reaction, making the work of beneficence, in all its branches, twice blessed. He who gives to the needy blesses others, and is blessed himself in a still greater degree. (CS 13.4)

The Glory of the Gospel

That man might not lose the blessed results of benevolence, our Redeemer formed the plan of enlisting him as His coworker. God could have reached His object in saving sinners without the aid of man; but He knew that man could not be happy without acting a part in the great work. By a chain of circumstances which would call forth his charities, He bestows upon man the best means of cultivating benevolence, and keeps him habitually giving to help the poor and to advance His cause. By its necessities a ruined world is drawing forth from us talents of means and of influence, to present to men and women the truth, of which they are in perishing need. And as we heed these calls, by labor and by acts of benevolence, we are assimilated to the image of Him who for our sakes became poor. In bestowing, we bless others, and thus accumulate

true riches. (CS 13.5)

It is the glory of the gospel that it is founded upon the principle of restoring in the fallen race the divine image by a constant manifestation of benevolence. This work began in the heavenly courts. There God gave to human beings an unmistakable evidence of the love with which He regarded them. He "so loved the world, that He gave His only-begotten Son, that whosoever believeth in Him should not perish, but have everlasting life." *John 3:16.* The gift of Christ reveals the Father's heart. It testifies that, having undertaken our redemption, He will spare nothing, however dear, which is necessary to the completion of His work. (CS 14.1)

The spirit of liberality is the spirit of heaven. Christ's self-sacrificing love is revealed upon the cross. That man might be saved, He gave all that He had, and then gave Himself. The cross of Christ appeals to the benevolence of every follower of the blessed Saviour. The principle there illustrated is to give, give. This, carried out in actual benevolence and good works, is the true fruit of the Christian life. The principle of worldlings is to get, get, and thus they expect to secure happiness; but, carried out in all its bearings, the fruit is misery and death. (CS 14.2)

The light of the gospel shining from the cross of Christ rebukes selfishness, and encourages liberality and benevolence. It should not be a lamented fact that there are increasing calls to give. God in His providence is calling His people out from their limited sphere of action, to enter upon greater enterprises. Unlimited effort is demanded at this time when moral darkness is covering the world. Many of God's people are in danger of being ensnared by worldliness and covetousness. They should understand that it is His mercy that multiplies the demands for their means. Objects that call benevolence into action must be placed before them, or they cannot pattern after the character of the great Exemplar. (CS 14.3)

The Blessings of Stewardship

In commissioning His disciples to go "into all the world, and preach the gospel to every creature," Christ assigned to men the work of extending the knowledge of His grace. But while some go forth to preach, He calls upon others to answer His claims upon them for offerings, with which to support His cause in the earth. He has placed means in the hands of men, that His divine gifts may flow through human channels in doing the work appointed us in saving our fellow men. This is one of God's ways of exalting man. It is just the work that man needs; for it will stir the deepest sympathies of his heart, and call into exercise the highest capabilities of the mind. (CS 15.1)

Every good thing of earth was placed here by the bountiful hand of God as an expression of His love to man. The poor are His, and the cause of religion is His. The gold and the silver are the Lord's; and He could rain them from heaven if He chose. But instead of this He has made man His steward, entrusting him with means, not to be hoarded, but to be used in benefiting others. He thus makes man the medium through which to distribute His blessings on earth. God planned the system of beneficence, in order that man might become like his Creator, benevolent and unselfish in character, and finally be a partaker with Christ of the eternal, glorious reward. (CS 15.2)

Meeting Around the Cross

The love expressed on Calvary should be revived, strengthened, and diffused among our churches. Shall we not do all we can to give power to the principles which Christ brought to this world? Shall we not strive to establish and give efficiency to the benevolent enterprises which are now called for without delay? As you stand before the cross, and see the Prince of heaven dying for you, can you seal your heart, saying, "No; I have nothing to give"? (CS 16.1)

Christ's believing people are to perpetuate His love. This love is to draw them together around the cross. It is to divest them of all selfishness, and bind them to God and to one another. (CS 16.2)

Meet around the cross of Calvary in self-sacrifice and self-denial. God will bless you as you do your best. As you approach the throne of grace, as you find yourself bound to this throne by the golden chain let down from heaven to earth, to draw men from the pit of sin, your heart will go out in love for your brethren and sisters who are without God and without hope in the world.– *Testimonies for the Church 9:253-256.* (CS 16.3)

Chapter 2
Our Bountiful Benefactor

The power of God is manifested in the beating of the heart, in the action of the lungs, and in the living currents that circulate through the thousand different channels of the body. We are indebted to Him for every moment of existence, and for all the comforts of life. The powers and abilities that elevate man above the lower creation, are the endowment of the Creator. (CS 17.1)

He loads us with His benefits. We are indebted to Him for the food we eat, the water we drink, the clothes we wear, the air we breathe. Without His special providence, the air would be filled with pestilence and poison. He is a bountiful benefactor and preserver. (CS 17.2)

The sun which shines upon the earth, and glorifies all nature, the weird, solemn radiance of the moon, the glories of the firmament, spangled with brilliant stars, the showers that refresh the land, and cause vegetation to flourish, the precious things of nature in all their varied richness, the lofty trees, the shrubs and plants, the waving grain, the blue sky, the green earth, the changes of day and night, the renewing seasons, all speak to man of his Creator's love. (CS 17.3)

He has linked us to Himself by all these tokens in heaven and in earth. He watches over us with more tenderness than does a mother over an afflicted child. "Like as a father pitieth his children, so the Lord pitieth them that fear Him."- *Review and Herald, September 18, 1888.* (CS 17.4)

Continual Recipients to Give Continually

As we are continually receiving the blessings of God, so are we to be continually giving. When the heavenly Benefactor ceases to give to us, then

we may be excused; for we shall have nothing to bestow. God has never left us without evidence of His love, in that He did us good.... (CS 17.5)

We are sustained every moment by God's care, and upheld by His power. He spreads our tables with food. He gives us peaceful and refreshing sleep. Weekly He brings to us the Sabbath, that we may rest from our temporal labors, and worship Him in His own house. He has given us His word to be a lamp to our feet and a light to our path. In its sacred pages we find the counsels of wisdom; and as oft as we lift our hearts to Him in penitence and faith, He grants us the blessings of His grace. Above all else is the infinite gift of God's dear Son, through whom flow all other blessings for this life and for the life to come. (CS 18.1)

Surely goodness and mercy attend us at every step. Not till we wish the infinite Father to cease bestowing His gifts on us, should we impatiently exclaim, Is there no end of giving? Not only should we faithfully render to God our tithes, which He claims as His own, but we should bring a tribute to His treasury as an offering of gratitude. Let us with joyful hearts bring to our Creator the first fruits of all His bounties,—our choicest possessions, our best and holiest service.- *The Review and Herald, February 9, 1886.* (CS 18.2)

Only Way to Manifest Gratitude

The Lord does not need our offerings. We cannot enrich Him by our gifts. Says the psalmist: "All things come of Thee, and of Thine own have we given Thee." Yet God permits us to show our appreciation of His mercies by self-sacrificing efforts to extend the same to others. This is the only way in which it is possible for us to manifest our gratitude and love to God. He has provided no other.- *The Review and Herald, December 6,*

1887. (CS 18.3)

Paul's Argument Against Selfishness

Paul sought to uproot the plant of selfishness from the hearts of his brethren; for the character cannot be complete in Christ when self-love and covetousness are retained. The love of Christ in their hearts would lead them to help their brethren in their necessities. By pointing them to the sacrifice Christ had made in their behalf, he sought to arouse their love. (CS 19.1)

"I speak not by commandment," he said, "but by occasion of the forwardness of others, and to prove the sincerity of your love. For ye know the grace of our Lord Jesus Christ, that, though He was rich, yet for your sakes He became poor, that ye through His poverty might be rich." (CS 19.2)

Here is the apostle's mighty argument. It is not the commandment of Paul, but of the Lord Jesus Christ.... (CS 19.3)

How great was the gift of God to man, and how like our God to make it! With a liberality that can never be exceeded He gave, that He might save the rebellious sons of men and bring them to see His purpose and discern His love. Will you, by your gifts and offerings, show that you think nothing too good for Him who "gave His only-begotten Son"?– *The Review and Herald, May 15, 1900.* (CS 19.4)

The spirit of liberality is the spirit of heaven. The spirit of selfishness is the spirit of Satan.– *The Review and Herald, October 17, 1882.* (CS 19.5)

Chapter 3
Why God Employs Men as His Almoners

God is not dependent upon men for the advancement of His cause. He might have made angels the ambassadors of His truth. He might have made known His will, as He proclaimed the law from Sinai with His own voice. But in order to cultivate a spirit of benevolence in us, He has chosen to employ men to do this work. (CS 20.1)

Every act of self-sacrifice for the good of others will strengthen the spirit of beneficence in the giver's heart, allying him more closely to the Redeemer of the world, who "was rich, yet for our sakes became poor, that we through His poverty might be rich." And it is only as we fulfill the divine purpose in our creation that life can be a blessing to us. All the good gifts of God to man will prove only a curse, unless he employs them to bless his fellow men, and for the advancement of God's cause in the earth.– *The Review and Herald, December 7, 1886.* (CS 20.2)

The Fruit of Seeking Gain

It is this increasing devotion to money getting, the selfishness which the desire for gain begets, that deadens the spirituality of the church, and removes the favor of God from her. When the head and hands are constantly occupied with planning and toiling for the accumulation of riches, the claims of God and humanity are forgotten. (CS 20.3)

If God has blessed us with prosperity, it is not that our time and attention should be diverted from Him and given to that which He has lent us. The giver is greater than the gift. We have been bought with a price, we are not our own. Have we forgotten that infinite price paid for our redemption? Is gratitude dead in the heart? Does not the cross of Christ put to shame a life of selfish ease and indulgence? ... We are reaping the fruits of this infinite self-sacrifice; and yet, when labor is to be done, when our

money is wanted to aid the work of the Redeemer in the salvation of souls, we shrink from duty and pray to be excused. Ignoble sloth, careless indifference, and wicked selfishness seal our senses to the claims of God. (CS 20.4)

Oh, must Christ, the Majesty of heaven, the King of glory, bear the heavy cross, and wear the thorny crown, and drink the bitter cup, while we recline at ease, glorify ourselves, and forget the souls He died to redeem by His precious blood? No; let us give while we have the power. Let us do while we have the strength. Let us work while it is day. Let us devote our time and our means to the service of God, that we may have His approbation, and receive His reward.– *The Review and Herald, October 17, 1882.* (CS 21.1)

Our Greatest Conflict With Self

In this life our possessions are limited, but the great treasure that God offers in His gift to the world, is unlimited. It comprehends every human desire, and goes far beyond our human calculations. In the great day of final decision, when every man shall be judged according to his deeds, every voice of self-justification will be hushed; for it will be seen that in His gift to the human race the Father gave all He had to give, and that they are without excuse who have refused to accept the gracious offering. (CS 21.2)

We have no enemy without that we need to fear. Our great conflict is with unconsecrated self. When we conquer self, we are more than conquerors through Him who has loved us. My brethren, there is eternal life for us to win. Let us fight the good fight of faith. Not in the future, but now, is our probation. While it lingers, "seek ye first the kingdom of God, and His righteousness; and all these things,"–the things which now so often serve Satan's purpose as snares to deceive and destroy,–"shall be added unto you."– *The*

A Foul Blot

We should never forget that we are placed on trial in this world, to determine our fitness for the future life. None can enter heaven whose characters are defiled by the foul blot of selfishness. Therefore, God tests us here, by committing to us temporal possessions, that our use of these may show whether we can be entrusted with eternal riches.– *The Review and Herald, May 16, 1893.* **(CS 22.1)**

Our Possessions Only in Trust

However large, however small the possessions of any individual, let him remember that it is his only in trust. For his strength, skill, time, talents, opportunities, and means, he must render an account to God. This is an individual work; God gives to us, that we may become like Him, generous, noble, beneficent, by giving to others. Those who, forgetful of their divine mission, seek only to save or to spend in the indulgence of pride or selfishness, may secure the gains and pleasures of this world; but in God's sight, estimated by their spiritual attainments, they are poor, wretched, miserable, blind, naked. **(CS 22.2)**

When rightly employed, wealth becomes a golden bond of gratitude and affection between man and his fellow men, and a strong tie to bind his affections to his Redeemer. The infinite gift of God's dear Son calls for tangible expressions of gratitude from the recipients of His grace. He who receives the light of Christ's love, is thereby placed under the strongest obligation to shed the blessed light upon other souls in darkness.– *The Review and Herald, May 16, 1882.* **(CS 22.3)**

To Awaken Attributes of Christ's Character

The Lord permits suffering and calamity to come upon men and women to call us out of our selfishness, to awaken in us the attributes of His character,–compassion, tenderness, and love. **(CS 23.1)**

Divine love makes its most touching appeals when it calls upon us to manifest the same tender compassion that Christ manifested. He was a man of sorrows, and acquainted with grief. In all our afflictions He is afflicted. He loves men and women as the purchase of His own blood, and He says to us, "A new commandment I give unto you, That ye love one another; as I have loved you, that ye also love one another."– *The Review and Herald, September 13, 1906.* **(CS 23.2)**

The Highest Honor, the Greatest Joy

God is the source of life and light and joy to the universe. Like rays of light from the sun, blessings flow out from Him to all the creatures He has made. In His infinite love He has granted men the privilege of becoming partakers of the divine nature, and, in their turn, of diffusing blessings to their fellow men. This is the highest honor, the greatest joy, that it is possible for God to bestow upon men. Those are brought nearest to their Creator who thus become participants in labors of love. He who refuses to become a "laborer together with God,"–the man who for the sake of selfish indulgence ignores the wants of his fellow men, the miser who heaps up his treasures here,–is withholding from himself the richest blessing that God can give him.– *The Review and Herald, December 6, 1887.* **(CS 23.3)**

Chapter 4

The Conflicting Principles of Christ and Satan

Human beings belong to one great family,–the family of God. The Creator designed that they should respect and love one another, ever manifesting a pure, unselfish interest in one another's welfare. But Satan's aim has been to lead men to self first; and yielding themselves to his control, they have developed a selfishness that has filled the world with misery and strife, setting human beings at variance with one another. (CS 24.1)

Selfishness is the essence of depravity, and because human beings have yielded to its power, the opposite of allegiance to God is seen in the world today. Nations, families, and individuals are filled with a desire to make self a center. Man longs to rule over his fellow men. Separating himself in his egotism from God and his fellow beings, he follows his unrestrained inclinations. He acts as if the good of others depended on their subjection to his supremacy. (CS 24.2)

Selfishness has brought discord into the church, filling it with unholy ambition.... Selfishness destroys Christlikeness, filling man with self-love. It leads to continual departure from righteousness. Christ says, "Be ye therefore perfect, even as your Father which is in heaven is perfect." But self-love is blind to the perfection which God requires.... (CS 24.3)

Christ came to this world to reveal the love of God. His followers are to continue the work which He began. Let us strive to help and strengthen one another. Seeking the good of others is the way in which true happiness can be found. Man does not work against his own interest by loving God and his fellow men. The more unselfish his spirit, the happier he is, because he is fulfilling God's purpose for him. The breath of God is breathed through him, filling him with gladness. To him life is a sacred trust, precious in his sight because given by God to be spent in ministering to others.– *The Review and Herald, June 25, 1908.* (CS 24.4)

An Unequal Contest

Selfishness is the strongest and most general of human impulses, the struggle of the soul between sympathy and covetousness is an unequal contest; for while selfishness is the strongest passion, love and benevolence are too often the weakest, and as a rule the evil gains the victory. Therefore in our labors and gifts for God's cause, it is unsafe to be controlled by feeling or impulse. (CS 25.1)

To give or to labor when our sympathies are moved, and to withhold our gifts or service when the emotions are not stirred, is an unwise and dangerous course. If we are controlled by impulse or mere human sympathy, then a few instances where our efforts for others are repaid with ingratitude, or where our gifts are abused or squandered, will be sufficient to freeze up the springs of beneficence. Christians should act from fixed principle, following the Saviour's example of self-denial and self-sacrifice.– *The Review and Herald, December 7, 1886.* (CS 25.2)

The Keynote of Christ's Teaching

Self-sacrifice is the keynote of Christ's teachings. Often this is enjoined upon believers in language that seems authoritative, because there is no other way to save men than to cut them away from their life of selfishness. Christ gave, in His life on earth, a true representation of the power of the gospel.... To every soul who will suffer with Him in resistance of sin, in labor for His cause, in self-denial for the good of others, He promises a part in the eternal reward of the righteous. Through the exercise of the spirit that characterized His lifework, we are to become partakers of His nature. Partaking in this life of sacrifice for the sake of others, we shall share with Him in the life to come the "far more exceeding and eternal weight of glory."– *The Review and Herald, September 28, 1911.* (CS 25.3)

The Fruits of Selfishness

Those who allow a covetous spirit to take possession of them cherish and develop those traits of character which will place their names on the record books of heaven as idolaters. All such are classed with thieves, revilers, and extortioners, none of whom, the word of God declares, shall inherit the kingdom of God. "The wicked boasteth of his heart's desire, and blesseth the covetous, whom the Lord abhorreth." Covetous attributes are ever opposed to the exercise of Christian beneficence. The fruits of selfishness always reveal themselves in a neglect of duty, and in a failure to use God's entrusted gifts for the advancement of His work.– *The Review and Herald, December 1, 1896.* (CS 26.1)

Death to All Piety

Christ is our example. He gave His life as a sacrifice for us, and He asks us to give our lives as a sacrifice for others. Thus we may cast out the selfishness which Satan is constantly striving to implant in our hearts. This selfishness is death to all piety, and can be overcome only by manifesting love to God and to our fellow men. Christ will not permit one selfish person to enter the courts of heaven. No covetous person can pass through the pearly gates; for all covetousness is idolatry.– *The Review and Herald, July 11, 1899.* (CS 26.2)

Chapter 5
Beneficence Where Christ Abides

When the perfect love of God is in the heart, wonderful things will be done. Christ will be in the heart of the believer as a well of water springing up unto everlasting life. But those who manifest indifference to the suffering ones of humanity will be charged with indifference to Jesus Christ in the person of His suffering saints. Nothing saps spirituality from the soul more quickly than to enclose it in selfishness and self-caring. (CS 27.1)

Those who indulge self and neglect to care for the souls and bodies of those for whom Christ has given His life, are not eating of the bread of life, nor drinking of the water of the well of salvation. They are dry and sapless, like a tree that bears no fruit. They are spiritual dwarfs, who consume their means on self; but "whatsoever a man soweth, that shall he also reap." (CS 27.2)

Christian principles will always be made visible. In a thousand ways the inward principles will be made manifest. Christ abiding in the soul is as a well that never runs dry.– *The Review and Herald, January 15, 1895.* (CS 27.3)

When Christ Is Enthroned in the Heart

When God entrusts man with riches, it is that he may adorn the doctrine of Christ our Saviour by using his earthly treasure in advancing the kingdom of God in our world. He is to represent Christ, and therefore is not to live to please and glorify himself, to receive honor because he is rich. (CS 27.4)

When the heart is cleansed from sin, Christ is placed on the throne that self-indulgence and love of earthly treasure once occupied. The image of Christ is seen in the expression of the countenance. The work of sanctification is carried forward in the soul. Self-righteousness is banished. There is seen the putting on of the new man, which after Christ is created in righteousness and true holiness.– *The Review and Herald, September 11, 1900.* (CS 27.5)

Covetousness and Avarice Overcome

The rich should consecrate their all to God, and he who is sanctified through the truth in body, soul, and spirit, will also devote his property to God, and will become an agent whereby other souls will be reached. In his experience and example it will be made manifest that the grace of Christ has power to overcome covetousness and avarice, and the rich man who renders unto God His entrusted goods, will be accounted a faithful steward, and can present to others the fact that every dollar of their accumulated property is stamped with the image and superscription of God.– *The Review and Herald, September 19, 1893.* (CS 28.1)

Chapter 6
Preaching Practical Sermons

Giving for the necessity of the saints and for the advancement of the kingdom of God, is preaching practical sermons, which testify that those who give have not received the grace of God in vain. A living example of an unselfish character, which is after the example of Christ, has great power upon men. Those who do not live for self, will not use up every dollar meeting their supposed wants, and supplying their conveniences, but will bear in mind that they are Christ's followers, and that there are others who are in need of food and clothing. (CS 29.1)

Those who live to gratify appetite and selfish desire, will lose the favor of God, and will lose the heavenly reward. They testify to the world that they have not genuine faith, and when they seek to impart to others a knowledge of present truth, the world will regard their words as sounding brass and a tinkling cymbal. Let everyone show his faith by his works. "Faith without works is dead," "being alone." "Wherefore show ye to them and before the churches, the proof of your love, and of our boasting in your behalf."– *The Review and Herald, August 21, 1894.* (CS 29.2)

The Most Difficult Sermon

The most difficult sermon to preach and the hardest to practice is self-denial. The greedy sinner, self, closes the door to the good which might be done, but which is not done because money is invested for selfish purposes. But it is impossible for anyone to retain the favor of God and enjoy communion with the Saviour, and at the same time be indifferent to the interests of his fellow beings who have no life in Christ, who are perishing in their sins. Christ has left us a wonderful example of self-sacrifice.... (CS 29.3)

As we follow Him in the path of self-denial, lifting the cross and bearing it after Him to His Father's home, we shall reveal in our lives the beauty of the Christ life. At the altar of self-sacrifice,–the appointed place of meeting between God and the soul,–we receive from the hand of God the celestial torch which searches the heart, revealing the need of an abiding Christ.– *The Review and Herald, January 31, 1907.* (CS 30.1)

Expands the Heart, Unites With Christ

The offerings of the poor, given through self-denial to aid in extending the precious light of saving truth, will not only be a sweet-smelling savor to God, and wholly acceptable to Him as a consecrated gift, but the very act of giving expands the heart of the giver, and unites him more fully to the Redeemer of the world. He was rich; but for our sakes He became poor, that we through His poverty might be made rich. The smallest sums given cheerfully by those who are in limited circumstances are fully as acceptable to God, and even of more value in His sight, than the offerings of the rich who can bestow their thousands, and yet exercise no self-denial and feel no lack.– *The Review and Herald, October 31, 1878.* (CS 30.2)

Giving With Cheerful Alacrity

The spirit of Christian liberality will strengthen as it is exercised, and will not need to be unhealthfully stimulated. All who possess this spirit, the spirit of Christ, will with cheerful alacrity press their gifts into the Lord's treasury. Inspired by love for Christ and for the souls for whom He has died, they feel an intense earnestness to act their part with fidelity.– *The Review and Herald, May 16, 1893.* (CS 30.3)

For Further Study

Section 2

God's Work and Its Support

Chapter 7
The Lord's Work to Be Maintained

The last years of probation are passing into eternity. The great day of the Lord is right upon us. Every energy we possess should now be used to arouse those dead in trespasses and sins.... (CS 35.1)

It is time that we gave heed to the teaching of the word of God. All His injunctions are given to do us good. He calls upon those who stand under the bloodstained banner of Prince Immanuel to give evidence that they realize their dependence on God and their accountability to Him, by returning to Him a certain portion of that which He entrusts to them. This money is to be used in advancing the work that must be done to fulfill the commission given by Christ to His disciples.... (CS 35.2)

God's people are called to a work that requires money and consecration. The obligations resting upon us hold us responsible to work for God to the utmost of our ability. He calls for undivided service, for the entire devotion of heart, soul, mind, and strength. (CS 35.3)

There are only two places in the universe where we can place our treasures,–in God's storehouse or in Satan's; and all that is not devoted to God's service is counted on Satan's side, and goes to strengthen his cause. The Lord designs that the means entrusted to us shall be used in building up His kingdom. His goods are entrusted to His stewards that they may be carefully traded upon, and bring back a revenue to Him in the saving of souls. These souls in their turn will become stewards of trust, cooperating with Christ to further the interests of God's cause. (CS 35.4)

Receiving to Impart

Wherever there is life in a church, there is increase and growth. There is also a constant interchange, taking and giving out, receiving and returning to the Lord His own. To every true believer God imparts light and blessing, and this the believer imparts to others in the work that he does for the Lord. As he gives of that which he receives, his capacity for receiving is increased. Room is made for fresh supplies of grace and truth. Clearer light, increased knowledge, are his. On this giving and receiving depend the life and growth of the church. He who receives, but never gives, soon ceases to receive. If the truth does not flow from him to others, he loses his capacity to receive. We must impart the goods of heaven, if we would receive fresh blessing. (CS 36.1)

The Lord does not propose to come to this world, and lay down gold and silver for the advancement of His work. He supplies men with resources, that by their gifts and offerings they may keep His work advancing. The one purpose above all others for which God's gifts should be used is the sustaining of workers in the harvest field. And if men will become channels through which heaven's blessing can flow to others, the Lord will keep the channel supplied. It is not returning to the Lord His own that makes men poor; withholding tends to poverty.... (CS 36.2)

A Time for Economy and Sacrifice

God calls upon His people to awake to their responsibilities. A flood of light is shining from His word, and there must be a meeting of neglected obligations. When these are met, by giving to the Lord His own in tithes and offerings, the way will be opened for the world to hear the message that the Lord designs it to hear. If our people had the love of God in the heart, if every church member were imbued with the spirit of self-sacrifice, there would be no lack of funds for home and foreign missions; our resources would be multiplied; a thousand doors of usefulness would be opened; and we should be invited to enter. Had the purpose of God been carried out in giving the message of mercy to the world, Christ would have come, and the saints would have received their welcome into the city of God. (CS 36.3)

If ever there was a time when sacrifices should be made, it is now. My brethren and sisters, practice economy in your homes. Put away the idols that you have placed before God. Give up your selfish pleasures. Do not, I beg of you, spend means in embellishing your houses; for your money belongs to God, and to Him you must give an account for its use. Do not use the Lord's money to gratify the fancies of your children. Teach them that God has a claim on all they possess, and that nothing can ever cancel this claim. (CS 37.1)

Money is a needed treasure. Do not lavish it upon those who need it not. Someone needs your willing gifts. There are those in the world who are hungry, starving. You may say, I cannot feed them all. But by practicing Christ's lessons of economy, you can feed one. "Gather up the fragments that remain, that nothing be lost." These words were spoken by Him whose power wrought a miracle to supply the needs of a hungry multitude. (CS 37.2)

If you have extravagant habits, cut them away from your life at once. Unless you do this, you will be bankrupt for eternity. Habits of economy, industry, and sobriety, are a better portion for your children than a rich dowry. (CS 37.3)

We are pilgrims and strangers on the earth. Let us not spend our means in gratifying desires that God would have us repress. Let us fitly represent our faith by restricting our wants. Let our church members arise as one man, and work earnestly, as those who are walking in the full light of truth for these last days.... (CS 38.1)

Of what value is untold wealth, if it is hoarded in expensive mansions, or in bank stock? What do these weigh in the scale in comparison with the salvation of the souls for whom Christ, the Son of the infinite God, has died?– *The Review and Herald, December 24,* 1903. (CS 38.2)

A Privilege and a Responsibility

The most solemn truths ever entrusted to mortals have been given to us to proclaim to the world. The proclamation of these truths is our work. The world is to be warned, and God's people are to be true to the trust committed to them. They are not to engage in speculations, neither are they to enter into business enterprises with unbelievers; for this would hinder them in doing the work given them. (CS 38.3)

Christ says of His people, "Ye are the light of the world." It is not a small matter that the counsels and purposes and plans of God have been so clearly opened to us. It is a wonderful privilege to be able to understand the will of God as revealed in the sure word of prophecy. This places on us a heavy responsibility. God expects us to impart to others the knowledge He has given us. It is His purpose that divine and human instrumentalities shall unite in the proclamation of the warning message.– *The Review and Herald, July 28, 1904.* (CS 38.4)

Support Foreign Missions

The sympathies of God's people should be aroused in every church throughout our land, and there should be unselfish action to meet the necessities of different mission fields. Men should testify to their interest in the cause of God by giving of their substance. If such an interest were manifested, the bond of Christian brotherhood would exist and increase in strength between all the members of Christ's family. (CS 38.5)

This work of faithfully bringing in all the tithes, that there may be meat in the house of God, would supply laborers for both home and foreign fields. Although books and publications upon present truth are pouring out their treasures of knowledge to all parts of the world, yet missionary posts must be established at different points. The living preacher must proclaim the words of life and salvation. There are open fields inviting workers to enter. The harvest is ripe, and the earnest Macedonian cry for laborers is heard from every part of the world.– *The Review and Herald, February 19,*

1889. (CS 39.1)

The Work Must Not Stop

[An appeal made by Mrs. White in 1886. Written from Europe.] If we indeed have the truth for these last days, it must be carried to every nation, kindred, tongue, and people. Erelong the living and the dead are to be judged according to the deeds done in the body, and the law of God is the standard by which they are to be tested. Then they must now be warned; God's holy law must be vindicated, and held up before them as a mirror. To accomplish this work, means is needed. I know that times are hard, money is not plenty; but the truth must be spread, and money to spread it must be placed in the treasury.... (CS 39.2)

Shall We Abandon the Work?

Our message is world wide; yet many are doing literally nothing, many more so very little, with so great a want of faith, that it is next to nothing. Shall we abandon the fields we have already opened in foreign countries? Shall we drop part of the work in our home missions? Shall we grow pale at a debt of a few thousand dollars? Shall we falter and become laggards now, in the very last scenes of this earth's history? My heart says, No, no. I cannot contemplate this question without a burning zeal to have the work go. We would not deny our faith, we would not deny Christ, yet we shall do this unless we move forward as the providence of God opens the way. (CS 39.3)

The work must not stop for want of means. More means must be invested in it. Brethren in America, in the name of my Master I bid you wake up! You that are placing your talents of means in a napkin, and hiding them in the earth, who are building houses and adding land to land, God calls upon you, "Sell that ye have, and give alms." There is a time coming when commandment keepers can neither buy nor sell. Make haste to dig out your buried talents. If God has entrusted you with money, show yourselves faithful to your trust; unwrap your napkin, and send your talents to the exchangers, that when Christ shall come, He may receive His own with interest. (CS 40.1)

Cheerful Liberality in the Closing Work

In the last extremity, before this work shall close, thousands will be cheerfully laid upon the altar. Men and women will feel it a blessed privilege to share in the work of preparing souls to stand in the great day of God, and they will give hundreds as readily as dollars are given now. (CS 40.2)

If the love of Christ were burning in the hearts of His professed people, we would see the same spirit manifested today. Did they but realize how near is the end of all work for the salvation of souls, they would sacrifice their possessions as freely as did the members of the early church. They would work for the advancement of God's cause as earnestly as worldly men labor to acquire riches. Tact and skill would be exercised, and earnest and unselfish labor put forth to acquire means, not to hoard, but to pour into the treasury of the Lord. (CS 40.3)

What if some become poor in investing their means in the work? Christ for your sakes became poor; but you are securing for yourselves eternal riches, a treasure in heaven that faileth not. Your means is far safer there than if deposited in the bank, or invested in houses and lands. It is laid up in bags that wax not old. No thief can approach it, no fire consume it.... (CS 41.1)

In obeying the Saviour's injunction, our example will preach louder than words. The highest display of the power of truth is seen when those who profess to believe it give evidence of their faith by their works. Those who believe this solemn truth should possess such a spirit of self-sacrifice as will rebuke the worldly ambition of the money worshiper.– *Historical Sketches of the Foreign Missions of the Seventh-day Adventists, 291-293.* (CS 41.2)

Chapter 8
Wholehearted Attachment to the Church

Every believer should be wholehearted in his attachment to the church. Its prosperity should be his first interest, and unless he feels under sacred obligations to make his connection with the church a benefit to it in preference to himself, it can do far better without him. It is in the power of all to do something for the cause of God. There are those who spend a large amount for needless luxuries; they gratify their appetites, but feel it a great tax to contribute means to sustain the church. They are willing to receive all the benefit of its privileges, but prefer to leave others to pay the bills. Those who really feel a deep interest in the advancement of the cause, will not hesitate to invest money in the enterprise whenever and wherever it is needed.– *Testimonies for the Church 4:18*. (CS 42.1)

Those who rejoice in the precious light of truth should feel a burning desire to have it sent everywhere. There are a few faithful standard-bearers who never flinch from duty or shirk responsibilities. Their hearts and purses are always open to every call for means to advance the cause of God. Indeed, some seem ready to exceed their duty, as though fearful that they will lose an opportunity of investing their portion in the bank of heaven. (CS 42.2)

There are others who will do as little as possible. They hoard their treasure, or lavish means upon themselves, grudgingly doling out a mere pittance to sustain the cause of God. If they make a pledge or a vow to God, they afterward repent of it, and will avoid the payment of it as long as they can, if not altogether. They make their tithe as small as possible, as if afraid that that which they return to God is lost. Our various institutions may be embarrassed for means, but this class act as though it made no difference to them whether they prosper or not. And yet these are God's instrumentalities with

which to enlighten the world.– *Testimonies for the Church 4:477, 478*. (CS 42.3)

The Baptismal Vow

Everyone who connects himself with the church makes in that act a solemn vow to work for the interest of the church, and to hold that interest above every worldly consideration. It is his work to preserve a living connection with God, to engage with heart and soul in the great scheme of redemption, and to show, in his life and character, the excellency of God's commandments in contrast with the customs and precepts of the world. Every soul that has made a profession of Christ has pledged himself to be all that it is possible for him to be as a spiritual worker, to be active, zealous, and efficient in his Master's service. Christ expects every man to do his duty; let this be the watchword throughout the ranks of His followers.... (CS 43.1)

All are to show their fidelity to God by the wise use of His entrusted capital, not in means alone, but in any endowment that will tend to the upbuilding of His kingdom. Satan will employ every possible device to prevent the truth from reaching those who are buried in error; but the voice of warning and entreaty must come to them. And while only a few are engaged in this work, thousands ought to be as much interested as they.– *Testimonies for the Church 5:460-462*. (CS 43.2)

The Task Before Us

There is a world to be warned. To us has been entrusted this work. At any cost we must practice the truth. We are to stand as self-sacrificing minutemen, willing to suffer the loss of life itself, if need be, in the service of God. There is a great work to be done in a short time. We need to understand our work, and to do it with fidelity. Everyone who is finally crowned victor will, by noble, determined effort to serve God, have earned the right to be clothed with Christ's righteousness. To enter the crusade against Satan, bearing aloft the bloodstained banner of the cross of Christ–this is the duty of every Christian. (**CS 43.3**)

This work calls for self-sacrifice. Self-denial and the cross stand all along the way of life. "He that will come after Me," Christ said, "let him deny himself, and take up his cross, and follow Me." Those who secure the treasures of this world are obliged to toil and sacrifice. Should those who are seeking for an eternal reward think that they need make no sacrifices?– *The Review and Herald, January 31, 1907.* (**CS 44.1**)

Wait Not for Appeals

Our people are not to wait for more appeals, but are to lay right hold of the work, making those things which appear impossibilities, possibilities. Let each one ask himself, Has not the Lord entrusted me with means for the advancement of His cause? ... (**CS 44.2**)

Let us be honest with the Lord. All the blessings that we enjoy come from Him; and if He has entrusted us with the talent of means, that we may help to do His work, shall we hold back? Shall we say, No, Lord; my children would not be pleased, and therefore I shall venture to disobey God, burying His talent in the earth?

(**CS 44.3**)

There should be no delay. The cause of God demands your assistance. We ask you, as the Lord's stewards, to put His means into circulation, to provide facilities by which many will have the opportunity of learning what is truth. (**CS 44.4**)

The temptation may come to you to invest your money in land. Perhaps your friends will advise you to do this. But is there not a better way of investing your means? Have you not been bought with a price? Has not your money been entrusted to you to be traded upon for Him? Can you not see that He wants you to use your means in helping to build meeting- houses, in helping to establish sanitariums, where the sick shall receive physical and spiritual healing, and in helping to start schools, in which the youth shall be trained for service, that workers may be sent to all parts of the world? (**CS 45.1**)

God Himself originates the plans for the advancement of His work, and He has provided His people with a surplus of means, that when He calls for help, they may cheerfully respond. If they will be faithful in bringing to His treasury the means lent them, His work will make rapid advancement. Many souls will be won to the truth, and the day of Christ's coming will be hastened.– *The Review and Herald, July 14, 1904.* (**CS 45.2**)

Chapter 9
The Voice of Consecration

Is this the language of your heart? "I am wholly Thine, my Saviour; Thou hast paid the ransom for my soul, and all that I am or ever hope to be is Thine. Help me to acquire means, not to expend foolishly, not to indulge pride, but to use to Thine own name's glory." (CS 46.1)

In all you do, let your thought be, "Is this the way of the Lord? Will this please my Saviour? He gave His life for me; what can I give back to God? I can only say, 'Of Thine own, O lord, I freely give Thee.'" Unless the name of God is written in your forehead,–written there because God is the center of your thoughts,–you will not be meet for the inheritance in light. It is your Creator who has poured out to you all heaven in one wondrous gift,–His only-begotten Son.... (CS 46.2)

God lays His hand upon the tithe, as well as upon gifts and offerings, and says, "That is Mine. When I entrusted you with My goods, I specified that a portion should be your own, to supply your necessities, and a portion should be returned to Me." (CS 46.3)

As you gathered in your harvest, storing barns and granary for your own comfort, did you return to God a faithful tithe? Have you presented to Him your gifts and offerings, that His cause may not suffer? Have you looked after the fatherless and the widow? This is a branch of home missionary work that should by no means be neglected. (CS 46.4)

Are there not around you poor and suffering ones who need warmer clothing, better food, and, above everything else, that which will be most highly prized,– sympathy and love? What have you done for the widows, the distressed, who call upon you to aid them in educating and training their children or grandchildren? How have you treated these cases? Have you tried to help the orphans? When anxious, soul-burdened parents or grandparents have asked you, and even begged you, to consider their case, have you turned them away with unfeeling, unsympathetic refusals? If so, may the Lord pity your future; for "with what measure ye mete, it shall be measured to you again." Can we be surprised that the Lord withholds His blessing, when His gifts are selfishly perverted and misapplied? (CS 46.5)

God is constantly bestowing upon you the blessings of this life; and if He asks you to dispense His gifts by helping the various branches of His work, it is for your own temporal and spiritual interest to do so, and thus acknowledge God as the giver of every blessing. God, as the Master Worker, cooperates with men in securing the means necessary for their sustenance; and He requires them to cooperate with Him in the salvation of souls. He has placed in the hands of His servants the means wherewith to carry forward His work in home and foreign missions. But if only half the people do their duty, the treasury will not be supplied with the necessary funds, and many parts of the work of God must be left incomplete.– *The Review and Herald, December 23, 1890.* (CS 47.1)

Answering Christ's Prayer for Unity

Never can the church reach the position that God desires it to reach until it is bound up in sympathy with its missionary workers. Never can the unity for which Christ prayed exist until spirituality is brought into missionary service, and until the church becomes an agency for the support of missions. The efforts of the missionaries will not accomplish what they should until the church members in the home field show, not only in word, but in deed, that they realize the obligation resting on them to give these missionaries their hearty support. (**CS 47.2**)

God calls for workers. Personal activity is needed. But conversion comes first; seeking for the salvation of others, next.– *The Review and Herald, September 10, 1903.* (**CS 48.1**)

Empty the Heart of Selfishness

It is to be regretted that the church today feels so little inclination to express thanksgiving to the Lord for enriching her with His grace, for giving her His talents of means, that she may have wherewith to supply His treasury. (**CS 48.2**)

The barren portions of the Lord's vineyard cry to God, saying, "Men have neglected to care for me." By allowing their fellow beings to remain in the bondage of want and degradation, men and women allow Satan to reproach God for permitting His children to suffer for the necessaries of life. God is insulted by the indifference of those to whom He has entrusted His goods. His stewards refuse to notice the distress which they might relieve. Thus they bring a reproach upon God. (**CS 48.3**)

Let no one trifle with his responsibilities. If you are not trading upon dollars, but only upon cents, remember that the blessing of God rests upon unwearied diligence. He does not despise the day of small things. A wise use of the littles will bring a wonderful increase. One talent wisely used will bring two to God. Interest is expected in proportion to the entrusted capital. God accepts according to what a man hath, and not according to that he hath not. (**CS 48.4**)

God calls for what you owe Him in tithes and offerings. He calls for consecration in every line of His work. Act faithfully your part at your appointed post of duty. Work earnestly, remembering that Christ is by your side, planning, devising, and constructing for you. "God is able to make all grace abound toward you; that ye, always having all sufficiency in all things, may abound to every good work." Give cheerfully, gladly, willingly, thankful that you are able to do something to advance God's kingdom in the world. Empty the heart of selfishness, and brace the mind for Christian activity. If you are in close connection with God, you will be willing to make any sacrifice to place eternal life within the reach of the perishing. (**CS 48.5**)

Spiritual Prosperity and Christian Liberality

In the name of the Lord, I beseech my brethren and sisters, at this crisis in our work, to come up to the help of the Lord, to the help of the Lord against the mighty. Withholding from God always brings a curse. Spiritual prosperity is closely bound up with Christian liberality. Hunger only for the exaltation of imitating the divine beneficence of the Redeemer. You have the precious assurance that your treasure is going before you to the heavenly courts. (**CS 49.1**)

Would you make your property secure? Place it in the hand that bears the nail prints of the crucifixion. Retain all in your possession, and it will be to your eternal loss. Give it to God, and from that moment it bears His inscription. It is sealed with His immutability. Would you enjoy your substance? Then use it to bless the suffering. Would you increase your possessions? "Honor the Lord with thy substance, and with the first fruits of all thine increase: so shall thy barns be filled with plenty, and thy presses shall burst out with new wine." (**CS 49.2**)

God Will Refill the Hand

If all will act their part, the barrenness of the Lord's vineyard will no longer speak in condemnation of those who profess to follow Christ. Medical missionary work is to open the door for the gospel of present truth. The third angel's message is to be heard in all places. Economize! Strip yourselves of pride. Give to God your earthly treasure. Give what you can now, and as you cooperate with Christ, your hand will open to impart still more. And God will refill your hand, that the treasure of truth may be taken to many souls. He will give to you that you may give to others.– *The Review and Herald, December 10, 1901.* (**CS 50.1**)

Chapter 10
A Call to Greater Earnestness

The world and the churches are breaking God's law, and the warning must be given, "If any man worship the beast and his image, and receive his mark in his forehead, or in his hand, the same shall drink of the wine of the wrath of God, which is poured out without mixture into the cup of His indignation." With such a curse hanging over the transgressors of God's holy Sabbath, should we not show greater earnestness, greater zeal? Why are we so indifferent, so selfish, so engrossed in temporal interests? Is our interest separated from Jesus? Has the truth become too pointed, too close in its application to our souls; and like the disciples of Christ who were offended, have we turned away to the beggarly elements of the world? We spend money for selfish purposes, and gratify our own desires, while souls are dying without a knowledge of Jesus and the truth. How long shall this continue? (CS 51.1)

All should have a living faith,–a faith which works by love, and purifies the soul. Men and women are ready to do anything to indulge self, but how little are they willing to do for Jesus, and for their fellow men who are perishing for the want of the truth!... (CS 51.2)

Invest Now in the Bank of Heaven

Has not the time come when we should begin to cut down our possessions? May God help you who can do something now to make an investment in the bank of heaven. We do not ask a loan, but a freewill offering,–a return to the Master of His own goods which He has lent you. If you love God supremely, and your neighbor as yourself, we believe you will give tangible proofs of the same in freewill offerings for our mission work. There are souls to be saved, and may you be coworkers with Jesus Christ in saving these souls for whom Christ has given His life. The Lord will bless you in the good fruit you may bear to His glory. May the same Holy Spirit which inspired the Bible take possession of your hearts, leading you to love His word, which is spirit and life. May it open your eyes to discover the things of the Spirit of God. The reason there is so much dwarfed religion today is because people have not brought practical self-denial and self-sacrifice into their lives.– *The Review and Herald, January 8, 1889.* (CS 51.3)

Latter Rain Postponed

The great outpouring of the Spirit of God, which lightens the whole earth with His glory, will not come until we have an enlightened people, that know by experience what it means to be laborers together with God. When we have entire, wholehearted consecration to the service of Christ, God will recognize the fact by an outpouring of His Spirit without measure; but this will not be while the largest portion of the church are not laborers together with God. God cannot pour out His Spirit when selfishness and self-indulgence are so manifest; when a spirit prevails that, if put into words, would express that answer of Cain,–"Am I my brother's keeper?"– *The Review and Herald, July 21, 1896.* (CS 52.1)

Subordinate Every Earthly Interest

My dear brethren and sisters,

I speak to you in words of love and tenderness. Every earthly interest must be made subordinate to the great work of redemption. Remember that in the lives of the followers of Christ must be seen the same devotion, the same subjection to God's work of every social claim and every earthly affection, that was seen in His life. God's claims must ever be made paramount.

"He that loveth father or mother more than Me is not worthy of Me." Christ's life is our lesson book. His example is to inspire us to put forth untiring, self-sacrificing effort for the good of others.... (CS 52.2)

Every power of God's servants is to be kept in continual exercise to bring many sons and daughters to God. In His service there is to be no indifference, no selfishness. Any departure from self-denial to self-indulgence, any relaxation of earnest supplication for the Holy Spirit's working, means so much power given to the enemy. Christ is reviewing His church. How many there are whose religious life is their own condemnation! (CS 53.1)

God demands that which we do not give,–unreserved consecration. If every Christian had been true to the pledge made on accepting Christ, so many in the world would not have been left to perish in sin. Who will answer for the souls who have gone to the grave unprepared to meet their Lord? Christ offered Himself as a complete sacrifice in our behalf. How earnestly He worked to save sinners! How untiring were His efforts to prepare His disciples for service! But how little we have done! And the influence of the little that we have done has been terribly weakened by the neutralizing effect of what we have left undone, or undertaken and never brought to completion, and by our habits of listless indifference. How much we have lost by failing to press forward to accomplish our God-given work! As professed Christians, we ought to be appalled by the outlook.– *The Review and Herald, December 30, 1902.* (CS 53.2)

The Spirit of Sacrifice

The plan of salvation was laid in a sacrifice so broad and deep and high that it is immeasurable. Christ did not send His angels to this fallen world, while He remained in heaven; but He Himself went without the camp, bearing the reproach. He became a man of sorrows, and acquainted with grief; Himself took our infirmities, and bore our weaknesses. And the absence of self-denial in His professed followers, God regards as a denial of the Christian name. Those who profess to be one with Christ, and indulge their selfish desires for rich and expensive clothing, furniture, and food, are Christians only in name. To be a Christian is to be Christlike. (CS 54.1)

And yet how true are the words of the apostle: "For all seek their own, not the things which are Jesus Christ's." Many Christians do not have works corresponding to the name they bear. They act as if they had never heard of the plan of redemption wrought out at infinite cost. The majority aim to make a name for themselves in the world; they adopt its forms and ceremonies, and live for the indulgence of self. They follow out their own purposes as eagerly as do the world, and thus they cut off their power to help in establishing the kingdom of God.... (CS 54.2)

The work of God, which should be going forward with tenfold its present strength and efficiency, is kept back, like a spring season held by the chilling blast of winter, because some of God's professed people are appropriating to themselves the means that should be dedicated to His service. Because Christ's self-sacrificing love is not interwoven in the life practices, the church is weak where it should be strong. By its own course it has put out its light, and robbed millions of the gospel of Christ.... (CS 54.3)

How can those for whom Christ has sacrificed so much, continue to enjoy His gifts selfishly? His love and self-denial are without a parallel; and when this love enters into the experience of His followers, they will identify their interests with those of their Redeemer. Their work will be to build up the kingdom of Christ. They will consecrate themselves and their possessions to Him, and use both as His cause may require. (CS 55.1)

This is nothing more than Jesus expects of His followers. No individual who has before him so great an object as the salvation of souls will be at a loss to devise ways and means for denying self. This will be an individual work. All that it is in our power to bestow will flow into the Lord's treasury, to be used for the proclamation of truth, that the message of Christ's soon coming and the claims of His law may be sounded to all parts of the world. Missionaries must be sent out to do this work. (CS 55.2)

The love of Jesus in the soul will be revealed in word and deed. The kingdom of Christ will be paramount. Self will be laid a willing sacrifice on the altar of God. Everyone who is truly united with Christ will feel the same love for souls that caused the Son of God to leave His royal throne, His high command, and for our sake become poor, that we through His poverty might be made rich.– *The Review and Herald, October 13, 1896.* (**CS 55.3**)

A Call for Consecrated Families

God calls for personal effort from those that know the truth. He calls for Christian families to go into communities that are in darkness and error, to go into foreign fields, to become acquainted with a new class of society, and to work wisely and perseveringly for the cause of the Master. To answer this call, self-sacrifice must be experienced. (**CS 55.4**)

While many are waiting to have every obstacle removed, souls are dying without hope and without God in the world. Many, very many, for the sake of worldly advantage, for the sake of acquiring knowledge of the sciences, will venture into pestilential regions, and will go into countries where they think they can obtain commercial advantage; but where are the men and women who will change their location, and move their families into regions that are in need of the light of the truth, in order that their example may tell upon those who shall see in them the representatives of Christ? (**CS 56.1**)

The Macedonian cry is coming from every quarter of the world, and men are saying, "Come over, ... and help us," and why is there not a decided response? Thousands ought to be constrained by the Spirit of Christ to follow the example of Him who has given His life for the life of the world. Why decline to make decided, self-denying efforts, in order to instruct those who know not the truth for this time? The Chief Missionary came to our world, and He has gone before us to show us the way in which we should work. No one can mark out a precise line for those who would be witnesses for Christ.

(**CS 56.2**)

Those who have means are doubly responsible; for this means has been entrusted to them of God, and they are to feel their accountability to forward the work of God in its various branches. The fact that the truth binds souls by its golden links to the throne of God, should inspire men to work with all their God-given energy, to trade upon their Lord's goods in regions beyond, disseminating the knowledge of Christ far hence among the Gentiles. (**CS 56.3**)

Many to whom God has entrusted means with which to bless humanity, have let it prove a snare to them, instead of letting it prove a blessing to themselves and others. Can it be that the property that God has given to you shall be permitted to become a stumbling block? Will you let His entrusted means, which has been given you to trade upon, bind you away from the work of God? Will you allow the trust which God has reposed in you as His faithful steward, serve to lessen your influence and usefulness, by keeping you from being laborers together with God? Will you permit yourself to be detained at home, in order to hold together the means which God has entrusted to you to put into the bank of heaven? You cannot plead that there is nothing to do; for there is everything to do. Will you be content to enjoy the comforts of your home, and not try to tell perishing souls how they may obtain the mansions Christ has gone to prepare for those who love Him? Will you not sacrifice your possessions, in order that others may obtain an immortal inheritance?– *The Review and Herald, July 21, 1896.* (**CS 56.4**)

Chapter 11
Selling Homes and Property

God calls upon those who have possessions in lands and houses, to sell, and to invest the money where it will be supplying the great want in the missionary field. When once they have experienced the real satisfaction that comes from thus doing, they will keep the channel open, and the means the Lord entrusts to them will be constantly flowing into the treasury, that souls may be converted. These souls will, in their turn, practice the same self-denial, economy, and simplicity, for Christ's sake, that they, too, may bring their offerings to God. Through these talents, wisely invested, still other souls may be converted; and thus the work goes on, showing that the gifts of God are appreciated. The Giver is acknowledged, and glory redounds to Him through the faithfulness of His stewards. (CS 58.1)

When we make these earnest appeals in behalf of the cause of God, and present the financial wants of our missions, conscientious souls who believe the truth are deeply stirred. Like the poor widow, whom Christ commended, who gave her two mites into the treasury, they give, in their poverty, to the utmost of their ability. Such often deprive themselves even of the apparent necessities of life; while there are men and women who, possessing houses and lands, cling to their earthly treasure with selfish tenacity, and do not have faith enough in the message and in God to put their means into His work. To these last are especially applicable the words of Christ, "Sell that ye have, and give alms." (CS 58.2)

Expect Individual Guidance

There are poor men and women who are writing to me for advice as to whether they shall sell their homes, and give the proceeds to the cause. They say the appeals for means stir their souls, and they want to do something for the Master who has done everything for them. I would say to such, "It may not be your duty to sell your little homes just now; but go to God for yourselves; the Lord will certainly hear your earnest prayers for wisdom to understand your duty."– *Testimonies for the Church 5:733, 734.* (CS 59.1)

Possessions to Decrease Rather Than Increase

It is now that our brethren should be cutting down their possessions instead of increasing them. We are about to move to a better country, even a heavenly. Then let us not be dwellers upon the earth, but be getting things into as compact a compass as possible. (CS 59.2)

The time is coming when we cannot sell at any price. The decree will soon go forth prohibiting men to buy or sell of any man save he that hath the mark of the beast.– *Testimonies for the Church 5:152.* (CS 59.3)

Preparation for Time of Trouble

Houses and lands will be of no use to the saints in the time of trouble, for they will then have to flee before infuriated mobs, and at that time their possessions cannot be disposed of to advance the cause of present truth. I was shown that it is the will of God that the saints should cut loose from every encumbrance before the time of trouble comes, and make a covenant with God through sacrifice. If they have their property on the altar, and earnestly inquire of God for duty, He will teach them when to dispose of these things. Then they will be free in the time of trouble, and have no clogs to weigh them down. (CS 59.4)

I saw that if any held on to their property, and did not inquire of the Lord as to their duty,

He would not make duty known, and they would be permitted to keep their property, and in the time of trouble it would come up before them like a mountain to crush them, and they would try to dispose of it, but would not be able. I heard some mourn like this: "The cause was languishing, God's people were starving for the truth, and we made no effort to supply the lack; now our property is useless. O that we had let it go, and laid up treasure in heaven!" (**CS 60.1**)

I saw that a sacrifice did not increase, but it decreased and was consumed. I also saw that God had not required all of His people to dispose of their property at the same time, but if they desired to be taught, He would teach them, in a time of need, when to sell and how much to sell. Some have been required to dispose of their property in times past to sustain the advent cause, while others have been permitted to keep theirs until a time of need. Then, as the cause needs it, their duty is to sell.– *Early Writings, 56, 57.* (**CS 60.2**)

No Cord to Bind to Earth

The work of God is to become more extensive, and if His people follow His counsel, there will not be much means in their possession to be consumed in the final conflagration. All will have laid up their treasure where moth and rust cannot corrupt; and the heart will not have a cord to bind it to earth.– *Testimonies for the Church 1:197.* (**CS 60.3**)

For Further Study

Section 3
God's Reserves—the Tithe

Chapter 12
A Test of Loyalty

"Honor the Lord with thy substance, and with the first fruits of all thine increase: so shall thy barns be filled with plenty, and thy presses shall burst out with new wine." (CS 65.1)

This scripture teaches that God, as the Giver of all our benefits, has a claim upon them all; that His claim should be our first consideration; and that a special blessing will attend all who honor this claim. (CS 65.2)

Herein is set forth a principle that is seen in all God's dealings with men. The Lord placed our first parents in the Garden of Eden. He surrounded them with everything that could minister to their happiness, and He bade them acknowledge Him as the possessor of all things. In the garden He caused to grow every tree that was pleasant to the eye or good for food; but among them He made one reserve. Of all else, Adam and Eve might freely eat; but of this one tree God said, "Thou shalt not eat of it." Here was the test of their gratitude and loyalty to God. (CS 65.3)

So the Lord has imparted to us heaven's richest treasure in giving us Jesus. With Him He has given us all things richly to enjoy. The productions of the earth, the bountiful harvests, the treasures of gold and silver, are His gifts. Houses and lands, food and clothing, He has placed in the possession of men. He asks us to acknowledge Him as the Giver of all things; and for this reason He says, Of all your possessions I reserve a tenth for Myself, besides gifts and offerings, which are to be brought into My storehouse. This is the provision God has made for carrying forward the work of the gospel. (CS 65.4)

It was by the Lord Jesus Christ Himself, who gave His life for the life of the world, that this plan for systematic giving was devised. He who left the royal courts, who laid aside His honor as Commander of the heavenly hosts, who clothed His divinity with humanity in order to uplift the fallen race; He who for our sake became poor that we through His poverty might be rich, has spoken to men, and in His wisdom has told them His own plan for sustaining those who bear His message to the world.– *The Review and Herald, February 4, 1902.* (CS 66.1)

God's Reserves of Time and Means

The very same language is used concerning the Sabbath as in the law of the tithe: "The seventh day is the Sabbath of the Lord thy God." Man has no right nor power to substitute the first day for the seventh. He may pretend to do this; "nevertheless the foundation of God standeth sure." The customs and teachings of men will not lessen the claims of the divine law. God has sanctified the seventh day. That specified portion of time, set apart by God Himself for religious worship, continues as sacred today as when first hallowed by our Creator. (CS 66.2)

In like manner a tithe of our income is "holy unto the Lord." The New Testament does not reenact the law of the tithe, as it does not that of the Sabbath; for the validity of both is assumed, and their deep spiritual import explained.... While we as a people are seeking faithfully to give to God the time which He has reserved as His own, shall we not also render to Him that portion of our means which He claims?– *The Review and Herald, May 16, 1882.* (CS 66.3)

Possessions as Well as Income to Be Tithed

As did Abraham, they are to pay tithe of all they possess and all they receive. A faithful tithe is the Lord's portion. To withhold it is to rob God.

Every man should freely and willingly and gladly bring tithes and offerings into the storehouse of the Lord, because in so doing there is a blessing. There is no safety in withholding from God His own portion.– *Manuscript 159, 1899.* (**CS 66.4**)

For Every Dispensation

Such [referring to the experience of Abraham and Jacob in paying tithe] was the practice of patriarchs and prophets before the establishment of the Jews as a nation. But when Israel became a distinct people, the Lord gave them definite instruction upon this point: "All the tithe of the land, whether of the seed of the land, or of the fruit of the tree, is the Lord's: it is holy unto the Lord." This law was not to pass away with the ordinances and sacrificial offerings that typified Christ. As long as God has a people upon the earth, His claims upon them will be the same. (**CS 67.1**)

A tithe of all our increase is the Lord's. He has reserved it to Himself, to be employed for religious purposes. It is holy. Nothing less than this has He accepted in any dispensation. A neglect or postponement of this duty, will provoke the divine displeasure. If all professed Christians would faithfully bring their tithes to God, His treasury would be full.– *The Review and Herald, May 16, 1882.* (**CS 67.2**)

Designed as a Great Blessing

The special system of tithing was founded upon a principle which is as enduring as the law of God. This system of tithing was a blessing to the Jews, else God would not have given it them. So also will it be a blessing to those who carry it out to the end of time. Our heavenly Father did not originate the plan of systematic benevolence to enrich Himself, but to be a great blessing to man. He saw that this system of beneficence was just what man needed.– *Testimonies for the Church 3:404, 405.* (**CS 67.3**)

Nine Tenths Worth More Than the Ten

Many have pitied the lot of the Israel of God in being compelled to give systematically, besides making liberal offerings yearly. An all-wise God knew best what system of benevolence would be in accordance with His providence, and has given His people directions in regard to it. It has ever proved that nine tenths are worth more to them than ten tenths.– *Testimonies for the Church 3:546.* (**CS 68.1**)

A Marked Change From Jewish Days

Of all our income we should make the first appropriation to God. In the system of beneficence enjoined upon the Jews, they were required either to bring to the Lord the first fruits of all His gifts, whether in the increase of their flocks or herds, or in the produce of their fields, orchards, or vineyards, or they were to redeem it by substituting an equivalent. How changed the order of things in our day! The Lord's requirements and claims, if they receive any attention, are left till the last. Yet our work needs tenfold more means now than was needed by the Jews. (**CS 68.2**)

The great commission given to the apostles was to go throughout the world and preach the gospel. This shows the extension of the work, and the increased responsibility resting upon the followers of Christ in our day. If the law required tithes and offerings thousands of years ago, how much more essential are they now! If the rich and poor were to give a sum proportionate to their property in the Jewish economy, it is doubly essential now.– *Testimonies for the Church 4:474.* (**CS 68.3**)

Chapter 13
Founded Upon Eternal Principles

The tithing system reaches back beyond the days of Moses. Men were required to offer to God gifts for religious purposes before the definite system was given to Moses, even as far back as the days of Adam. In complying with God's requirements, they were to manifest in offerings their appreciation of His mercies and blessings to them. This was continued through successive generations, and was carried out by Abraham, who gave tithes to Melchizedek, the priest of the most high God. (CS 69.1)

The same principle existed in the days of Job. Jacob, when at Bethel, an exile and penniless wanderer, lay down at night, solitary and alone, with a rock for his pillow, and there promised the Lord, "Of all that Thou shalt give me I will surely give the tenth unto Thee." God does not compel men to give. All that they give must be voluntary. He will not have His treasury replenished with unwilling offerings.– *Testimonies for the Church 3:393*. (CS 69.2)

Paul's Recognition of the System

In his first letter to the church at Corinth, Paul gave the believers instruction regarding the general principles underlying the support of God's work in the earth. Writing of his apostolic labors in their behalf, he inquired: (CS 69.3)

"Who goeth a warfare any time at his own charges? who planteth a vineyard, and eateth not of the fruit thereof? or who feedeth a flock, and eateth not of the milk of the flock? Say I these things as a man? or saith not the law the same also? For it is written in the law of Moses, Thou shalt not muzzle the mouth of the ox that treadeth out the corn. Doth God take care for oxen? or saith He it altogether for our sakes? For our sakes, no doubt, this is written: that he that ploweth should plow in hope; and that he that thresheth in hope should be partaker of his hope. (CS 69.4)

"If we have sown unto you spiritual things," the apostle further inquired, "is it a great thing if we shall reap your carnal things? If others be partakers of this power over you, are not we rather? Nevertheless we have not used this power; but suffer all things, lest we should hinder the gospel of Christ. Do ye not know that they which minister about holy things live of the things of the temple? and they which wait at the altar are partakers with the altar? Even so hath the Lord ordained that they which preach the gospel should live of the gospel." *1 Corinthians 9:7-14*. (CS 70.1)

The apostle here referred to the Lord's plan for the maintenance of the priests who ministered in the temple. Those who were set apart to this holy office were supported by their brethren, to whom they ministered spiritual blessings. "Verily they that are of the sons of Levi, who receive the office of the priesthood, have a commandment to take tithes of the people according to the law." *Hebrews 7:5*. The tribe of Levi was chosen by the Lord for the sacred offices pertaining to the temple and the priesthood. Of the priest it was said, "The Lord thy God hath chosen him ... to stand to minister in the name of the Lord." *Deuteronomy 18:5*. One tenth of all the increase was claimed by the Lord as His own.... (CS 70.2)

It was to this plan for the support of the ministry that Paul referred when he said, "Even so hath the Lord ordained that they which preach the gospel should live of the gospel." And later, in writing to Timothy, the apostle said, "The laborer is worthy of his reward." *1 Timothy 5:18*. – *The Acts of the Apostles, 335, 336*. (CS 70.3)

God's Claim Upon Us

God has a claim on us and all that we have. His claim is paramount to every other. And in acknowledgment of this claim, He bids us render to Him a fixed proportion of all that He gives us. The tithe is this specified portion. By the Lord's direction it was consecrated to Him in the earliest times.... (**CS 71.1**)

When God delivered Israel from Egypt to be a special treasure unto Himself, He taught them to devote a tithe of their possessions to the service of the tabernacle. This was a special offering, for a special work. All that remained of their property was God's, and was to be used to His glory. But the tithe was set apart for the support of those who ministered in the sanctuary. It was to be given from the first fruits of all the increase, and, with gifts and offerings, it provided ample means for supporting the ministry of the gospel for that time. (**CS 71.2**)

God requires no less of us than He required of His people anciently. His gifts to us are not less, but greater, than they were to Israel of old. His service requires, and ever will require, means. The great missionary work for the salvation of souls is to be carried forward. In the tithe, with gifts and offerings, God has made ample provision for this work. He intends that the ministry of the gospel shall be fully sustained. He claims the tithe as His own, and it should ever be regarded as a sacred reserve, to be placed in His treasury for the benefit of His cause, for the advancement of His work, for sending His messengers into "regions beyond," even to the uttermost parts of the earth. (**CS 71.3**)

God has laid His hand upon all things, both man and his possessions; for all belong to Him. He says, I am the owner of the world; the universe is Mine, and I require you to consecrate to My service the first fruits of all that I, through My blessing, have caused to come into your hands. God's word declares, "Thou shalt not delay to offer the first of thy ripe fruits." "Honor the Lord with thy substance, and with the first fruits of all thine increase." This tribute He demands as a token of our loyalty to Him. (**CS 72.1**)

We belong to God; we are His sons and daughters,–His by creation, and His by the gift of His only-begotten Son for our redemption. "Ye are not your own; for ye are bought with a price: therefore glorify God in your body, and in your spirit, which are God's." The mind, the heart, the will, and the affections belong to God; the money that we handle is the Lord's. Every good that we receive and enjoy is the result of divine benevolence. God is the bountiful giver of all good, and He desires that there shall be an acknowledgment, on the part of the receiver, of these gifts that provide for every necessity of the body and the soul. God demands only His own. The primary portion is the Lord's, and must be used as His entrusted treasure. The heart that is divested of selfishness will awaken to a sense of God's goodness and love, and be moved to a hearty acknowledgment of His righteous requirements.– *The Review and Herald, December 8, 1896.* (**CS 72.2**)

Chapter 14
A Plan Beautiful in Simplicity

God's plan in the tithing system is beautiful in its simplicity and equality. All may take hold of it in faith and courage, for it is divine in its origin. In it are combined simplicity and utility, and it does not require depth of learning to understand and execute it. All may feel that they can act a part in carrying forward the precious work of salvation. Every man, woman, and youth may become a treasurer for the Lord, and may be an agent to meet the demands upon the treasury.... (CS 73.1)

Great objects are accomplished by this system. If one and all would accept it, each would be made a vigilant and faithful treasurer for God; and there would be no want of means with which to carry forward the great work of sounding the last message of warning to the world. The treasury will be full if all adopt this system, and the contributors will not be left the poorer. Through every investment made, they will become more wedded to the cause of present truth. They will be "laying up in store for themselves a good foundation against the time to come, that they may lay hold on eternal life."– *Testimonies for the Church 3:388, 389.* (CS 73.2)

For Rich and Poor

In the Bible system of tithes and offerings the amounts paid by different persons will of course vary greatly, since they are proportioned to the income. With the poor man, the tithe will be a comparatively small sum, and his gifts will be according to his ability. But it is not the greatness of the gift that makes the offering acceptable to God; it is the purpose of the heart, the spirit of gratitude and love that it expresses. Let not the poor feel that their gifts are so small as to be unworthy of notice. Let them give according to their ability, feeling that they are servants of God, and that He will accept their offering. (CS 73.3)

The one to whom God has entrusted a large capital will not, if he loves and fears God, find it a burden to meet the demands of an enlightened conscience according to the claims of God. The rich will be tempted to indulge in selfishness and avarice, and to withhold from the Lord His own. But he who is true to God will, when tempted, answer to Satan, "It is written," "Will a man rob God?" "What shall it profit a man, if he shall gain the whole world, and lose his own soul? Or what shall a man give in exchange for his soul?"– *The Review and Herald, May 16, 1893.* (CS 74.1)

Bound by Covenant Relations

In the great work of warning the world, those who have the truth in the heart, and are sanctified through the truth, will act their assigned part. They will be faithful in the payment of tithes and offerings. Every church member is bound by covenant relation with God to deny himself of every extravagant outlay of means. Let not the want of economy in the home life render us unable to act our part in strengthening the work already established, and in entering new territory.– *The Review and Herald, January 17, 1907.* (CS 74.2)

I entreat my brethren and sisters throughout the world to awaken to the responsibility that rests upon them to pay a faithful tithe.... Keep a faithful account with your Creator. Realize fully the importance of being just with Him who has divine foreknowledge. Let everyone search His heart diligently. Let him look up his accounts, and find out how he stands as related to God. (CS 74.3)

He who gave His only-begotten Son to die for you, has made a covenant with you. He gives you His blessings, and in return He requires you to bring Him your tithes and offerings. No one will ever dare to say that there was no way in which he could understand in regard to this matter. God's plan regarding tithes and offerings is definitely stated in the third chapter of Malachi. God calls upon His human agents to be true to the contract He has made with them. "Bring ye all the tithes into the storehouse," He says, "that there may be meat in Mine house."– *The Review and Herald, December 3, 1901.* (**CS 75.1**)

Not a Rigorous Law

Some will pronounce this one of the rigorous laws binding upon the Hebrews. But this was not a burden to the willing heart that loved God. It was only when their selfish natures were strengthened by withholding, that men lost sight of eternal considerations, and valued their earthly treasures above souls.– *Testimonies for the Church 3:396.* (**CS 75.2**)

No Burden Save to the Disobedient

Christians are required by the Scriptures to enter upon a plan of active benevolence which will keep in constant exercise an interest in the salvation of their fellow men. The moral law enjoined the observance of the Sabbath, which was not a burden, except when that law was transgressed and they were bound by the penalties involved in breaking it. The tithing system was no burden to those who did not depart from the plan. The system enjoined upon the Hebrews has not been repealed or relaxed by the One who originated it. Instead of being of no force now, it was to be more fully carried out and more extended, as salvation through Christ alone should be more fully brought to light in the Christian age.– *Testimonies for the Church 3:391, 392.* (**CS 75.3**)

A Meager Pittance

I speak of the tithing system; yet how meager it looks to my mind! How small the estimate! How vain the endeavor to measure with mathematical rules, time, money, and love against a love and sacrifice that is measureless and incomputable! Tithes for Christ! Oh, meager pittance, shameful recompense for that which cost so much!– *Testimonies for the Church 4:119.* (**CS 76.1**)

Chapter 15
A Question of Honesty

A close, selfish spirit seems to prevent men from giving to God His own. The Lord made a special covenant with men, that if they would regularly set apart the portion designated for the advancement of Christ's kingdom, the Lord would bless them abundantly, so that there would not be room to receive His gifts. But if men withhold that which belongs to God, the Lord plainly declares, "Ye are cursed with a curse." ... (CS 77.1)

Those who realize their dependence upon God, will feel that they must be honest with their fellow men, and, above all, they must be honest with God, from whom come all the blessings of life. The evasion of the positive commands of God concerning tithes and offerings, is registered in the books of heaven as robbery toward Him. (CS 77.2)

No man who is dishonest with God or with his fellow men can truly prosper. The most high God, the possessor of heaven and earth, says, "Thou shalt not have in thy bag divers weights, a great and a small. Thou shalt not have in thine house divers measures, a great and a small. But thou shalt have a perfect and just weight, a perfect and just measure shalt thou have: that thy days may be lengthened in the land which the Lord thy God giveth thee. For all that do such things, and all that do unrighteously, are an abomination unto the Lord thy God." Through the prophet Micah, the Lord again expresses His abhorrence of dishonesty: "Are there yet the treasures of wickedness in the house of the wicked, and the scant measure that is abominable? Shall I count them pure with the wicked balances? ... Therefore also will I make thee sick in smiting thee, in making thee desolate because of thy sins."– *The Review and Herald, December 17, 1889.* (CS 77.3)

Forfeiting Peace of Conscience

When we deal unjustly with our fellow men or with our God, we despise the authority of God, and ignore the fact that Christ has purchased us with His own life. The world is robbing God upon the wholesale plan. The more He imparts of wealth, the more thoroughly do men claim it as their own, to be used as they shall please. But shall the professed followers of Christ follow the customs of the world? Shall we forfeit peace of conscience, communion with God, and fellowship with our brethren, because we fail to devote to His cause the portion He has claimed as His own? (CS 78.1)

Let those who claim to be Christians, bear in mind that they are trading on the capital entrusted them of God, and that they are required to faithfully follow the directions of the Scriptures in regard to its disposal. If your heart is right with God, you will not embezzle your Lord's goods, and invest them in your own selfish enterprises.... (CS 78.2)

Brethren and sisters, if the Lord has blessed you with means, do not look upon it as your own. Regard it as yours in trust for God, and be true and honest in paying tithes and offerings. When a pledge is made by you, be sure that God expects you to pay as promptly as possible. Do not promise a portion to the Lord, and then appropriate it to your own use, lest your prayers become an abomination unto Him. It is the neglect of these plainly revealed duties that brings darkness upon the church.– *The Review and Herald, December 17, 1889.* (CS 78.3)

No Better Than Sacrilege

That which has been set apart according to the Scriptures as belonging to the Lord, constitutes the revenue of the gospel, and is no longer ours.

It is no better than sacrilege for a man to take from God's treasury in order to serve himself or to serve others in their secular business. Some have been at fault in diverting from the altar of God that which has been especially dedicated to Him. All should regard this matter in the right light. Let no one, when brought into a strait place, take money consecrated to religious purposes, and use it for his advantage, soothing his conscience by saying that he will repay it at some future time. Far better cut down the expenses to correspond with the income, to restrict the wants, and live within the means, than to use the Lord's money for secular purposes.– *Testimonies for the Church 9:246, 247.*

Chapter 16
Regularity and System

The directions given by the Holy Spirit through the apostle Paul in regard to gifts, present a principle that applies also to tithing: "Upon the first day of the week let every one of you lay by him in store, as God hath prospered him." Parents and children are here included. Not only the rich, but the poor, are addressed. "Every man according as he purposeth in his heart [through the candid consideration of God's prescribed plan], so let him give; not grudgingly, or of necessity: for God loveth a cheerful giver." The gifts are to be made in consideration of the great goodness of God to us. (CS 80.1)

And what more appropriate time could be chosen for setting aside the tithe and presenting our offerings to God? On the Sabbath we have thought upon His goodness. We have beheld His work in creation as an evidence of His power in redemption. Our hearts are filled with thankfulness for His great love. And now, before the toil of a week begins, we return to Him His own, and with it an offering to testify our gratitude. Thus our practice will be a weekly sermon, declaring that God is the possessor of all our property, and that He has made us stewards to use it to His glory. Every acknowledgment of our obligation to God will strengthen the sense of obligation. Gratitude deepens as we give it expression, and the joy it brings is life to soul and body.- *The Review and Herald, February 4, 1902.* (CS 80.2)

First the Tithe–Then Offerings

This matter of giving is not left to impulse. God has given us definite instruction in regard to it. He has specified tithes and offerings as the measure of our obligation. And He desires us to give regularly and systematically.... Let each regularly examine his income, which is all a blessing from God, and set apart the tithe as a separate fund, to be sacredly the Lord's. This fund should not in any case be devoted to any other use; it is to be devoted solely to support the ministry of the gospel. After the tithe is set apart, let gifts and offerings be apportioned, "as God hath prospered" you.- *The Review and Herald, May 9, 1893.* (CS 80.3)

Meeting God's Claims First

Not only does the Lord claim the tithe as His own, but He tells us how it should be reserved for Him. He says, "Honor the Lord with thy substance, and with the first fruits of all thine increase." This does not teach that we are to spend our means on ourselves, and bring to the Lord the remnant, even though it should be otherwise an honest tithe. Let God's portion be first set apart.- *The Review and Herald, February 4, 1902.* (CS 81.1)

We are not to consecrate to Him what remains of our income after all our real or imaginary wants are satisfied; but before any portion is consumed, we should set apart that which God has specified as His. (CS 81.2)

Many persons will meet all inferior demands and dues, and leave to God only the last gleanings, if there be any. If not, His cause must wait till a more convenient season.- *The Review and Herald, May 16, 1882.* (CS 81.3)

Chapter 17
The Message of Malachi

The reproof and warning and promise of the Lord are given in definite language in *Malachi 3:8:* "Will a man rob God? Yet ye have robbed Me. But ye say, Wherein have we robbed Thee?" The Lord answers, "In tithes and offerings. Ye are cursed with a curse: for ye have robbed Me, even this whole nation." **(CS 82.1)**

The Lord of heaven challenges those whom He has supplied with His bounties to prove Him. "Bring ye all the tithes into the storehouse, that there may be meat in Mine house, and prove Me now herewith, saith the Lord of hosts, if I will not open you the windows of heaven, and pour you out a blessing, that there shall not be room enough to receive it." **(CS 82.2)**

This message has lost none of its force. It is just as fresh in its importance as God's gifts are fresh and continual. There is no difficulty in understanding our duty in the light of this message, given through God's holy prophet. We are not left to stumble along in darkness and disobedience. The truth is plainly stated, and it can be clearly understood by all who wish to be honest in the sight of God. A tithe of all our income is the Lord's. He lays His hand upon that portion which He has specified that we shall return to Him, and says, I allow you to use My bounties after you have laid aside the tenth, and have come before Me with gifts and offerings. **(CS 82.3)**

The Lord calls for His tithe to be given in to His treasury. Strictly, honestly, and faithfully, let this portion be returned to Him. Besides this, He calls for your gifts and offerings. No one is compelled to present his tithe or his gifts and offerings to the Lord. But just as surely as God's word is given to us, just so surely will He require His own with usury at the hand of every human being. If men are unfaithful in rendering to God His own, if they disregard God's charge to His stewards, they will not long have the blessing of that which the Lord has entrusted to them.... **(CS 82.4)**

The Lord has given to every man his work. His servants are to act in partnership with Him. If they choose, men may refuse to connect themselves with their Maker; they may refuse to give themselves to His service, and trade upon His entrusted goods; they may fail to exercise frugality and self-denial, and may forget that the Lord requires a return of what He has given them. All such are unfaithful stewards. **(CS 83.1)**

A faithful steward will do all he possibly can in the service of God; the one object before him will be the great need of the world. He will realize that the message of truth is to be given, not only in his own neighborhood, but in the regions beyond. When men cherish this spirit, the love of the truth and the sanctification they will receive through the truth, will banish avarice, overreaching, and every species of dishonesty.– *The Review and Herald Supplement, December 1, 1896.* **(CS 83.2)**

A Daring Repudiation

"I understand that you are also proclaiming that we should not pay tithe. My brother, take off thy shoes from off thy feet; for the place whereon you are standing is holy ground. The Lord has spoken in regard to paying tithes. He has said, 'Bring ye all the tithes into the storehouse, that there may be meat in Mine house.' ... **(CS 83.3)**

"Very recently I have had direct light from the Lord upon this question, that many Seventh-day Adventists were robbing God in tithes and offerings, and it was plainly revealed to me that Malachi has stated the case as it really is. Then how dare any man even think in his heart that a suggestion to withhold tithes and offerings is from the Lord? Where, my brother, have you stepped out of the path? O get your feet back in the straight path again."– *Testimonies to Ministers and Gospel Workers, 60.* (**CS 83.4**)

Robbing God

To have your name on the church book does not make you a Christian. You are to bring your gifts to the altar of sacrifice, cooperating with God to the utmost of your ability, that through you He may reveal the beauty of His truth. Withhold nothing from the Saviour. All is His. You would have nothing to give did He not first give to you. (**CS 84.1**)

Selfishness has come in, and has appropriated to itself that which belongs to God. This is covetousness, which is idolatry. Men monopolize that which God has lent them, as though it were their own property, to do with as they please. When their power to grasp wealth is gratified, they think that their possessions make them of value in the sight of God. This is a snare, a deception of Satan. What does outward pomp and show avail? What do men and women gain by pride and self-indulgence? "What shall it profit a man, if he shall gain the whole world, and lose his own soul? Or what shall a man give in exchange for his soul?" Worldly treasure is fleeting. Only through Christ can we obtain eternal riches. The wealth that He gives is beyond all computation. Having found God, you are supremely rich in the contemplation of His treasure. "Eye hath not seen, nor ear heard, neither have entered into the heart of man, the things which God hath prepared for them that love Him." (**CS 84.2**)

Ask yourself the question, What am I doing with the Lord's talents? Are you placing yourselves where the words are applicable to you, "Ye are cursed with a curse: for ye have robbed Me, even this whole nation"? (**CS 85.1**)

We are living in a time of solemn privilege and sacred trust, a time in which our destiny is being decided for life or for death. Let us come to our senses. You who claim to be children of God, bring your tithes to His treasury. Make your offerings willingly and abundantly, according as God has prospered you. Remember that the Lord has entrusted you with talents, upon which you

are to trade diligently for Him. Remember also that the faithful servant takes no credit to himself. All the praise and glory is given to the Lord: Thou deliveredst unto me thy pound. No gain could have been made unless there had first been a deposit. There could have been no interest without the principal. The capital was advanced by the Lord. Success in trading comes from Him, and to Him belongs the glory. (**CS 85.2**)

Oh, if all who have a knowledge of the truth would only obey the teaching of this truth! Why is it that men, standing on the very threshold of the eternal world, are so blinded? There is not a dearth of means, generally speaking, among Seventh-day Adventists. But many Seventh-day Adventists fail to realize the responsibility which rests upon them to cooperate with God and Christ for the saving of souls. They do not show forth to the world the great interest God has in sinners. They do not make the most of the opportunities granted them. The leprosy of selfishness has taken hold of the church. The Lord Jesus Christ will heal the church of this terrible disease if she will be healed. The remedy is found in the fifty-eighth chapter of Isaiah.– *The Review and Herald, December 10, 1901.* (**CS 85.3**)

A Serious Matter

It is a serious thing to embezzle the Lord's goods, to practice robbery toward God; for in so doing the perceptions become perverted and the heart hardened. How barren is the religious experience, how clouded is the understanding, of one who loves not God with pure, unselfish love, and who fails, therefore, to love his neighbor as himself.... (**CS 86.1**)

The last great day will reveal to them and to the whole universe what good might have been done, had they not followed their selfish inclinations, and thus robbed God in tithes and offerings. They might have placed their treasure in the bank of heaven, and preserved it in bags that wax not old; but instead of doing this, they expended it upon themselves and their children, and seemed to feel afraid that the Lord would get any of their money or their influence, and thus they met with eternal loss. Let them contemplate the consequence of withholding from God. The slothful servant, who puts not out his Lord's money to usury, loses an eternal inheritance in the kingdom of glory.– *The Review and Herald, January 22, 1895.* (**CS 86.2**)

To defraud God is the greatest crime of which man can be guilty; and yet this sin is deep and widespread.– *The Review and Herald, October 13, 1896.* (**CS 86.3**)

Every Dollar Charged

Will you withhold from God His own? Will you divert from the treasury the portion of means which the Lord claims as His? If so, you are robbing God, and every dollar is charged against you in the books of heaven.– *The Review and Herald, December 23, 1890.* (**CS 86.4**)

Why the Blessing is Withheld from Some

Hasten, my brethren and sisters, to bring to God a faithful tithe, and to bring Him also a willing thank offering. There are many who will not be blessed till they make restitution of the tithe which they have withheld. God is waiting for you to redeem the past. The hand of the holy law is laid upon every soul who enjoys God's benefits. Let those who have kept back their tithe make an accurate reckoning, and bring to the Lord that of which they have robbed His work. Make restitution, and bring the Lord peace offerings. "Let him take hold of My strength, that he may make peace with Me; and he shall make peace with Me." If you acknowledge that you have done wrong in misappropriating His goods, and freely and fully repent, He will forgive your transgression.– *The Review and Herald, December 10, 1901.* (**CS 87.1**)

Darkness Brought Into the Churches

Some fail to educate the people to do their whole duty. They preach that part of our faith which will not create opposition and displease their hearers; but they do not declare the whole truth.

The people enjoy their preaching; but there is a lack of spirituality, because the claims of God are not met. His people do not give Him in tithes and offerings that which is His own. This robbery of God, which is practiced by both rich and poor, brings darkness into the churches; and the minister who labors with them, and who does not show them the plainly revealed will of God, is brought under condemnation with the people, because he neglects his duty.– *The Review and Herald, April 8, 1884.* (**CS 87.2**)

Selfish Withholding Recorded

God reads the covetous thought in every heart that purposes to withhold from Him. Those who are selfishly neglectful in paying their tithes, and bringing their gifts and offerings to the treasury, God sees. The Lord Jehovah understands it all. As a book of remembrance is written before Him of them that fear the Lord, and that think upon His name, so there is a record kept of all who are appropriating to themselves the gifts which God entrusted to them to use for the salvation of souls.– *The Review and Herald, May 16, 1893.* (**CS 87.3**)

Great Loss to the Unfaithful Steward

The promise to those who honor God with their substance still stands upon record on the sacred page. If the Lord's people had faithfully obeyed His directions, the promise would have been fulfilled to them. But when men disregard the claims of God, plainly set before them, the Lord permits them to follow their own way, and reap the fruit of their doings. Whoever appropriates to his own use the portion that God has reserved, is proving himself an unfaithful steward. He will lose not only that which he has withheld from God, but also that which was committed to him as his own.– *The Review and Herald, February 4, 1902.* (**CS 88.1**)

Chapter 18
Let Us Prove the Lord

"Bring ye all the tithes into the storehouse, that there may be meat in Mine house, and prove Me now herewith, saith the Lord of hosts, if I will not open you the windows of heaven, and pour you out a blessing, that there shall not be room enough to receive it." Shall we obey God, and bring in all our tithes and offerings, that there may be meat to supply the demands of souls hungering for the bread of life? God invites you to prove Him now, as the old year draws to its close, and let the new year find us with God's treasuries replenished.... (CS 89.1)

He tells us that He will open the windows of heaven, and pour us out a blessing, that there shall not be room enough to receive it. He pledges His word, "I will rebuke the devourer for your sakes, and he shall not destroy the fruits of your ground; neither shall your vine cast her fruit before the time in the field, saith the Lord of hosts." Thus His word is our assurance that He will so bless us that we shall have still larger tithes and offerings to bestow. "Return unto Me, and I will return unto you, saith the Lord of hosts." (CS 89.2)

Brethren, will you comply with the conditions? Will you offer willingly, gladly, and abundantly? The foreign missions call for means from America. Shall they call in vain? Home missions are in great need of money; they have been established in faith, in different parts of the field. Shall they be left to languish and die? Shall we not arouse? God help His people to do their very best. (CS 89.3)

No Risk to Run

O, what gracious, full, complete assurances are given us, if we will only do what God requires us to do! Take hold of this matter as though you believed the Lord would do just as He has promised. Let us venture something upon God's word. In their zeal to be rich, many run great risks; eternal considerations are overlooked, and noble principles are sacrificed; yet they may lose all in the game. But in complying with the heavenly invitations we have no such risk to run. We must take God at His word, and in simplicity of faith walk out upon the promise, and give to the Lord His own.– *The Review and Herald, December 18, 1888.* (CS 90.1)

A Reason for Adversity

Many who profess to be Christians provide abundantly for themselves, supplying all their imaginary wants, while they give no heed to the wants of the Lord's cause. They have thought it gain to rob God by retaining all, or a selfish proportion, of His gifts as their own. But they meet with loss instead of gain. Their course results in the withdrawal of mercies and blessings. By their selfish, avaricious spirit, men have lost much. If they had fully and freely acknowledged God's requirements and met His claims, His blessing would have been manifest in increasing the productions of the earth. The harvests would have been greater. The wants of all would have been abundantly supplied. The more we give, the more we shall receive.– *The Review and Herald, December 8, 1896.* (CS 90.2)

Promises With God's Commands

Duty is duty, and should be performed for its own sake. But the Lord has compassion upon us in our fallen condition, and accompanies His commands with promises. He calls upon His people to prove Him, declaring that He will reward obedience with the richest blessings.... He encourages us to give to Him, declaring that the returns He makes to us will be proportionate to our gifts to Him. "He which soweth bountifully shall reap also bountifully." God is not unrighteous to forget your work and your labor of love. (**CS 90.3**)

How tender, how true God is with us! He has given us in Christ the richest blessings. Through Him He has put His signature upon the contract He has made with us.– *The Review and Herald, December 3, 1901.* (**CS 91.1**)

Chapter 19

Appropriating God's Reserve Funds

The Lord has of late given me special testimonies to bear in regard to the warnings and promises He has given through Malachi. After I had spoken with great plainness to the church in Sydney [Australia], and was putting on my wraps in the dressing room, the question was asked me, "Sister White, do you think my father should pay tithes? He has met with great loss recently, and he says that as soon as he cancels his debt, he will pay tithes." I asked, "How do you regard our obligations to God, who gives us life and breath, and all the blessings we enjoy? Would you have our indebtedness to God continually increasing? Would you rob Him of the portion which He has never given us to use for any other purpose than to advance His work, to sustain His servants in the ministry? For the answer to your question the prophet Malachi asks, 'Will a man rob God? ... But ye say, Wherein have we robbed Thee?'–as though there was a willingness to misunderstand this subject. The answer comes: 'In tithes and offerings. Ye are cursed with a curse: for ye have robbed Me, even this whole nation.' After such a statement, would I dare say to you, You need not pay tithes as long as you are in debt? Shall I tell you to be sure to pay all you owe any man, although you rob God to do so?" (CS 92.1)

If all would take the Scripture just as it reads, and open their hearts to understand the word of the Lord, they would not say, "I cannot see the tithing question. I cannot see that in my circumstances I should pay tithes." "Will a man rob God?" The consequence of doing so is plainly stated, and I would not risk the consequence. All who will take a wholehearted, decided position to obey God; who will not take the Lord's reserved funds–His own money–to settle their debts; who will render to the Lord the portion that He claims as His own, will receive the blessing of God which is promised to all who

obey Him.– *Special Testimony to Battle Creek Church, 8-10* [August, 1896]. (CS 92.2)

The True Reason for Withholding

I saw that some have excused themselves from aiding the cause of God because they were in debt. Had they closely examined their own hearts, they would have discovered that selfishness was the true reason why they brought no freewill offering to God. Some will always remain in debt. Because of their covetousness, the prospering hand of God will not be with them to bless their undertakings. They love this world better than they love the truth. They are not being fitted up and made ready for the kingdom of God.– *Testimonies for the Church 1:225.* (CS 93.1)

Withheld Tithes Because of Lack of Confidence

The tithe is sacred, reserved by God for Himself. It is to be brought into His treasury to be used to sustain the gospel laborers in their work. For a long time the Lord has been robbed because there are those who do not realize that the tithe is God's reserved portion. (CS 93.2)

Some have been dissatisfied, and have said, "I will not longer pay my tithe; for I have no confidence in the way things are managed at the heart of the work." But will you rob God because you think the management of the work is not right? Make your complaint, plainly and openly, in the right spirit, to the proper ones. Send in your petitions for things to be adjusted and set in order; but do not withdraw from the work of God, and prove unfaithful, because others are not doing right.– *Testimonies for the Church 9:249.* (CS 93.3)

The First Duty to God

Some have felt under sacred obligations to their children. They must give each a portion, but feel themselves unable to raise means to aid the cause of God. They make the excuse that they have a duty to their children. This may be right, but their first duty is to God.... Let no one throw in his claims and lead you to rob God. Let not your children steal your offering from God's altar for their own benefit.– *Testimonies for the Church 1:220.* (**CS 94.1**)

Chapter 20

The Response of an Aroused Conscience

A decided advancement in spirituality, piety, charity, and activity, has been made as the result of the special meetings in the-church. Discourses were preached on the sin of robbing God in tithes and offerings.... (CS 95.1)

Many confessed that they had not paid tithes for years; and we know that God cannot bless those who are robbing Him, and that the church must suffer in consequence of the sins of its individual members. There are a large number of names on our church books; and if all would be prompt in paying an honest tithe to the Lord, which is His portion, the treasury would not lack for means.... (CS 95.2)

As the sin of robbing God was presented, the people received clearer views of their duty and privilege in this matter. One brother said that for two years he had not paid his tithes, and he was in despair; but as he confessed his sin, he began to gather hope. "What shall I do?" he asked. (CS 95.3)

I said, "Give your note to the treasurer of the church; that will be businesslike." (CS 95.4)

He thought that was a rather strange request; but he sat down, and began to write, "For value received, I promise to pay–" He looked up, as if to say, Is that the proper form in which to write out a note to the Lord? (CS 95.5)

"Yes," he continued, "for value received. Have I not been receiving the blessings of God day after day? Have not the angels guarded me? Has not the Lord blessed me with all spiritual and temporal blessings? For value received, I promise to pay the sum of $571.50 to the church treasurer." After doing all he could do on his part, he was a happy man. In a few days he took up his note, and paid his tithe into the treasury. He had also made a Christmas donation of $125. (CS 95.6)

Another brother gave a note for $1,000, expecting to meet it in a few weeks; and another gave a note for $300.– *The Review and Herald, February 19, 1889.* (CS 96.1)

The Back Tithe is God's Property

Many have long neglected to deal honestly with their Maker. Failing to lay aside the tithe weekly, they have let it accumulate, until it amounts to a large sum, and now they are very reluctant to make the matter right. This back tithe they keep, using it as their own. But it is God's property, which they have refused to put into His treasury.– *The Review and Herald, December 23, 1890.* (CS 96.2)

The Careless and Indifferent to Redeem Their Honor

Let those who have become careless and indifferent, and are withholding their tithes and offerings, remember that they are blocking the way, so that the truth cannot go forth to the regions beyond. I am bidden to call upon the people of God to redeem their honor by rendering to God a faithful tithe.– *Manuscript 44, 1905.* (CS 96.3)

Payment by Note

Friday morning I spoke on the subject of tithing. This subject has not been presented to the churches as it should have been, and the neglect, together with financial depression, has caused a marked falling off in the tithes the past year. At this conference the subject has been carefully canvassed in meeting after meeting.... (CS 96.4)

One brother, a noble-looking man, a delegate from Tasmania, came to me and said, "I am glad I heard you speak today upon tithing. I did not know it was so important a matter. I dare not neglect it longer." He is now figuring up the amount of his tithe for the last twenty years, and says he shall pay it all as fast as he is able, for he cannot have robbery of God registered in the books of heaven meet him in the judgment. **(CS 96.5)**

One sister belonging to the Melbourne church, has brought in eleven pounds [$54] back tithe which she had not understood that it devolved on her to pay. As they have received the light, many have made confession in regard to their indebtedness to God, and expressed their determination to meet this debt.... I proposed that they place in the treasury their note promising to pay the full amount of an honest tithe as soon as they could obtain the money to do so. Many heads bowed assent, and I am confident that next year we shall not, as now, have an empty treasury.– *Manuscript 4, 1893.* **(CS 97.1)**

Pale at Thought of Withheld Tithe

Many, many have lost the spirit of self-denial and sacrifice. They have been burying their money in temporal possessions. There are men whom God has blessed, whom He is testing to see what response they will make to His benefits. They have withheld their tithes and offerings until their debt to the Lord God of hosts has become so great that they grow pale at the thought of rendering to the Lord His own,–a just tithe. Make haste, brethren, you have now the opportunity to be honest with God; delay not.– *General Conference Daily Bulletin, February 28, 1893.* **(CS 97.2)**

Facing the New Year

What of your stewardship? Have you during the past year robbed God in tithes and offerings? Look at your well-filled barns, at your cellars stored with the good things the Lord has given you, and ask yourselves whether you have returned to the Giver that which belongs to Him. If you have robbed the Lord, make restitution. As far as possible, make the past right, and then ask the Saviour to pardon you. Will you not return to the Lord His own, before this year, with its burden of record, has passed into eternity?– *The Review and Herald, December 23, 1902.* **(CS 97.3)**

Restitution With Contrition

Wherever there has been any neglect on your part to give back to the Lord His own, repent with contrition of soul, and make restitution, lest His curse rest upon you.... When you have done what you can on your part, withholding nothing that belongs to your Maker, you may ask Him to provide means to send the message of truth to the world.– *The Review and Herald, January 20, 1885.* **(CS 98.1)**

Jacob's Fidelity

Jacob made his vow [*Genesis 28:20-22*] while refreshed by the dews of grace, and invigorated by the presence and assurance of God. After the divine glory had passed away, he had temptations, like men in our time; but he was faithful to his vow, and would not harbor thoughts as to the possibility of being released from the pledge which he had made. He might have reasoned much as men do now, that this revelation was only a dream, that he was unduly excited when he made his vow, and that therefore it need not be kept; but he did not. **(CS 98.2)**

Long years intervened before Jacob dared to return to his own country; but when he did, he faithfully discharged his debt to his Master. He had become a wealthy man, and a very large amount of property passed from his possessions to the treasury of the Lord. **(CS 98.3)**

Many in our day fail where Jacob made a success. Those to whom God has given the greatest amount have the strongest inclination to retain what they have, because they must give a sum proportionate to their property. Jacob gave the tenth of all that he had, and then reckoned the use of the tenth, and gave the Lord the benefit of that which he had used for his own interest during the time he was in a heathen land, and could not pay his vow. This was a large amount, but he did not hesitate; that which he had vowed to God he did not regard as his, but as the Lord's. **(CS 99.1)**

According to the amount bestowed will be the amount required. The larger the capital entrusted, the more valuable is the gift which God requires to be returned to Him. If a

Christian has ten or twenty thousand dollars, God's claims are imperative upon him, not only to give his proportion according to the tithing system, but to present his sin offerings and thank offerings to God.– *Testimonies for the Church 4:466, 467*. (**CS 99.2**)

Prayer Not a Substitute for Tithing

Prayer is not intended to work any change in God; it brings us into harmony with God. It does not take the place of duty. Prayer offered ever so often and ever so earnestly will never be accepted by God in the place of our tithe. Prayer will not pay our debts to God.– *Messages to Young People, 248*. (**CS 99.3**)

Before It Is Too Late

It will not be long before probation will close. If you do not now serve the Lord with fidelity, how will you meet the record of your unfaithful dealing? Not long hence, a call will be made for a settlement of accounts, and you will be asked, "How much owest thou unto my Lord?" If you have refused to deal honestly with God, I beseech you to think of your deficiency, and if possible to make restitution. If this cannot be done, in humble penitence pray that God for Christ's sake will pardon your great debt. Begin now to act like Christians. Make no excuse for failing to give the Lord His own. Now, while mercy's sweet voice is still heard, while it is not yet too late for wrongs to be righted, while it is called today, if ye will hear His voice, harden not your hearts.– *The Review and Herald Supplement, December 1, 1896*. (**CS 99.4**)

Chapter 21
The Use of the Tithe

God has given special direction as to the use of the tithe. He does not design that His work shall be crippled for want of means. That there may be no haphazard work and no error, He has made our duty on these points very plain. The portion that God has reserved for Himself is not to be diverted to any other purpose than that which He has specified. Let none feel at liberty to retain their tithe, to use according to their own judgment. They are not to use it for themselves in an emergency, nor to apply it as they see fit, even in what they may regard as the Lord's work. (CS 101.1)

The minister should, by precept and example, teach the people to regard the tithe as sacred. He should not feel that he can retain and apply it according to his own judgment, because he is a minister. It is not his. He is not at liberty to devote to himself whatever he thinks is his due. He should not give his influence to any plans for diverting from their legitimate use the tithes and offerings dedicated to God. They are to be placed in His treasury and held sacred for His service as He has appointed. (CS 101.2)

God desires all His stewards to be exact in following divine arrangements. They are not to offset the Lord's plans by performing some deed of charity, or giving some gift or some offering, when or how they, the human agents, shall see fit. It is a very poor policy for men to seek to improve on God's plan, and invent a makeshift, averaging up their good impulses on this and that occasion, and offsetting them against God's requirements. God calls upon all to give their influence to His own arrangement. He has made His plan known; and all who would cooperate with Him must carry out this plan, instead of daring to attempt an improvement on it. (CS 101.3)

The Lord instructed Moses, for Israel, "Thou shalt command the children of Israel, that they bring thee pure oil olive beaten for the light, to cause the lamp to burn always." *Exodus 27:20.* This was to be a continual offering that the house of God might be properly supplied with that which was necessary for His service. His people today are to remember that the house of worship is the Lord's property, and that it is to be scrupulously cared for. But the funds for this work are not to come from the tithe. (CS 102.1)

A very plain, definite message has been given to me for our people. I am bidden to tell them that they are making a mistake in applying the tithe to various objects which, though good in themselves, are not the object to which the Lord has said that the tithe should be applied. Those who make this use of the tithe are departing from the Lord's arrangement. God will judge for these things. (CS 102.2)

Other Lines to Be Sustained, but Not From Tithes

One reasons that the tithe may be applied to school purposes. Still others reason that canvassers and colporteurs should be supported from the tithe. But a great mistake is made when the tithe is drawn from the object for which it is to be used–the support of the ministers.... (CS 102.3)

The tithe is the Lord's, and those who meddle with it will be punished with the loss of their heavenly treasure unless they repent. Let the work no longer be hedged up because the tithe has been diverted into various channels other than the one to which the Lord has said it should go. Provision is to be made for these other lines of work. They are to be sustained, but not from the tithe. God has not changed; the tithe is still to be used for the support of the ministry.– *Testimonies for the Church 9:247-250.*

(**CS 102.4**)

Includes Bible Teachers

Our conferences look to the schools for educated and well-trained laborers, and they should give the schools a most hearty and intelligent support. Light has been plainly given that those who minister in our schools, teaching the word of God, explaining the Scriptures, educating the students in the things of God, should be supported by the tithe money. This instruction was given long ago, and more recently it has been repeated again and again.– *Testimonies for the Church 6:215.* (**CS 103.1**)

Not a Poor Fund

The tithe is set apart for a special use. It is not to be regarded as a poor fund. It is to be especially devoted to the support of those who are bearing God's message to the world; and it should not be diverted from this purpose.– *The Review and Herald Supplement, December 1, 1896.* (**CS 103.2**)

Not for Church Expense

I was shown that it is wrong to use the tithe for defraying the incidental expenses of the church. In this there has been a departure from correct methods. It would be far better to dress less expensively, cut down your indulgences, practice self-denial, and meet these outgoings. By so doing you will have a clear conscience. But you are robbing God every time that you put your hands into the treasury for funds to meet the running expenses of the church.– *Special Testimony to Battle Creek Church, 6, 7* [August, 1896]. (**CS 103.3**)

Chapter 22
Education by Ministers and Church Officers

Those who go forth as ministers have a solemn responsibility devolving upon them which is strangely neglected. Some enjoy preaching, but they do not give personal labor to the churches. There is great need of instruction concerning the obligations and duties to God, especially in regard to paying an honest tithe. Our ministers would feel sadly aggrieved if they were not promptly paid for their labor; but will they consider that there must be meat in the treasure house of God wherewith to sustain the laborers? If they fail to do their whole duty in educating the people to be faithful in paying to God His own, there will be a shortage of means in the treasury to carry forward the Lord's work. (CS 104.1)

The overseer of the flock of God should faithfully discharge his duty. If he takes the position that because this is not pleasant to him, he will leave it for someone else to do, he is not a faithful worker. Let him read in Malachi the words of the Lord charging the people with robbery toward God in withholding the tithes. The mighty God declares, "Ye are cursed with a curse." *Malachi 3:9.* When the one who ministers in word and doctrine sees the people pursuing a course that will bring this curse upon them, how can he neglect his duty to give them instruction and warning? Every church member should be taught to be faithful in paying an honest tithe.– *Testimonies for the Church 9:250, 251.* (CS 104.2)

Instructing New Converts

A laborer should never leave some portion of the work undone because it is not agreeable to perform, thinking that the minister coming next will do it for him. When this is the case, if a second minister follows the first, and presents the claims that God has upon His people, some draw back, saying, "The minister who brought us the truth did not mention these things." And they become offended because of the word. Some refuse to accept the tithing system; they turn away, and no longer walk with those who believe and love the truth. When other lines are opened before them, they answer, "It was not so taught us," and they hesitate to move forward. How much better it would have been if the first messenger of truth had faithfully and thoroughly educated these converts in regard to all essential matters, even if fewer had been added to the church under his labors. God would be better pleased to have six thoroughly converted to the truth than to have sixty make a profession and yet not be truly converted. (CS 104.3)

It is part of the minister's work to teach those who accept the truth through his efforts, to bring the tithe to the storehouse, as an acknowledgment of their dependence upon God. The new converts should be fully enlightened as to their duty to return to the Lord His own. The command to pay tithe is so plain that there is no semblance of excuse for disregarding it. He who neglects to give instruction on this point, leaves undone a most important part of his work. (CS 105.1)

Ministers must also impress upon the people the importance of bearing other burdens in connection with the work of God. No one is exempt from the work of benevolence. The people must be taught that every department of the cause of God should enlist their support and engage their interest. The great missionary field is open before us, and this subject must be agitated, agitated, again and again. The people must be made to understand that it is not the hearers, but the doers of the word, who will gain eternal life. And they are to be taught also that those who become partakers of the grace of Christ are not only to communicate of their substance for the advancement of the truth, but are to give themselves to God without reserve.– *Gospel Workers, 369-371.* (CS 105.2)

The Pastor's Duty

Let the church appoint pastors or elders who are devoted to the Lord Jesus, and let these men see that officers are chosen who will attend faithfully to the work of gathering in the tithe. If the pastors show that they are not fitted for their charge, if they fail to set before the church the importance of returning to God His own, if they do not see to it that the officers under them are faithful, and that the tithe is brought in, they are in peril. They are neglecting a matter which involves a blessing or a curse to the church. They should be relieved of their responsibility, and other men should be tested and tried. (CS 106.1)

The Lord's messengers should see that His requirements are faithfully discharged by the members of the churches. God says that there should be meat in His house, and if the money in the treasury is tampered with, if it is regarded as right for individuals to make what use they please of the tithe, the Lord cannot bless. He cannot sustain those who think that they can do as they please with that which is His.– *The Review and Herald Supplement, December 1, 1896.* (CS 106.2)

The Responsibility of Church Officers

It is the duty of the elders and officers of the church to instruct the people on this important matter, and to set things in order. As laborers together with God, the officers of the church should be sound upon this plainly revealed question. The ministers themselves should be strict to carry out to the letter the injunctions of God's word. Those who hold positions of trust in the church should not be negligent, but they should see that the members are faithful in performing this duty.... Let the elders and officers of the church follow the direction of the Sacred Word, and urge upon their members the necessity of faithfulness in the payment of pledges, tithes, and offerings.– *The Review and Herald, December 17, 1889.* (CS 106.3)

Teaching the Poor to be Liberal

Frequently those who receive the truth are among the poor of this world; but they should not make this an excuse for neglecting those duties which devolve upon them in view of the precious light they have received. They should not allow poverty to prevent them from laying up a treasure in heaven. The blessings within reach of the rich are also within their reach. If they are faithful in using what little they do possess, their treasure in heaven will increase according to their fidelity. It is the motive with which they work, not the amount they do, that makes their offering valuable in the sight of Heaven.– *Gospel Workers, 222.* (CS 107.1)

For Further Study

Tithes and Offerings in Israel, *Patriarchs and Prophets, 525-529*

Tithing Reaches Back Beyond Days of Moses, *Testimonies for the Church 3:393*

As Enduring as the Law of God, *Testimonies for the Church 3:404*

Like the Sabbath, the Tithe Is Sacred, *Testimonies for the Church 3:395, 396*

A Distinct Arrangement Made by Jesus Christ Himself, *Testimonies for the Church 6:384*

Not Repealed or Relaxed, *Testimonies for the Church 3:392*

Left to the Conscience and Benevolence of Men, *Testimonies for the Church 3:394*

An Acknowledgment of the Claims of Creation and Redemption, *Testimonies for the Church 6:479-481*

God Lays His Hand Upon Our Possessions–"Consecrate to Me the Tithes," *Testimonies for the Church 9:245*; A Matter of Simple Honesty, *Education, 138, 139*

The Spirit of Covetousness Abhorrent to God, *The Acts of the Apostles, 339*

Liberality Not a Natural Grace, but One to Be Cultivated, *Testimonies for the Church 5:271, 272*

The Message in Malachi, *Testimonies for the Church 6:384-390* 6T 384-390

None to Rob God by Following Inclinations

of the Selfish Heart, *Testimonies for the Church* 5:481

By Using the Tithe for Secular Debts, Man Becomes Double Debtor, *Testimonies for the Church 6:390, 391; Testimonies for the Church 1:220*

When We Are in Harmony With God, None Will Be Preferred Before Him, *Testimonies for the Church 6:103, 104*

The Message Greatly Hindered by Withheld Tithes, *Testimonies for the Church 9:52*

What Would Result From Faithfulness in Tithe Paying, *Testimonies for the Church 3:389; Testimonies for the Church 6:385; Testimonies for the Church 4:474-476; The Acts of the Apostles, 338*

An Abundance to Carry Forward God's Work, *Testimonies for the Church 5:150*

A Test as to Whether Worthy of Eternal Life, *Testimonies for the Church 3:408*

Adversity Because of Selfish Withholding, *Testimonies for the Church 1:221, Testimonies for the Church 4:484, 620; Testimonies for the Church 2:661, 662; Testimonies for the Church 5:151, 152*

No Excuse for Ignorance or Neglect, *Testimonies for the Church 6:387; Testimonies to Ministers and Gospel Workers, 305, 306*

Regarded as Robbery in Book of Heaven, *Testimonies for the Church 3:394*

Not Returning to God, but Withholding, Tends to Poverty, *Testimonies for the Church 6:449*

When Tithe Is Paid the Remainder Is Blessed, *Testimonies for the Church 4:477*

Nine Tenths Worth More Than Ten Tenths, *Testimonies for the Church 3:404*

Promises of Prosperity to the Faithful, *Testimonies for the Church 5:267, 268*

Claiming the Promise in Malachi, *Testimonies to Ministers and Gospel Workers, 308*

Bring Withheld Tithes With Confession, *Testimonies for the Church 9:51, 52*

Appeal for Tithes to Be Brought in Before End of Year, *Testimonies to Ministers and Gospel Workers, 305-307*

Repentance and Restitution Called For, *Testimonies for the Church 3:394, 395*

The Tithe Exclusively for the Ministry, *Testimonies for the Church 9:249, 250; Gospel Workers, 226*

Bible Teachers to Be Paid From Tithe, *Testimonies for the Church 6:134, 135*

Duty of Conference Presidents and Ministry to Educate, *Testimonies for the Church 5:374, 375; Testimonies for the Church 9:250; Testimonies to Ministers and Gospel Workers, 305-307*

Teach by Precept and Example, *Testimonies for the Church 9:246*

Those Who Fail to Teach Not Held Guiltless, *Testimonies for the Church 3:296, 270; Testimonies to Ministers and Gospel Workers, 307*

The Poor to Be Taught Systematic Benevolence, *Gospel Workers, 222, 223*

In Case of Doubt Exceed Rather Than Fall Short of Duty's Requirement, *Testimonies for the Church 4:485*

Section 4

To Every Man According to His Ability

Chapter 23
The Principles of Stewardship

Are we as individuals searching the word of God carefully and prayerfully, lest we shall depart from its precepts and requirements? The Lord will not look upon us with pleasure if we withhold anything, small or great, that should be returned to Him. If we desire to spend money to gratify our own inclinations, let us think of the good we might do with that money. Let us lay aside for the Master small and large sums, that the work may be built up in new places. If we spend selfishly the money so much needed, the Lord does not, cannot, bless us with His commendation. (CS 111.1)

As stewards of the grace of God, we are handling the Lord's money. It means much, very much to us to be strengthened by His rich grace day by day, to be enabled to understand His will, to be found faithful in that which is least as well as in that which is great. When this is our experience, the service of Christ will be a reality to us. God demands this of us, and before angels and men we should reveal our gratitude for what He has done for us. God's benevolence to us we should reflect back in praise and deeds of mercy.... (CS 111.2)

Do all church members realize that all they have is given them to be used and improved to God's glory? God keeps a faithful account with every human being in our world. And when the day of reckoning comes, the faithful steward takes no credit to himself. He does not say, "My pound;" but, "Thy pound hath gained" other pounds. He knows that without the entrusted gift no increase could have been made. He feels that in faithfully discharging his stewardship he has but done his duty. The capital was the Lord's, and by His power he was enabled to trade upon it successfully. His name only should be glorified. Without the entrusted capital he knows that he would have been bankrupt for eternity.

(CS 111.3)

The approval of the Lord is received almost with surprise, it is so unexpected. But Christ says to him, "Well done, thou good and faithful servant: thou hast been faithful over a few things, I will make thee ruler over many things: enter thou into the joy of thy Lord."– *The Review and Herald, September 12, 1899.* (CS 112.1)

How God Proves His Stewards

How inclined is man to set his affections on earthly things! His attention is absorbed in houses and lands, and his duty to his fellow man is neglected; his own salvation is treated as a matter of little consequence, and the claims of God upon him are forgotten. Men grasp the treasures of earth as tenaciously as if they could hold on to them forever. They seem to think that they have a right to do with their means just as it pleases them, no matter what the Lord has commanded, or what may be the need of their fellow men. (CS 112.2)

They forget that all they claim as theirs, has simply been entrusted to them. They are stewards of the grace of God. God has committed this treasure to them to prove them, that they may manifest their attitude to His cause, and show the thoughts of their heart toward Him. They are not only trading for time, but for eternity, with their Lord's money, and the use or abuse of their talent will determine their position and trust in the world to come.– *The Review and Herald, February 14, 1888.* (CS 112.3)

A Practical Question

The idea of stewardship should have a practical bearing upon all the people of God.... Practical benevolence will give spiritual life to thousands of nominal professors of the truth who now mourn over their darkness. It will transform them from selfish, covetous worshipers of mammon, to earnest, faithful coworkers with Christ in the salvation of sinners.– *Testimonies for the Church 3:387.* **(CS 112.4)**

In the Master's Stead

A steward identifies himself with his master. He accepts the responsibilities of a steward, and he must act in his master's stead, doing as his master would do were he presiding. His master's interests become his. The position of a steward is one of dignity, because his master trusts him. If in any wise he acts selfishly, and turns the advantages gained by trading with his lord's goods to his own advantage, he has perverted the trust reposed in him.– *Testimonies for the Church 9:246.* **(CS 113.1)**

A selfish use of riches proves one unfaithful to God, and unfits the steward of means for the higher trust of heaven.– *Testimonies for the Church 6:391.* **(CS 113.2)**

Chapter 24
Our Talents

The parable of the talents, rightly understood, will bar out covetousness, which God calls idolatry.– *Testimonies for the Church 3:387.* (CS 114.1)

God has lent men talents–an intellect to originate, a heart to be the place of His throne, affection to flow out in blessings to others, a conscience to convict of sin. Each one has received something from the Master, and each one is to do his part in supplying the needs of God's work. (CS 114.2)

God desires His workers to look to Him as the Giver of all they possess, to remember that all that they have and are comes from Him who is wonderful in counsel and excellent in working. The delicate touch of the physician's hand, his power over nerve and muscle, his knowledge of the delicate organism of the body, are the wisdom of divine power, to be used in behalf of suffering humanity. The skill with which the carpenter uses the hammer, the strength with which the blacksmith makes the anvil ring, come from God. He has entrusted men with talents, and He desires them to look to Him for counsel. Thus they may use His gifts with unerring aptitude, testifying that they are workers together with God. (CS 114.3)

Property is a talent. To His people the Lord sends the message, "Sell that ye have, and give alms." All that we have is the Lord's, without any question. He calls upon us to awake, to bear a share of the burdens of His cause, that prosperity may attend His work. Every Christian is to act his part as a faithful steward. The methods of God are sensible and right, and we are to trade on our pence and our pounds, returning our freewill offerings to Him to sustain His work, to bring souls to Christ. Large and small sums should flow into the Lord's treasury.... (CS 114.4)

Speech is a talent. Of all the gifts bestowed on the human family, none should be more appreciated than the gift of speech. It is to be used to declare God's wisdom and wondrous love. Thus the treasures of His grace and wisdom are to be communicated. (CS 115.1)

An indwelling Saviour is revealed by the words. But the Holy Spirit does not abide in the heart of him who is peevish if others do not agree with his ideas and plans. From the lips of such a man there come scathing remarks, which grieve the Spirit away, and develop attributes that are satanic rather than divine. The Lord desires those connected with His work to speak at all times with the meekness of Christ. If you are provoked, do not become impatient. Manifest the gentleness of which Christ has given us an example in His life.... (CS 115.2)

Strength is a talent, and is to be used to glorify God. Our bodies belong to Him. He has paid the price of redemption for the body as well as for the soul.... We can serve God better in the vigor of health than in the palsy of disease; therefore we should cooperate with God in the care of our bodies. Love for God is essential for life and health. Faith in God is essential for health. In order to have perfect health, our hearts must be filled with love and hope and joy in the Lord.... (CS 115.3)

Influence is a talent, and it is a power for good when the sacred fire of God's kindling is brought into our service. The influence of a holy life is felt at home and abroad. The practical benevolence, the self-denial and self-sacrifice, which mark the life of a man, have an influence for good upon those with whom he associates.... (CS 115.4)

According to the Ability of the Recipient

In the Lord's plan there is a diversity in the

distribution of talents. To one man is given one talent, to another five, to another ten. These talents are not bestowed capriciously, but according to the ability of the recipient. (CS 116.1)

According to the talents bestowed will be the returns called for. The heaviest obligation rests upon him who has been made a steward of the greatest abilities. A man who has ten pounds is held responsible for all that ten pounds would do if used aright. He who has only ten pence is accountable for only that amount.... (CS 116.2)

It is the faithfulness with which the endowment has been used that wins the Lord's commendation. If we desire to be acknowledged as good and faithful servants, we must do thorough, consecrated work for the Master. He will reward diligent, honest service. If men will put their trust in Him, if they will recognize His compassion and benevolence, and will walk humbly before Him, He will cooperate with them. He will increase their talents. (CS 116.3)

"Occupy Till I Come"

God has left us in charge of His goods in His absence. Each steward has his own special work to do for the advancement of God's kingdom. No one is excused. The Lord bids us all, "Occupy till I come." By His own wisdom He has given us direction for the use of His gifts. The talents of speech, memory, influence, property, are to accumulate for the glory of God and the advancement of His kingdom. He will bless the right use of His gifts. (CS 116.4)

We claim to be Christians, waiting for the second appearing of our Lord in the clouds of heaven. Then what shall we do with our time, our understanding, our possessions, which are not ours, but are entrusted to us to test our honesty? Let us bring them to Jesus. Let us use our treasures for the advancement of His cause.

Thus we shall obey the injunction, "Lay not up for yourselves treasures upon earth, where moth and rust doth corrupt, and where thieves break through and steal: but lay up for yourselves treasures in heaven, where neither moth nor rust doth corrupt, and where thieves do not break through nor steal: for where your treasure is, there will your heart be also."– *The Review and Herald, April 9, 1901.* (CS 116.5)

To Every Man His Work

It has come to be understood that talents are given only to a certain favored class, to the exclusion of others who, of course, are not called upon to share in the toils or rewards. But it is not so represented in the parable. When the Master of the house called His servants, He gave to every man his work. The whole family of God are included in the responsibility of using their Lord's goods.... (CS 117.1)

To a greater or less degree, all are placed in charge of the talents of their Lord. The spiritual, mental, and physical ability, the influence, station, possessions, affections, sympathies, all are precious talents to be used in the cause of the Master for the salvation of souls for whom Christ died.– *The Review and Herald, October 26, 1911.* (CS 117.2)

Why Talents Are Bestowed

The people of God should realize the fact that God has not given them talents for the purpose of enriching themselves with earthly goods, but in order that they may lay up in store a good foundation against the time to come, even for eternal life.– *The Review and Herald, January 8, 1895.* (CS 117.3)

Chapter 25
Responsibilities of the Man With One Talent

Some who have been entrusted with only one talent, excuse themselves because they have not as large a number of talents as those to whom are entrusted many talents. They, like the unfaithful steward, hide the one talent in the earth. They are afraid to render to God that which He has entrusted to them. They engage in worldly enterprises, but invest little, if anything, in the cause of God. They expect those who have large talents, to bear the burden of the work, while they feel that they are not responsible for its success and advancement.... (CS 118.1)

Many who are professing to love the truth are doing this very work. They are deceiving their own souls; for Satan has blinded their eyes. In robbing God, they have robbed themselves more. They have deprived themselves of the heavenly treasure through their covetousness, and because of their evil heart of unbelief. (CS 118.2)

Because they have but one talent, they are afraid to trust it with God, and they hide it in the earth. They feel relieved of responsibility. They love to see the truth progress, but do not think that they are called upon to practice self-denial, and aid in the work through their own individual effort and with their means, although they have not a large amount.... (CS 118.3)

All Entrusted With Talents

All, both high and low, rich and poor, have been trusted by the Master with talents; some more, and some less, according to their several ability. The blessing of God will rest upon the earnest, loving, diligent workers. Their investment will be successful, and will secure souls to the kingdom of God, and for themselves an immortal treasure. All are moral agents, and are entrusted with goods of heaven. The amount of talents is proportioned according to the capabilities possessed by each. (CS 118.4)

God gives to every man his work, and He expects corresponding returns, according to their various trusts. He does not require the increase from ten talents of the man to whom He has given only one talent. He does not expect the man of poverty to give alms as the man who has riches. He does not expect of the feeble and suffering, the activity and strength which the healthy man has. The one talent, used to the best account, God will accept "according to that a man hath, and not according to that he hath not." (CS 119.1)

God calls us servants, which implies that we are employed by Him to do a certain work, and to bear responsibilities. He has lent us capital for investment. It is not our property; and we displease God if we hoard up, or spend as we choose, our Lord's goods. We are responsible for the use or abuse of that which God has thus lent us. If this capital which the Lord has placed in our hands lies dormant, or we bury it in the earth, be it only one talent, we shall be called to an account by the Master. He requires, not ours, but His own, with usury. (CS 119.2)

Every talent which returns to the Master, will be scrutinized. The doings and trusts of God's servants will not be considered an unimportant matter. Every individual will be dealt with personally, and will be required to give an account of the talents entrusted to him, whether he has improved or abused them. The reward bestowed will be proportionate to the talents improved. The punishment awarded will be according as the talents have been abused.– *The Review and Herald, February 23, 1886.* (CS 119.3)

Entrusted Talents to Be Used

None should mourn that they have not larger talents. When they use to the glory of God the talents He has given them, they will improve. It is no time now to bemoan our position in life, and excuse our neglect to improve our abilities because we have not another's ability and position, saying, O, if I had his gift and ability, I might invest a large capital for my Master. If such persons use their one talent wisely and well, that is all the Master requires of them.... **(CS 120.1)**

I hope efforts will be made in every church to arouse those who are doing nothing. May God make these realize that He will require of them the one talent with improvement; and if they neglect to gain other talents besides the one, they will meet with the loss of that one talent and their own souls also. We hope to see a change in our churches. The Householder is preparing to return and call His stewards to account for the talents He has entrusted to them. God pity the do-nothings then! Those who hear the welcome plaudit, "Well done, good and faithful servant," will have well done in the improvement of their abilities and means to the glory of God.– *The Review and Herald, March 14, 1878.* **(CS 120.2)**

Unimproved Talents

Some are willing to give according to what they have, and feel that God has no further claims upon them, because they have not a great amount of means. They have no income that they can spare from the necessities of their families. But there are many of this class who might ask themselves the question, Am I giving according to what I might have had? God designed that their powers of body and mind should be put to use. Some have not improved to the best account the ability that God has given them. Labor is apportioned to man. It was connected with the curse, because made necessary by sin. The physical, mental, and moral well-being of man makes a life of useful labor necessary. "Be not slothful in business," is the injunction of the inspired apostle Paul. **(CS 120.3)**

No person, whether rich or poor, can glorify God by a life of indolence. All the capital that many poor men have is time and physical strength; and this is frequently wasted in love of ease and in careless indolence, so that they have nothing to bring to their Lord in tithes and in offerings. If Christian men lack wisdom to labor to the best account, and to make a judicious appropriation of their physical and mental powers, they should have meekness and lowliness of mind to receive advice and counsel of their brethren, that their better judgment may supply their own deficiencies. Many poor men who are now content to do nothing for the good of their fellow men, and for the advancement of the cause of God, might do much if they would. They are as accountable to God for their capital of physical strength as is the rich man for his capital of money.– *Testimonies for the Church 3:400.* **(CS 121.1)**

Accountability for Physical Strength

I saw that those who have no property, but have strength of body, are accountable to God for their strength. They should be diligent in business and fervent in spirit; they should not leave those that have possessions to do all the sacrificing. I saw that they can sacrifice, and that it is their duty to do so, as well as those who have property. But often those that have no possessions do not realize that they can deny themselves in many ways, can lay out less upon their bodies, and to gratify their tastes and appetites, and find much to spare for the cause, and thus lay up a treasure in heaven.– *Testimonies for the Church 1:115.* **(CS 121.2)**

Those who have physical strength are to employ that strength in the service of God. They are to labor with their hands, and earn means to use in the cause of God. Those who can obtain work are to work faithfully, and to improve the opportunities they see to help those who cannot obtain labor.– *The Review and Herald, August 21, 1894.* **(CS 122.1)**

Indolence Not to Be Encouraged

The word of God teaches that if a man will not work, neither shall he eat. The Lord does not require the hard-working man to support those who are not diligent. There is a waste of time, a lack of effort, which brings to poverty and want. If these faults are not seen and corrected by those who indulge in them, all that might be done in their behalf is like putting treasure into a basket with holes. But there is an unavoidable poverty; and we are to manifest tenderness and compassion toward those who are unfortunate.–

The Review and Herald, January 3, 1899. **(CS 122.2)**

Chapter 26
Robbing God of Rightful Service

There are men in the ranks of Sabbathkeepers who are holding fast their earthly treasure. It is their god, their idol; and they love their money, their farms, their cattle, and their merchandise better than they love their Saviour, who for their sakes became poor, that they, through His poverty, might be made rich. They exalt their earthly treasures, considering them of greater value than the souls of men. Will such have the "Well done" spoken to them? No; never. The irrevocable sentence, "Depart," will fall upon their startled senses. Christ has no use for them. They have been slothful servants, hoarding the means God has given them, while their fellow men have perished in darkness and error. (CS 123.1)

My soul feels to the very depths on this point. Will the men of means sleep on until it is too late? until God shall reject them and their treasures, saying, "Go to now, ye rich men, weep and howl for your miseries that shall come upon you. Your riches are corrupted, and your garments are moth-eaten. Your gold and silver is cankered; and the rust of them shall be a witness against you." What a revelation will be made in the day of God, when hoarded treasures, and wages kept back by fraud, cry against their possessors, who were professedly good Christians, and flattered themselves that they were keeping the law of God, when they loved gain better than they loved the purchase of Christ's blood, the souls of men. (CS 123.2)

Now is the time for all to work.... What will many answer in the day of God, when He inquires, What have ye done for Me, who gave My riches, My honor, My command, and My life to save you from ruin? The do-nothings will be speechless in that day. They will see the sin of their neglect. They have robbed God of the service of a lifetime. They have not influenced any for good. They have not brought one soul to Jesus. They felt content to do nothing for the Master; and they meet no reward, but eternal loss. They perish with the wicked, although they professed to be followers of Christ.– *The Review and Herald, March 14, 1878.* (CS 123.3)

The Great Sin of Professed Christians

Every man, of whatever trade or profession, should make the cause of God his first interest; he should not only exercise his talents to advance the Lord's work, but should cultivate his ability to this end. Many a man devotes months and years to the acquirement of a trade or profession that he may become a successful worker in the world; and yet he makes no special effort to cultivate those talents which would render him a successful laborer in the vineyard of the Lord. He has perverted his powers, misused his talents. He has shown disrespect to his heavenly Master. This is the great sin of the professed people of God. They serve themselves, and serve the world. They may have the name of being shrewd, successful financiers; but they neglect to increase by use the talents which God has given them for His service. The worldly tact is becoming stronger by exercise; the spiritual is becoming weaker through inactivity.– *The Review and Herald, January 1, 1884.* (CS 124.1)

The Sin of Neglect

If those whose talents are rusting from inaction would seek the aid of the Spirit of God, and go to work, we should see much more accomplished. Urgent appeals for help would stir hearts; and the response would be made, "We will do what we can in our weakness and ignorance, looking to the Great Teacher for wisdom." Can it be that amid all these open doors for usefulness, these pathetic pleadings for help, men and women will sit with folded hands, or employ those hands only in selfish labor for earthly objects? **(CS 124.2)**

"Ye are the light of the world," said Jesus to His disciples. But how few are conscious of their own power and influence; how few realize what they might do to be a help and a blessing to others. They wrap their talent in a napkin, and bury it in the earth, and flatter themselves that they possess a commendable humility. But the books of heaven testify against these idlers, as slothful, wicked servants who are grievously sinning against God by neglecting the work which He has given them to do. They will make no plea of unfitness when the heavenly records are opened, revealing their glaring neglect. **(CS 125.1)**

Whatever the talent entrusted to us may be, we are required to use it in the service of God, and not in the service of mammon.... **(CS 125.2)**

Those who are hiding their talents in the earth are throwing away their opportunities to obtain a star-gemmed crown. Until the great disclosures of the final judgment shall be made, it will never be known how many men and women have done this, nor how many lives have gone out in darkness because God-given talents have been buried in business instead of being used in the service of the Giver.... **(CS 125.3)**

Men ... may be interested in mines which yield rich profit in silver and gold. They may devote a lifetime to securing earthly treasures; but they die, and leave it all behind. They cannot take one dollar with them to enrich them in the great beyond. Are these men wise? Are they not insane, to let the precious hours of probation pass without making a preparation for the future life? Those who are wise will lay up "a treasure in the heavens that faileth not,"–"a good foundation against the time to come, that they may lay hold on eternal life." If we would secure enduring riches, let us begin now to transfer our treasure to the other side, and our hearts will be where our treasure is.– *The Review and Herald, October 7, 1884.* **(CS 125.4)**

Chapter 27
Facing the Judgment Day

God does not compel anyone to love Him and obey His law. He has manifested unutterable love toward man in the plan of redemption. He has poured out the treasures of His wisdom, and has given the most precious gift of heaven that we might be constrained to love Him, and come into harmony with His will. If we refuse such love, and will not have Him to rule over us, we are working our own ruin, and we shall sustain an eternal loss at last. (CS 127.1)

God desires the willing service of our hearts. He has endowed us with reasoning faculties, with talents of ability, and with means and influence, to be exercised for the good of mankind, that we may manifest His spirit before the world. Precious opportunities and privileges are placed within our reach, and if we neglect them, we rob others, we defraud our own souls, and dishonor our Maker. We shall not want to meet these slighted opportunities and neglected privileges in the day of judgment. Our eternal interests for the future depend on the present diligent performance of duty in improving the talents that God has given into our trust for the salvation of souls.... (CS 127.2)

Position and influence, be they ever so exalted, should not be made an excuse for misappropriating the Lord's goods. The special favors of God should stimulate us to render wholehearted and affectionate service to Him; but many who are thus blessed forget the Giver, and become reckless, defiant, and profligate. They dishonor the God of heaven, and wield an influence that curses and destroys their associates. They do not seek to lessen the sufferings of the needy. They do not build up the work of God. They do not seek to redress the wrongs of the innocent, to plead the cause of the widow and the orphan, or to reveal a lofty pattern of character before high and low,

showing a spirit of beneficence and virtue. But on the contrary, they oppress the hireling; they keep back by fraud the just recompense for labor, cheat the innocent, rob the widow, and heap up treasure corroded with the blood of souls. They will have to render an account at the bar of God. This class are not doing the will of the Father in heaven, and they will hear the stern command, "Depart from Me, ye that work iniquity."– *The Review and Herald, February 14, 1888.* (CS 127.3)

Startling Revelations

What revelations will be made in the day of judgment! Many who have called themselves Christians will be found to have been not servants of God, but servants of themselves. Self has been their center; self-service has been their lifework. By living to please themselves and to gain all they could for themselves, they have crippled and dwarfed the capabilities and powers entrusted to them by God. They have not dealt honestly with God. Their lives have been one long system of robbery. These now complain against God and their fellow men, because they are not recognized and favored as they think they ought to be. But their unfaithfulness will be revealed in that day when the Lord judges the cases of all. He will return "and discern between the righteous and the wicked, between him that serveth God and him that serveth Him not." (CS 128.1)

In that day those who think that God will accept meager offerings and unwilling service will be disappointed. God will not put His superscription upon the work of any man, high or low, rich or poor, that is not done heartily, faithfully, and with an eye single to His glory. But those who have belonged to the family of God here below, who have striven to honor His name, have gained an experience that will make them as kings and priests unto God; and they will be accepted as faithful servants. To them the words will be spoken, "Well done, good and faithful servant:... enter thou into the joy of thy lord."– *The Review and Herald, January 5, 1897.* **(CS 128.2)**

Not Professing but Doing

When the cases of all come in review before God, the question, What did they profess? is never asked, but, What have they done? Have they been doers of the word? Have they lived for themselves? or have they been exercised in works of benevolence, in deeds of kindness, in love, preferring others before themselves, and denying themselves that they might bless others? **(CS 129.1)**

If the record shows that this has been their life, that their characters have been marked with tenderness, self-denial, and benevolence, they will receive the blessed assurance and benediction from Christ, "Well done," "Come, ye blessed of My Father, inherit the kingdom prepared for you from the foundation of the world." **(CS 129.2)**

Christ has been grieved and wounded by our marked selfish love, and indifference to the woes and needs of others.– *The Review and Herald, July 13, 1886.* **(CS 129.3)**

Promise to the Faithful Steward

It means much to sow beside all waters. It means a continual imparting of gifts and offerings. God will furnish facilities so that the faithful steward of His entrusted means shall be supplied with a sufficiency in all things, and be enabled to abound to every good work. "As it is written, He hath dispersed abroad; He hath given to the poor: His righteousness remaineth forever. Now He that ministereth seed to the sower both minister bread for your food, and multiply your seed sown, and increase the fruits of your

righteousness." *2 Corinthians 9:9, 10.* The seed sown with full, liberal hand, is taken charge of by the Lord. He who ministers seed to the sower gives His worker that which enables him to cooperate with the Giver of the seed.– *Testimonies for the Church 9:132.* **(CS 129.4)**

For Further Study

Our Day of Trust, *Testimonies for the Church 4:618, 619*

A Parable for Last-Day Christians, *Testimonies for the Church 1:197, 198*

All Talents to Be Improved, *Testimonies for the Church 2:659*

Accountability of All, Rich or Poor, *Testimonies for the Church 1:324, 325*

The Poor Frequently Neglect Opportunities to Do Good, *Testimonies for the Church 2:230*

The Unprofitable Steward, *Testimonies for the Church 5:282, 283*

What Is the "Joy of the Lord"? *Testimonies for the Church 3:386, 387*

Many Who Wrap Their Talent in a Napkin, *Testimonies for the Church 1:530*

The Unjust Steward, *Testimonies for the Church 1:538, 539*

"Make to Yourselves Friends," *Christ's Object Lessons, 372-375*

Trusts Proportionate to Capabilities, *Testimonies for the Church 2:245*

To Acquire the Heavenly Treasure the Earthly Must Be Sacrificed, *Testimonies for the Church 2:193*

A View of the Judgment, *Testimonies for the Church 4:384-387*

Hoarded Wealth Not Merely Useless, a Curse, *Christ's Object Lessons, 352*

Decisions of Judgment Turn on Practical Benevolence, *Testimonies to Ministers and Gospel Workers, 399, 400*

In Time of Trouble Hoarded Treasure an Offence, *Testimonies for the Church 1:169*

Businessmen, Farmers, Mechanics, Merchants, Lawyers, Responsible No Less Than Minister for the Talents Given, *Testimonies for the Church 4:469*

Section 5
Stewards of Wealth

Chapter 28
Wealth an Entrusted Talent

The followers of Christ are not to despise wealth; they are to look upon wealth as the Lord's entrusted talent. By a wise use of His gifts, they may be eternally benefited, but we are to bear the fact in mind that God has not given us riches to use just as we shall fancy, to indulge impulse, to bestow or withhold as we shall please. We are not to use riches in a selfish way, devoting them simply to our own enjoyment. This course would not be doing right toward God or toward our fellow men, and would bring at last only perplexity and trouble.... (CS 133.1)

The world favors the rich, and looks upon them as of greater value than the honest poor man; but the rich are developing their characters after the manner in which they use their entrusted gifts. They are making manifest whether or not it will be safe to trust them with eternal riches. Both the poor and the rich are deciding their own eternal destiny and proving whether they are fit subjects for the inheritance of the saints in light. Those who put their riches to a selfish use in this world are revealing attributes of character that show what they would do if they had greater advantages, and possessed the imperishable treasures of the kingdom of God. The selfish principles exercised on the earth are not the principles which will prevail in heaven. All men stand on an equality in heaven.... (CS 133.2)

Why is it that riches are called unrighteous mammon?–It is because Satan uses worldly treasure to ensnare, deceive, and delude souls, to accomplish their ruin. God has given directions as to how they are to appropriate His goods in relieving the wants of suffering humanity, in advancing His cause, in building up His kingdom in the world, in sending missionaries into regions beyond, in disseminating the knowledge of Christ in all parts of the world. If the God-entrusted means are not thus applied, will not God surely judge for these things? Souls are left to perish in their sins while church members who claim to be Christians are using God's sacred trust of means in gratifying unholy appetites, in indulging self. (CS 133.3)

How Means is Squandered

What a vast amount of God's entrusted capital is expended in purchasing tobacco, beer, and liquor! God has forbidden all these indulgences because they tear down the human structure. Through their indulgence health is sacrificed, and life itself is offered on Satan's shrine. Perverted appetite causes the brain to become enfeebled, so that men cannot think sharply and clearly, and devise plans that will succeed in temporal matters; and much less can they bring a cultivated intellect into their religious transactions. They are unable to discern sacred and eternal things above those which are common and temporal. (CS 134.1)

Satan has invented many ways in which to squander the means which God has given. Card playing, betting, gambling, horse racing, and theatrical performances are all of his own inventing, and he has led men to carry forward these amusements as zealously as though they were winning for themselves the precious boon of eternal life. Men lay out immense sums in following these forbidden pleasures; and the result is, their God-given power, which has been purchased by the blood of the Son of God, is degraded and corrupted. The physical, moral, and mental powers which are given to men of God, and which belong to Christ, are zealously used in serving Satan, and in turning men from righteousness and holiness. (CS 134.2)

Everything is devised that can possibly turn the mind from that which is noble and pure, and the boundary line is almost reached when the inhabitants of the earth will be as corrupt as were the inhabitants of the world before the flood.... (CS 135.1)

As in the Days of Noah

If we look at the picture of the days that were before the flood, and then turn our attention to the habits and practices of society today, we shall see that our earth is fast ripening for the plagues of the last days. Men have corrupted the earth by their sinful course of action. Satan is playing the game of life for the souls of men. Those who are doers of the words of Christ will find that they will have to watch and pray continually in order that they may not be led into temptation. (CS 135.2)

Many do not seem to appreciate the fact that the money they needlessly expend on amusements which only vex the soul and lay the foundation for the corruption of their morals, is money that belongs to the Lord. Those who use money for selfish gratification are pleasing and glorifying the enemy of all righteousness. If they turned their hearts to God, they would use their money to bless and uplift their fellow men, to relieve poverty and suffering. Starvation is in our world, nakedness, disease, and death; yet how few abate their sinful extravagance! Satan is inventing everything that he can possibly devise in order to keep men thoroughly occupied, so that they shall have no time to consider the question, "How is it with my soul?" (CS 135.3)

Christ's Interest in the Human Family

The owner of all our earthly treasures came to our world in human form. The Word was made flesh, and dwelt among us. We cannot appreciate how deeply interested He must be in the human family. He knows the value of every soul. What grief oppressed Him as He saw His purchased inheritance charmed with Satan's inventions! (CS 136.1)

The only satisfaction Satan takes in playing the game of life for the souls of men is the satisfaction he takes in hurting the heart of Christ. Though He was rich, for our sake Christ became poor, that we through His poverty might be made rich. Yet in view of this great fact, the majority of the world permit earthly possessions to eclipse heavenly attractions. They set their affections upon earthly things, and turn away from God. What a grievous sin it is that men will not come to their senses, and understand how foolish it is to permit inordinate affections for earthly things to expel the love of God from the heart. When the love of God is expelled, the love of the world quickly flows in to supply the vacuum. The Lord alone can cleanse the soul temple from the moral defilement. (CS 136.2)

Jesus gave His life for the life of the world, and He places an infinite value upon man. He desires that man shall appreciate himself, and consider his future well-being. If the eye is kept single, the whole body will be full of light. If the spiritual vision is clear, unseen realities will be looked upon in their true value, and beholding the eternal world will give added enjoyment to this world. (CS 136.3)

The Christian will be filled with joy in proportion as he is a faithful steward of his Lord's goods. Christ yearns to save every son and daughter of Adam. He lifts His voice in warning, in order to break the spell which has bound the soul in captivity to the slavery of sin. He beseeches men to turn from their infatuation. He brings the nobler world before their vision, and says, "Lay not up for yourselves treasure upon the earth." (CS 136.4)

The Subtle Temptations

Christ sees the danger; He knows the subtle temptations and power of the enemy; for He has experienced Satan's temptations. He gave His life to procure a period of probation for the sons and daughters of Adam. With the result of Adam's disobedience and transgressions before them, with greater light shining upon them, they are invited to come unto Him and find rest unto their souls. But the greater the light and the plainer the danger signal, the greater the condemnation of those will be who turn from light to darkness. The words of Christ are too serious in their import to be disregarded. (CS 137.1)

Men seem moved with an insane desire to procure earthly possessions. Every species of dishonesty is practiced in order to accumulate wealth. Men pursue their business affairs with intense zeal, as though success in this line would be a surety for obtaining heaven. They bind up the Lord's entrusted capital in worldly goods, and there is no means with which to advance the kingdom of God in the world by relieving the mental and physical distress of the world's inhabitants. Many who profess to be Christians fail to heed the command of Christ when He says, "Lay up for yourselves treasures in heaven, where neither moth nor rust doth corrupt, and where thieves do not break through nor steal: for where your treasure is, there will your heart be also." (**CS 137.2**)

The Lord will not compel men to deal justly, to love mercy, and to walk humbly with their God; He sets before the human agent good and evil, and makes plain what will be the sure result of following one course or the other. Christ invites us, saying, "Follow Me." But we are never forced to walk in His footsteps. If we do walk in His footsteps, it is the result of deliberate choice. As we see the life and character of Christ, strong desire is awakened to be like Him in character; and we follow on to know the Lord, and to know His goings forth are prepared as the morning. We then begin to realize that "the path of the just is as the shining light, that shineth more and more unto the perfect day."– *The Review and Herald, March 31, 1896.* (**CS 138.1**)

The Acquisition of Wealth Not a Sin

The Bible does not condemn the rich man because he is rich; it does not declare the acquisition of wealth to be a sin, nor does it say that money is the root of all evil. On the contrary, the Scriptures state that it is God who gives the power to get wealth. And this ability is a precious talent if consecrated to God and employed to advance His cause. The Bible does not condemn genius or art; for these come of the wisdom which God gives. We cannot make the heart purer or holier by clothing the body in sackcloth, or depriving the home of all that ministers to comfort, taste, or convenience. (**CS 138.2**)

The Scriptures teach that wealth is a dangerous possession only when placed in competition with the immortal treasure. It is when the earthly and temporal absorbs the thoughts, the affections, the devotion which God claims, that it becomes a snare. Those who are bartering the eternal weight of glory for a little of the glitter and tinsel of earth, the everlasting habitations for a home which can be theirs but a few years at best, are making an unwise choice. Such was the exchange made by Esau, when he sold his birthright for a mess of pottage; by Balaam, when he forfeited the favor of God for the rewards of the king of Midian; by Judas, when for thirty pieces of silver he betrayed the Lord of glory. (**CS 138.3**)

It is the love of money that the word of God denounces as the root of all evil. Money itself is the gift of God to men, to be used with fidelity in His service. God blessed Abraham, and made him rich in cattle, in silver, and in gold. And the Bible states, as an evidence of divine favor, that God gave David, Solomon, Jehoshaphat, Hezekiah, very much riches and honor. (**CS 139.1**)

Like other gifts of God, the possession of wealth brings its increase of responsibility, and its peculiar temptations. How many who have in adversity remained true to God, have fallen under the glittering allurements of prosperity. With the possession of wealth, the ruling passion of a selfish nature is revealed. The world is cursed today by the miserly greed and the self-indulgent vices of the worshipers of mammon.– *The Review and Herald, May 16, 1882.* (**CS 139.2**)

Financial Talent Needed

Those belonging to the higher ranks of society are to be sought out with tender affection and brotherly regard. This class has been too much neglected. It is the Lord's will that men to whom He has entrusted many talents shall hear the truth in a manner different from the way in which they have heard it in the past. Men in business, in positions of trust, men with large inventive faculties, and scientific insight, men of genius, are to be among the first to hear the gospel call. (**CS 139.3**)

There are men of the world who have God-given powers of organization, which are needed in the carrying forward of the work for these last days. All are not preachers; but men are needed who can take the management of the institutions where industrial work is carried on, men who in our conferences can act as leaders and educators. God needs men who can look ahead, and see what needs to be done, men who can act as faithful financiers, men who will stand as solid as a rock to principle in the present crisis and in the future perils that may arise.– *The Review and Herald, May 8, 1900.* **(CS 140.1)**

Chapter 29
Methods of Acquiring Wealth

There are those, even among Seventh-day Adventists, who are under the reproof of the word of God, because of the way they acquired their property and use it, acting as if they owned it, and created it, without an eye to the glory of God, and without earnest prayer to direct them in acquiring or using it. They are grasping at a serpent, which will sting them as an adder. (CS 141.1)

Of God's people He says, "Her merchandise and her hire shall be holiness to the Lord: it shall not be treasured nor laid up." But many who profess to believe the truth do not want God in their thoughts, any more than did the antediluvians or Sodomites. One sensible thought of God, awakened by the Holy Spirit, would spoil all their schemes. Self, self, self, has been their god, their alpha and their omega. (CS 141.2)

Christians are safe only in acquiring money as God directs, and using it in channels which He can bless. God permits us to use His goods with an eye single to His glory, to bless ourselves, that we may bless others. Those who have adopted the world's maxim, and discarded God's specifications, who grasp all they can obtain of wages or goods, are poor, poor indeed, because the frown of God is upon them. They walk in paths of their own choosing, and do dishonor to God, to truth, to His goodness, to His mercy, His character. (CS 141.3)

Now, in probationary time, we are all on test and trial. Satan is working with his deceiving enchantments and bribes, and some will think that by their schemes they have made a wonderful speculation. But lo, as they thought they were rising securely, and were carrying themselves loftily in selfishness, they learned that God can scatter faster than they can gather.– *Testimonies to Ministers and Gospel Workers, 335,*

336. (CS 141.4)

Integrity in Business

As we deal with our fellow men in petty dishonesty, or in more daring fraud, so will we deal with God. Men who persist in a course of dishonesty will carry out their principles until they cheat their own souls, and lose heaven and eternal life. They will sacrifice honor and religion for a small worldly advantage. There are such men right in our own ranks, and they will have to experience what it is to be born again, or they cannot see the kingdom of God. Honesty should stamp every action of our lives. Heavenly angels examine the work that is put into our hands; and where there has been a departure from the principles of truth, "wanting" is written in the records. (CS 142.1)

Says Jesus, "Lay not up for yourselves treasures upon earth, where moth and rust doth corrupt, and where thieves break through and steal." Treasures are those things which engross the mind, and absorb the attention, to the exclusion of God and the truth. (CS 142.2)

The love of money, which prompts the acquisition of earthly treasure, was the ruling passion in the Jewish age. High and eternal considerations were made subordinate to the considerations of securing earthly wealth and influence. Worldliness usurped the place of God and religion in the soul. Avaricious greed for wealth exerted such a fascinating, bewitching influence over the life, that it resulted in perverting the nobility, and corrupting the humanity of men, until they were drowned in perdition. Our Saviour gave a decided warning against hoarding up the treasures of earth. (CS 142.3)

All branches of business, all manner of

employments, are under the eye of God; and every Christian has been given ability to do something in the cause of the Master. Whether engaged in business in the field, in the warehouse, or in the counting room, men will be held responsible to God for the wise and honest employment of their talents. They are just as accountable to God for their work, as the minister who labors in word and doctrine is for his. If men acquire property in a manner that is not approved by the word of God, they obtain it at a sacrifice of the principles of honesty. An inordinate desire for gain will lead even the professed followers of Christ into imitation of the customs of the world. They will be influenced to dishonor their religion, by overreaching in trade, oppressing the widow and the orphan, and turning away the stranger from his right.– *The Review and Herald, September 18, 1888.* (CS 142.4)

Intelligence and Purity in Every Transaction

Holiness to the Lord was the great characteristic of the Redeemer's life on earth, and it is His will that this shall characterize the lives of His followers. His workers are to labor with unselfishness and faithfulness, and with reference to the usefulness and influence of every other worker. Intelligence and purity are to mark all their work, all their business transactions. He is the light of the world. In His work there are to be no dark corners where dishonest deeds are done. Injustice is in the highest degree displeasing to God.– *The Review and Herald, June 24, 1902.* (CS 143.1)

Temptation Resisted

God is very particular that all who profess to serve Him shall manifest the superiority of right principles. By the true follower of Christ every business transaction will be regarded as a part of his religion, just as prayer is a part of his religion.... (CS 143.2)

Satan is offering to every soul the kingdoms of this world in return for the carrying out of his will. This was the great inducement he presented to Christ in the wilderness of temptation. And so he says to many of Christ's followers. If you will follow my business methods, I will reward you with wealth. Every Christian is at some time brought to the test which will reveal his weak points of character. If the temptation is resisted, precious victories are gained. He must choose whether he will serve Christ or become a follower of the deceiver, and a worshiper of him.– *The Signs of the Times, February 24, 1909.* (CS 144.1)

The Registry in Heaven's Ledger

The customs of the world are no criterion for the Christian. He is not to imitate its sharp practices, its overreaching, its extortion. Every unjust act toward a fellow being is a violation of the golden rule. Every wrong done to the children of God, is done to Christ Himself in the person of His saints. Every attempt to take advantage of the ignorance, weakness, or misfortune of another, is registered as fraud in the ledger of heaven. He who truly fears God, would rather toil day and night, and eat the bread of poverty, than to indulge the passion for gain that oppresses the widow and fatherless or turns the stranger from his right. (CS 144.2)

The slightest departure from rectitude breaks down the barriers, and prepares the heart to do greater injustice. Just to that extent that a man would gain advantage for himself at the disadvantage of another, will his soul become insensible to the influence of the Spirit of God. Gain obtained at such a cost is a fearful loss.– *Prophets and Kings, 651, 652.* (CS 144.3)

A Sacrifice of Principle

We often see men who stand high in positions of trust, as Christ's followers, but who have made shipwreck of faith. A temptation comes to them and they sacrifice principle and their religious advantages to secure a coveted earthly treasure. The bait of Satan is taken. Christ conquered, thus making it possible for man to conquer also; but man places himself under the leadership of the god of this world, and steps from beneath the banner of Jesus Christ into the ranks of the enemy. All his powers are devoted to gain, and he worships other gods before the Lord. (CS 145.1)

The worldly man is not content with a present sufficiency, or with even an abundance.

He is always aiming to possess a larger stock, and turns every thought, every power, in this direction.– *The Review and Herald, March 1, 1887.* (**CS 145.2**)

Close and Selfish Dealing

I appeal to my brethren in faith, and urge them to cultivate tenderness of heart. Whatever may be your calling or position, if you cherish selfishness and covetousness, the displeasure of the Lord will be upon you. Do not make the work and cause of God an excuse for dealing closely and selfishly with anyone, even if transacting business that has to do with His work. God will accept nothing in the line of gain that is brought into His treasury through selfish transactions. Every act in connection with His work is to bear divine inspection. Every sharp transaction, every attempt to take advantage of a man who is under pressure of circumstances, every plan to purchase his land or property for a sum beneath its value, will not be acceptable to God, even though the money gained is made an offering to His cause. The price of the blood of the only-begotten Son of God has been paid for every man, and it is necessary to deal honestly, to deal with equity with every man, in order to carry out the principles of the law of God.... (**CS 145.3**)

If a brother who has labored disinterestedly for the cause of God, becomes enfeebled in body, and is unable to do his work, let him not be dismissed and be obliged to get along the best way he can. Give him wages sufficient to support him; for remember he belongs to God's family, and that you are all brethren.– *The Review and Herald, December 18, 1894.* (**CS 146.1**)

Chapter 30
Danger in Prosperity

Throughout the ages, riches and honor have been attended with much peril to humility and spirituality. It is when a man is prospered, when all his fellow men speak well of him, that he is in special danger. Man is human. Spiritual prosperity continues only so long as man depends wholly upon God for wisdom and for perfection of character. And those who feel most their need of dependence upon God are usually those who have the least amount of earthly treasure and human honor on which to depend. (CS 147.1)

The Commendation of Man

There is danger in the bestowal of rich gifts or of words of commendation upon human agencies. Those who are favored by the Lord need to be on guard constantly, lest pride spring up and obtain the supremacy. He who has an unusual following, he who has received many words of commendation from the messengers of the Lord, needs the special prayers of God's faithful watchmen, that he may be shielded from the danger of cherishing thoughts of self-esteem and spiritual pride. (CS 147.2)

Never is such a man to manifest self-importance, or attempt to act as a dictator or a ruler. Let him watch and pray, and keep his eye single to the glory of God. As his imagination takes hold upon things unseen, and he contemplates the joy of the hope that is set before him,–even the precious boon of life eternal,–the commendation of man will not fill his mind with thoughts of pride. And at times when the enemy makes special efforts to spoil him by flattery and worldly honor, his brethren should faithfully warn him of his dangers; for, if left to himself, he will be prone to make mistakes, and reveal human frailties.... (CS 147.3)

In the Valley of Humiliation

It is not the empty cup that we have trouble in carrying; it is the cup full to the brim that must be carefully balanced. Affliction and adversity may cause much inconvenience, and may bring great depression; but it is prosperity that is dangerous to spiritual life. Unless the human subject is in constant submission to the will of God, unless he is sanctified by the truth, and has the faith that works by love and purifies the soul, prosperity will surely arouse the natural inclination to presumption. (CS 148.1)

Our prayers need most to be offered for the men in high places. They need the prayers of the whole church, because they are entrusted with prosperity and influence. (CS 148.2)

In the valley of humiliation, where men depend on God to teach them and to guide their every step, there is comparative safety. But let everyone who has a living connection with God pray for the men in positions of responsibility,–for those who are standing on a lofty pinnacle, and who, because of their exalted position, are supposed to have much wisdom. Unless such men feel their need of an Arm stronger than the arm of flesh to lean upon, unless they make God their dependence, their view of things will become distorted, and they will fall.– *The Review and Herald, December 14, 1905.* (CS 148.3)

A Perversion of an Original Faculty

The desire to accumulate wealth is an original affection of our nature, implanted there by our heavenly Father for noble ends. If you ask the capitalist who has directed all his energies to the one object of securing wealth, and who is persevering and industrious to add to his property, with what design he thus labors, he could not give you a reason for this, a definite purpose for which he is gaining earthly treasures and heaping up riches. He cannot define any great aim or purpose he has in view, or any new source of happiness he expects to attain. He goes on accumulating because he has turned all his abilities and all his powers in this direction. (**CS 148.4**)

There is within the worldly man a craving for something that he does not have. He has, from force of habit, bent every thought, every purpose, in the direction of making provision for the future, and as he grows older, he becomes more eager than ever to acquire all that it is possible to gain. It is natural that the covetous man should become more covetous as he draws near the time when he is losing hold upon all earthly things. (**CS 149.1**)

All this energy, this perseverance, this determination, this industry after earthly power, is the result of the perversion of his powers to a wrong object. Every faculty might have been cultivated to the highest possible elevation by exercise, for the heavenly, immortal life, and for the far more exceeding and eternal weight of glory. The customs and practices of the worldly man in his perseverance and his energies, and in availing himself of every opportunity to add to his store, should be a lesson to those who claim to be children of God, seeking for glory, honor, and immortality. The children of the world are wiser in their generation than the children of the light, and herein is seen their wisdom. Their object is for earthly gain, and to this end they direct all their energies. O that this zeal would characterize the toiler for heavenly riches!– *The Review and Herald, March 1, 1887.* (**CS 149.2**)

The Handicap of Riches

Very few realize the strength of their love for money until the test is brought to bear upon them. Many who profess to be Christ's followers then show that they are unprepared for heaven. Their works testify that they love wealth more than their neighbor or their God. Like the rich young man, they inquire the way of life; but when it is pointed out and the cost estimated, and they see that the sacrifice of earthly riches is

demanded, they decide that heaven costs too much. The greater the treasures laid up on the earth, the more difficult it is for the possessor to realize that they are not his own, but are lent him to be used to God's glory. (**CS 150.1**)

Jesus here improves the opportunity to give His disciples an impressive lesson: "Then said Jesus unto His disciples, Verily I say unto you, That a rich man shall hardly enter into the kingdom of heaven." "It is easier for a camel to go through the eye of a needle, than for a rich man to enter into the kingdom of God." (**CS 150.2**)

Poor Rich Men and Rich Poor Men

Here the power of wealth is seen. The influence of the love of money over the human mind is almost paralyzing. Riches infatuate, and cause many who possess them to act as though they were bereft of reason. The more they have of this world, the more they desire. Their fears of coming to want increase with their riches. They have a disposition to hoard up means for the future. They are close and selfish, fearing that God will not provide for them. This class are indeed poor toward God. As their riches have accumulated, they have put their trust in them, and have lost faith in God and His promises. (**CS 150.3**)

The faithful, trusting poor man becomes rich toward God by judiciously using the little he has in blessing others with his means. He feels that his neighbor has claims upon him that he cannot disregard and yet obey the command of God, "Thou shalt love thy neighbor as thyself." He considers the salvation of his fellow men of greater importance than all the gold and silver the world contains. (**CS 151.1**)

Christ points out the way in which those who have wealth, and yet are not rich toward God, may secure the true riches. He says: "Sell that ye have and give alms;" and lay up treasure in heaven. The remedy He proposes is a transfer of their affections to the eternal inheritance. By investing their means in the cause of God to aid in the salvation of souls, and by relieving the needy, they become rich in good works, and are "laying up in store for themselves a good foundation against the time to come, that they may lay hold on eternal life." This will prove a safe investment. (CS 151.2)

But many show by their works that they dare not trust the bank of heaven. They choose to trust their means in the earth, rather than to send it before them to heaven. These have a great work to do to overcome covetousness and love of the world. Rich poor men, professing to serve God, are objects of pity. While they profess to know God, in works they deny Him. How great is the darkness of such! They profess faith in the truth, but their works do not correspond with their profession. The love of riches makes men selfish, exacting, and overbearing.– *The Review and Herald, January 15, 1880.* (CS 151.3)

A Question of Following Jesus

Jesus only required him [the rich young ruler] to go where He led the way. The thorny path of duty becomes easier to follow when we trace His divine footsteps before us, pressing down the briers. Christ would have accepted this talented and noble ruler, if he had yielded to His requirements, as readily as He accepted the poor fishermen whom He bade to follow Him. (CS 151.4)

The young man's ability to acquire property was not against him, provided he loved his neighbor as himself, and had not wronged another in acquiring his riches. That very ability, had it been employed in the service of God in seeking to save souls from ruin, would have been acceptable to the divine Master, and he might have made a diligent and successful worker for Christ. But he refused the exalted privilege of cooperating with Christ in the salvation of souls; he turned away from the glorious treasure promised him in the kingdom of God, and clung to the fleeting treasures of earth.... (CS 152.1)

The young ruler represents a large class who would be excellent Christians if there was no cross for them to lift, no humiliating burden for them to bear, no earthly advantages to resign, no sacrifice of property or feelings to make. Christ has entrusted to them capital of talents and means, and He expects corresponding returns. That which we possess is not our own, but is to be employed in serving Him from whom we have received all we have.– *The Review and*

Herald, March 21, 1878. (CS 152.2)

Faith Rare Among the Wealthy

A consistent faith is rare among rich men. Genuine faith, sustained by works, is rare. But all who possess this faith will be men who will not lack influence. They will copy after Christ in that disinterested benevolence and interest in the work of saving souls that He had. The followers of Christ should value souls as He valued them. Their sympathies should be with the work of their dear Redeemer, and they should labor to save the purchase of His blood at any sacrifice. What are money, houses, and lands, in comparison with even one soul?– *The Review and Herald, February 23, 1886.* (CS 152.3)

Riches Not a Ransom for the Transgressor

All the riches, even of the most wealthy, are not sufficient to hide the smallest sin from God. Neither riches nor intellect will be accepted as a ransom for the transgressor. Repentance, true humility, a broken heart, and a contrite spirit, alone will be acceptable to God. (CS 153.1)

There are many in our churches who should bring large offerings, and not content themselves with presenting a feeble pittance to Him who has done so much for them. Immeasurable blessings are falling upon them, but how little they return to the Giver! Let those who are indeed pilgrims and strangers upon the earth, now send their treasures before them to the heavenly country, in the much-needed gifts to the Lord's treasury.– *The Review and Herald, December 18, 1888.* (CS 153.2)

The Greatest Danger

I was shown that there is no lack of means among Sabbathkeeping Adventists. At present their greatest danger is in their accumulations of property. Some are continually increasing their cares and labors; they are overcharged. The result is, God and the wants of His cause are nearly forgotten by them; they are spiritually dead. They are required to make a sacrifice to God, an offering. A sacrifice does not increase, but decreases and consumes.... Much of the means among our people is only proving an injury to those who are holding on to it.– *Testimonies for the Church 1:492.* **(CS 153.3)**

Chapter 31

Satan's Wiles

As the people of God approach the perils of the last days, Satan holds earnest consultation with his angels as to the most successful plan of overthrowing their faith. He sees that the popular churches are already lulled to sleep by his deceptive power. By pleasing sophistry and lying wonders he can continue to hold them under his control. Therefore he directs his angels to lay their snares especially for those who are looking for the second advent of Christ and endeavoring to keep all the commandments of God. (CS 154.1)

Says the great deceiver: "We must watch those who are calling the attention of the people to the Sabbath of Jehovah; they will lead many to see the claims of the law of God; and the same light which reveals the true Sabbath, reveals also the ministration of Christ in the heavenly sanctuary, and shows that the last work for man's salvation is now going forward. Hold the minds of the people in darkness till that work is ended, and we shall secure the world and the church also.... (CS 154.2)

"Go, make the possessors of lands and money drunk with the cares of this life. Present the world before them in its most attractive light, that they may lay up their treasure here, and fix their affections upon earthly things. We must do our utmost to prevent those who labor in God's cause from obtaining means to use against us. Keep the money in our own ranks. The more means they obtain, the more they will injure our kingdom by taking from us our subjects. Make them care more for money than for the upbuilding of Christ's kingdom and the spread of the truths we hate, and we need not fear their influence; for we know that every selfish, covetous person will fall under our power, and will finally be separated from God's people."– *Testimonies to Ministers and Gospel Workers,*

472-474. (CS 154.3)

Worse Than Earthly Loss

Satan is the archdeceiver. The results to us of accepting his temptations are worse than any earthly loss that can be realized, yes, worse than death itself. Those who purchase success at the fearful cost of submission to the will and plans of Satan, will find that they have made a hard bargain. Everything in Satan's trade is secured at a high price. The advantages he presents are a mirage. The high hopes he holds out are secured at the loss of things that are good and holy and pure. Let Satan be always confounded by the word, "It is written." "Blessed is everyone that feareth the Lord: that walketh in His ways. For thou shalt eat the labor of thine hands: happy shalt thou be, and it shall be well with thee." ... (CS 155.1)

The path cast up for the ransomed of the Lord is far above all worldly schemes and practices. Those who walk in it are to show by their works the purity of their principles.– *The Signs of the Times, February 24, 1909.* (CS 155.2)

A Dwarfed Religious Experience

The wealthy are tempted to employ their means in self-indulgence, in the gratification of appetite, in personal adornment, or in the embellishment of their homes. For these objects professed Christians do not hesitate to spend freely, and even extravagantly. But when solicited to give to the Lord's treasury, to build up His cause, and to carry forward His work in the earth, many demur. The countenance that was all aglow with interest in plans for self-gratification, does not light up with joy when the cause of God appeals to their liberality. Perhaps, feeling that they cannot well do otherwise, they dole out a limited sum, far smaller than they freely spend for needless indulgence. But they manifest no real love for Christ, no earnest interest in the salvation of precious souls. What marvel that the Christian life of this class is at best but a dwarfed and sickly existence! Unless such persons change their course, their light will go out in darkness.–

The Review and Herald, May 16, 1882. **(CS 155.3)**

Chapter 32

Wealth Misused

Hoarded wealth is not merely useless; it is a curse. In this life it is a snare to the soul, drawing the affections away from the heavenly treasure. In the great day of God its witness to unused talents and neglected opportunities will condemn its possessor. (CS 157.1)

There are many who in their hearts charge God with being a hard master because He claims their possessions and their service. But we can bring to God nothing that is not already His. "All things come of Thee," said King David, "and of Thine own have we given Thee." All things are God's, not only by creation, but by redemption. All the blessings of this life and of the life to come are delivered to us stamped with the cross of Calvary.– *The Review and Herald, December 23, 1902.* (CS 157.2)

Transformed Through Love

Truth, set home to the heart by the Spirit of God, will crowd out the love of riches. The love of Jesus and the love of money cannot dwell in the same heart. The love of God so far surpasses the love of money that the possessor breaks away from his riches and transfers his affections to God. Through love he is then led to minister to the wants of the needy and to assist the cause of God. It is his highest pleasure to make a right disposition of his Lord's goods. He holds all that he has as not his own, and faithfully discharges his duty as God's steward. Then he can keep both the great commandments of the law: "Thou shalt love the Lord thy God with all thy heart, and with all thy soul, and with all thy mind." "Thou shalt love thy neighbor as thyself." (CS 157.3)

In this way it is possible for a rich man to enter the kingdom of God. "And everyone that hath forsaken houses, or brethren, or sisters, or father, or mother, or wife, or children, or lands, for My name's sake, shall receive a hundredfold, and shall inherit everlasting life." Here is the reward for those who sacrifice for God. They receive a hundredfold in this life, and shall inherit everlasting life.– *The Review and Herald, September 16, 1884.* (CS 158.1)

If the stewards of God do their duty, there is no danger that wealth will increase so rapidly as to prove a snare; for it will be used with practical wisdom and Christlike liberality.– *The Review and Herald, May 16, 1882.* (CS 158.2)

Property to Be Prized but Not Hoarded

He who is seeking for eternal riches should be striving for the heavenly treasure with far greater earnestness and perseverance, and with an intensity that is proportionate to the value of the object of which he is in pursuit. The worldly man is laboring for earthly, temporal things. He is laying up his treasure upon the earth, doing just that which Jesus has told him he must not do. (CS 158.3)

The sincere Christian appreciates the warning given by Jesus, and is a doer of His word, thus laying up his treasure in heaven, just as the world's Redeemer has told him he should do. He views an eternity of bliss worth a life of persevering and untiring effort. He is not misdirecting his efforts. He is setting his affections upon things above, where Christ sitteth at the right hand of God. Transformed by grace, his life is hid with Christ in God. (CS 158.4)

He has not lost by any means, the power of accumulation; but he employs his active energies in seeking for spiritual attainments; then all his entrusted talents will be appreciated as God's gifts to be employed to His glory. By him property will be prized, not hoarded, valued only inasmuch as it can be used to advance the truth, to work as Christ worked when He was upon the earth, to bless humanity. For this purpose he will use his powers, not to please or glorify self, but to strengthen every entrusted gift that he may do the highest service to God. Of him it can be said, "Not slothful in business; fervent in spirit; serving the Lord." (**CS 158.5**)

God does not condemn prudence and foresight in the use of the things of this life, but the feverish care, the undue anxiety, with respect to worldly things is not in accordance with His will.– *The Review and Herald, March 1, 1887.* (**CS 159.1**)

Chapter 33
Sympathy for the Poor

In view of what Heaven is doing to save the lost, how can those who are partakers of the riches of the grace of Christ withdraw their interest and their sympathies from their fellow men? How can they indulge in pride of rank or caste, and despise the unfortunate and the poor? (CS 160.1)

Yet it is too true that the pride of rank, and the oppression of the poor which prevail in the world, exist also among the professed followers of Christ. With many, the sympathies that ought to be exercised in full measure toward humanity, seem frozen up. Men appropriate to themselves the gifts entrusted to them wherewith to bless others. The rich grind the face of the poor, and use the means thus gained to indulge their pride and love of display even in the house of God. The poor are made to feel that it is too costly a thing for them to attend the service of God. The feeling exists with many that only the rich can engage in the public worship of God so as to make a good impression on the world. Were it not that the Lord has revealed His love to the poor and lowly who are contrite in heart, this world would be a sad place for the poor man.... (CS 160.2)

The world's Redeemer was the son of poor parents, and when in His infancy He was presented in the temple, His mother could bring only the offering appointed for the poor,–a pair of turtledoves or two young pigeons. He was the most precious gift of heaven to our world, a gift above all computation, yet it could be acknowledged only by the smallest offering. Our Saviour, during all His sojourn on earth, shared the lot of the poor and lowly. Self-denial and sacrifice characterized His life. (CS 160.3)

All the favors and blessings we enjoy are alone from Him; we are stewards of His grace and of His temporal gifts; the smallest talent and the humblest service may be offered to Jesus as a consecrated gift, and with the fragrance of His own merits He will present it to the Father. If the best we have is presented with a sincere heart, in love to God, from a longing desire to do service to Jesus, the gift is wholly acceptable. Everyone can lay up a treasure in the heavens. All can be "rich in good works, ready to distribute, willing to communicate; laying up in store for themselves a good foundation against the time to come, that they may lay hold on eternal life." (CS 161.1)

Bound By Ties of Sympathy

It is God's purpose that the rich and the poor shall be closely bound together by the ties of sympathy and helpfulness. He has a plan for us individually. To all who shall serve Him He has appointed a work. He bids us to interest ourselves in every case of suffering or need that shall come to our knowledge. (CS 161.2)

Our Lord Jesus Christ was rich, yet for our sake He became poor, that we through His poverty might be rich. He bids all whom He has entrusted with temporal blessings to follow His example. Jesus says, "Ye have the poor with you always, and whensoever ye will ye may do them good." The want and wretchedness in the world are constantly appealing to our compassion and sympathy, and the Saviour declares that ministry to the afflicted and suffering is the service most pleasing to Him. "Is it not," He says, "to deal thy bread to the hungry, and that thou bring the poor that are cast out to thy house? when thou seest the naked, that thou cover him; and that thou hide not thyself from thine own flesh?" We are to minister to the sick, to feed the hungry, to clothe the naked, and to instruct the ignorant. (CS 161.3)

There are many who complain of God because the world is so full of want and suffering.

But the Lord is a God of benevolence, and through His representatives, to whom He has entrusted His goods, He would have all the needs of His creatures supplied. He has made abundant provision for the wants of all, and if men did not abuse His gifts, and selfishly withhold them from their fellow men, none need suffer from want.– *The Review and Herald, June 20, 1893.* (CS 162.1)

No Caste in God's Sight

Never are we to be cold and unsympathetic, especially when dealing with the poor. Courtesy, sympathy, and compassion are to be shown to all. Partiality for the wealthy is displeasing to God. Jesus is slighted when His needy children are slighted. They are not rich in this world's goods, but they are dear to His heart of love. God recognizes no distinction of rank. With Him there is no caste. In His sight, men are simply men, good or bad. In the day of final reckoning, position, rank, or wealth will not alter by a hairsbreadth the case of anyone. By the all-seeing God, men will be judged by what they are in purity, in nobility, in love for Christ.... (CS 162.2)

Christ declared that the gospel is to be preached to the poor. Never does God's truth put on an aspect of greater loveliness than when brought to the needy and destitute. Then it is that the light of the gospel shines forth in its most radiant clearness, lighting up the hut of the peasant and the rude cottage of the laborer. Angels of God are there, and their presence makes the crust of bread and the cup of water a banquet. Those who have been neglected and abandoned by the world are raised to be sons and daughters of the Most High. Lifted above any position that earth can give, they sit in heavenly places in Christ Jesus. They may have no earthly treasure, but they have found the pearl of great price.– *The Review and Herald, July 21, 1910.* (CS 162.3)

Claims of the Widow and Fatherless

It is not wise to give indiscriminately to everyone who may solicit our aid; for we may thus encourage idleness, intemperance, and extravagance. But if one comes to your door and says he is hungry, do not turn him away empty. Give him something to eat, of such things as you have. You know not his circumstances, and it may be that his poverty is the result of misfortune. (CS 163.1)

But among all whose needs demand our interest, the widow and the fatherless have the strongest claims upon our tender sympathy and care. "Pure religion and undefiled before God and the Father is this, To visit the fatherless and widows in their affliction, and to keep himself unspotted from the world." (CS 163.2)

The father who has died in the faith, resting upon the eternal promise of God, left his loved ones in full trust that the Lord would care for them. And how does the Lord provide for these bereaved ones? He does not work a miracle in sending manna from heaven, He does not send ravens to bring them food; but He works a miracle upon human hearts, He expels selfishness from the soul, He unseals the fountain of benevolence. He tests the love of His professed followers by committing to their tender mercies the afflicted and bereaved ones, the poor and the orphan. These are in a special sense the little ones whom Christ looks upon, whom it is an offense to Him to neglect. Those who do neglect them are neglecting Christ in the person of His afflicted ones. (CS 163.3)

Every kind act done to them in the name of Jesus, is accepted by Him as if done to Himself, for He identifies His interest with that of suffering humanity, and He has entrusted to His church the grand work of ministering to Jesus by helping and blessing the needy and suffering. On all who shall minister to them with willing hearts, the blessing of the Lord will rest. (CS 164.1)

Until death shall be swallowed up in victory, there will be orphans to be cared for, who will suffer in more ways than one if the tender compassion and loving-kindness of our church members are not exercised in their behalf. The Lord bids us, "Bring the poor that are cast out to thy house." Christianity must supply fathers and mothers for these homeless ones. The compassion for the widow and the orphan manifested in prayers and deeds, will come up in remembrance before God, to be rewarded by and by.... (CS 164.2)

Mercy the Evidence of Our Union With God

God imparts His blessing to us, that we may give to others. And as long as we yield ourselves as the channels through which His love can flow, He will keep the channels supplied. When you ask God for your daily bread, He looks right into your heart to see if you will impart the same to others, more needy than yourself. When you pray, "God be merciful to me a sinner," He watches to see if you will manifest compassion to those with whom you associate. This is the evidence of our connection with God,–that we are merciful even as our Father who is in heaven is merciful. If we are His, we shall do with a cheerful heart just what He tells us to do, however inconvenient, however contrary it may be to our own feelings.... (CS 164.3)

It is in doing the works of Christ, ministering as He did to the suffering and afflicted, that we are to develop Christian character. It is for our good that God has called us to practice self-denial for Christ's sake, to bear the cross, to labor and sacrifice in seeking to save that which is lost. This is the Lord's process of refining, purging away the baser material, that the precious traits of character which were in Christ Jesus, may appear in the believer. All dross must be cleansed from the soul, through the sanctification of the truth.... (CS 165.1)

Through the grace of Christ our efforts to bless others are not only the means of our growth in grace, but they will enhance our future, eternal happiness. To those who have been coworkers with Christ it will be said, "Well done, good and faithful servant; thou hast been faithful over a few things, I will make thee ruler over many things: enter thou into the joy of thy Lord."– *The Review and Herald, June 27, 1893.* (CS 165.2)

Not to Be Supported in Idleness

The custom of supporting men and women in idleness by private gifts or church money encourages them in wrong habits. This course should be conscientiously avoided. Every man, woman, and child should be educated to practical, useful work. All should learn some trade. It may be tentmaking, it may be some other business, but all should be trained to use their powers to some purpose. And God is ready to increase the capabilities of all who will educate themselves to industrious habits. We are to be "not slothful in business; fervent in spirit; serving the Lord." God will bless all who will guard their influence in this respect.– *The Review and Herald, March 13, 1900.* (CS 165.3)

Diverting Means From the Mission Treasury

In many cases means which should be devoted to the missionary work is diverted into other channels, from mistaken ideas of benevolence. We may err in making gifts to the poor which are not a blessing to them, leading them to feel that they need not exert themselves and practice economy, for others will not permit them to suffer. We should not give countenance to indolence, or encourage habits of self-gratification by affording means for indulgence. While the worthy poor are not to be neglected, all should be taught, so far as possible, to help themselves. (CS 166.1)

The salvation of souls is the burden of our work. It was for this that Christ made the great sacrifice, and it is this that specially demands our beneficence.– *Historical Sketches of the Foreign Missions of the Seventh-day Adventists, 293.* (CS 166.2)

Self-Denial–Self-Sacrifice

In want and distress, God's children are calling to Him. Many are dying for want of the necessaries of life. Their cries have entered the ears of the Lord of Sabaoth. He will call to a strict account those who have neglected His needy ones. What will these selfish rich men do when the Lord asks them, "What did you do with the money I gave you to use for Me?" "These shall go away into everlasting punishment." The Lord will say to them, "Depart from Me, ye cursed; ... for I was an hungered, and ye gave Me no meat: I was thirsty, and ye gave Me no drink: I was a stranger, and ye took Me not in: naked, and ye clothed Me not: sick, and in prison, and ye visited Me not." (CS 166.3)

The wails of a world's sorrow are heard all around us. Sin is casting its shadow over us. Let us make ourselves ready to cooperate with the Lord. The pleasure and power of this world will pass away. No one can carry his earthly treasures into the eternal world. But the life spent in doing the will of God will abide forever. The result of that which is given to advance the work of God will be seen in the kingdom of God.– *The Review and Herald, January 31, 1907.* (**CS 166.4**)

For Further Study

Acquisition of Wealth a God-given Ability, *Testimonies for the Church 4:452, 458*

Wealth a Potential Blessing, *The Ministry of Healing, 212, 213*

Money of Value for Good It Can Do, *Christ's Object Lessons, 351*

The Ideal Christian Dispenses With One Hand, and Gains With the Other, *Testimonies for the Church 2:240*

Danger in Prosperity, *Prophets and Kings, 59, 60*

God Does Not Want Money Obtained by Dishonesty, *Testimonies for the Church 4:310, 311, 353*

Oppression of the Hireling, *Testimonies for the Church 1:175, 176, 480*

Overreaching in Trade, *Testimonies for the Church 4:494*

Close Dealing With Merchants, *Testimonies for the Church 2:238, 239*

Shrewdness to Be Kept Within Bounds, *Testimonies for the Church 4:540*

Immoderate Labor to Acquire Wealth, *Testimonies for the Church 2:654-656*

Men Act as Though Bereft of Reason, *Testimonies for the Church 2:662, 663*

Responsibilities of Christian Businessman, *Testimonies for the Church 4:468, 469*

Consecrated Business Ability Needed, *Testimonies for the Church 5:276*

Paul's Charge to the Rich, *Testimonies for the Church 1:540-542*

Satan Seeks to Retain Means in His Ranks, *Testimonies for the Church 2:675, 676 2; Early Writings, 266-269*

How to Thwart Satan's Designs, *Testimonies for the Church 1:142*

How to make Property Secure, *Testimonies for the Church 9:51*

Only Two Places for Deposit, *Testimonies for the Church 6:447, 448*

Tested by Invitation to the Gospel Feast, *Testimonies for the Church 3:383-385*

Riches and Idleness Not a Blessing, *Testimonies for the Church 2:259; Testimonies for the Church 6:452*

The Foolish Rich Man's Wasted Life, *Testimonies for the Church 3:546; Christ's Object Lessons, 256-259; Testimonies for the Church 5:260, 261*

Christ's Invitation to the Rich Young Ruler, *The Desire of Ages, 518-523*

Many Sabbathkeepers Like the Young Ruler, *Testimonies for the Church 1:170-172*

Providential Conversion of Men of Wealth, *Testimonies for the Church 9:114, 115; Testimonies for the Church 1:174, 175; Testimonies for the Church 6:258*

God Tests Man, Some by Granting, Others by Withholding, Wealth, *Testimonies for the Church 5:261*

Section 6
Liberality Abounding in Poverty

Chapter 34
Liberality Commended

The apostle Paul, in his ministry among the churches, was untiring in his efforts to inspire in the hearts of the new converts a desire to do large things for the cause of God. Often he exhorted them to the exercise of liberality. In speaking to the elders of Ephesus of his former labors among them, he said, "I have showed you all things, how that so laboring ye ought to support the weak, and to remember the words of the Lord Jesus, how He said, It is more blessed to give than to receive." *Acts 20:35.* (**CS 171.1**)

"He which soweth sparingly," he wrote to the Corinthians, "shall reap also sparingly; and he which soweth bountifully shall reap also bountifully. Every man according as he purposeth in his heart, so let him give; not grudgingly, or of necessity: for God loveth a cheerful giver." *2 Corinthians 9:6, 7.* (**CS 171.2**)

Nearly all the Macedonian believers were poor in this world's goods, but their hearts were overflowing with love for God and His truth, and they gladly gave for the support of the gospel. When general collections were taken up in the Gentile churches for the relief of the Jewish believers, the liberality of the converts in Macedonia was held up as an example to other churches. Writing to the Corinthian believers, the apostle called their attention to "the grace of God bestowed on the churches of Macedonia; how that in a great trial of affliction the abundance of their joy and their deep poverty abounded unto the riches of their liberality. For to their power, ... yea, and beyond their power they were willing of themselves; praying us with much entreaty that we would receive the gift, and take upon us the fellowship of the ministering to the saints." *2 Corinthians 8:1-4.* (**CS 171.3**)

The willingness to sacrifice on the part of the Macedonian believers came as a result of wholehearted consecration. Moved by the Spirit of God, they "first gave their own selves to the Lord" (*2 Corinthians 8:5*); then they were willing to give freely of their means for the support of the gospel. It was not necessary to urge them to give; rather, they rejoiced in the privilege of denying themselves even of necessary things in order to supply the needs of others. When the apostle would have restrained them, they importuned him to accept their offering. In their simplicity and integrity, and in their love for the brethren, they gladly denied self, and thus abounded in the fruit of benevolence. (**CS 172.1**)

When Paul sent Titus to Corinth to strengthen the believers there, he instructed him to build up that church in the grace of giving; and in a personal letter to the believers he also added his own appeal. "As ye abound in everything," he pleaded, "in faith, and utterance, and knowledge, and in all diligence, and in your love to us, see that ye abound in this grace also." "Now therefore perform the doing of it; that as there was a readiness to will, so there may be a performance also out of that which ye have. For if there be first a willing mind, it is accepted according to that a man hath, and not according to that he hath not." "And God is able to make all grace abound toward you; that ye, always having all sufficiency in all things, may abound to every good work: ... being enriched in everything to all bountifulness, which causeth through us thanksgiving to God." *2 Corinthians 8:7, 11, 12; 9:8-11.* (**CS 172.2**)

Unselfish liberality threw the early church into a transport of joy; for the believers knew that their efforts were helping to send the gospel message to those in darkness. Their benevolence testified that they had not received the grace of God in vain. What could produce such liberality but the sanctification of the Spirit? In the eyes of believers and unbelievers it was a miracle of grace.– *The Acts of the Apostles, 342-344.* (CS 172.3)

Liberality Rewarded

"So he [Elijah] arose and went to Zarephath. And when he came to the gate of the city, behold, the widow woman was there gathering of sticks: and he called to her, and said, Fetch me, I pray thee, a little water in a vessel, that I may drink. And as she was going to fetch it, he called to her, and said, Bring me, I pray thee, a morsel of bread in thine hand." (CS 173.1)

In this poverty-stricken home the famine pressed sore; and the pitifully meager fare seemed about to fail. The coming of Elijah on the very day when the widow feared that she must give up the struggle to sustain life, tested to the utmost her faith in the power of the living God to provide for her necessities. But even in her dire extremity, she bore witness to her faith by a compliance with the request of the stranger who was asking her to share her last morsel with him. (CS 173.2)

In response to Elijah's request for food and drink, the widow said, "As the Lord thy God liveth, I have not a cake, but a handful of meal in a barrel, and a little oil in a cruse: and, behold, I am gathering two sticks, that I may go in and dress it for me and my son, that we may eat it, and die." Elijah said to her: "Fear not; go and do as thou hast said: but make me thereof a little cake first, and bring it unto me, and after make for thee and for thy son. For thus saith the Lord God of Israel, The barrel of meal shall not waste, neither shall the cruse of oil fail, until the day that the Lord sendeth rain upon the earth." (CS 173.3)

No greater test of faith than this could have been required. The widow had hitherto treated all strangers with kindness and liberality. Now, regardless of the suffering that might result to herself and child, and trusting in the God of Israel to supply her every need, she met this supreme test of hospitality by doing "according to the saying of Elijah." (CS 173.4)

Wonderful was the hospitality shown to God's prophet by this Phoenician woman, and wonderfully were her faith and generosity

rewarded. "She, and he, and her house, did eat many days. And the barrel of meal wasted not, neither did the cruse of oil fail, according to the word of the Lord, which He spake by Elijah.".. (CS 174.1)

The widow of Zarephath shared her morsel with Elijah; and in return, her life and that of her son were preserved. And to all who, in time of trial and want, give sympathy and assistance to others more needy, God has promised great blessing. He has not changed. His power is no less now than in the days of Elijah.– *Prophets and Kings, 129-132.* (CS 174.2)

The Widow's Two Mites

Jesus was in the court where were the treasure chests, and He watched those who came to deposit their gifts. Many of the rich brought large sums, which they presented with great ostentation. Jesus looked upon them sadly, but made no comment on their liberal offerings. Presently His countenance lighted as He saw a poor widow approach hesitatingly, as though fearful of being observed. As the rich and haughty swept by, to deposit their offerings, she shrank back as if hardly daring to venture farther. And yet she longed to do something, little though it might be, for the cause she loved. She looked at the gift in her hand. It was very small in comparison with the gifts of those around her, yet it was her all. Watching her opportunity, she hurriedly threw in her two mites, and turned to hasten away. But in doing this she caught the eye of Jesus, which was fastened earnestly upon her. (CS 174.3)

The Saviour called His disciples to Him, and bade them mark the widow's poverty. Then His words of commendation fell upon her ear: "Of a truth I say unto you, that this poor widow hath cast in more than they all." Tears of joy filled her eyes as she felt that her act was understood and appreciated. Many would have advised her to keep her pittance for her own use; given into the hands of the well-fed priests, it would be lost sight of among the many costly gifts brought to the treasury. But Jesus understood her motive. She believed the service of the temple to be of God's appointment, and she was anxious to do her utmost to sustain it. She did what she could, and her act was to be a monument to her memory through all time, and her joy in eternity. Her heart went with her gift; its value was estimated, not by the worth of the coin, but by the love to God and the interest in His work that had prompted the deed. (**CS 175.1**)

Jesus said of the poor widow, She "hath cast in more than they all." The rich had bestowed from their abundance, many of them to be seen and honored by men. Their large donations had deprived them of no comfort, or even luxury; they had required no sacrifice, and could not be compared in value with the widow's mite. (**CS 175.2**)

The Motive Above the Amount

It is the motive that gives character to our acts, stamping them with ignominy or with high moral worth. Not the great things which every eye sees and every tongue praises does God account most precious. The little duties cheerfully done, the little gifts which make no show, and which to human eyes may appear worthless, often stand highest in His sight. A heart of faith and love is dearer to God than the most costly gift. (**CS 175.3**)

The poor widow gave her living to do the little that she did. She deprived herself of food in order to give those two mites to the cause she loved. And she did it in faith, believing that her heavenly Father would not overlook her great need. It was this unselfish spirit and childlike faith that won the Saviour's commendation.

(**CS 176.1**)

Among the poor there are many who long to show their gratitude to God for His grace and truth. They greatly desire to share with their more prosperous brethren in sustaining His service. These souls should not be repulsed. Let them lay up their mites in the bank of heaven. If given from a heart filled with love for God, these seeming trifles become consecrated gifts, priceless offerings, which God smiles upon and blesses.– *The Desire of Ages, 614-616.* (**CS 176.2**)

Mary's Acceptable Offering

It is the heart service that makes the gift valuable. When the Majesty of heaven became a babe, and was entrusted to Mary, she did not have much to offer for the precious gift. She brought to the altar only two turtledoves, the offering appointed for the poor; but they were an acceptable sacrifice to the Lord. She could not present rare treasures such as the wise men of the East came to Bethlehem to lay before the Son of God; yet the mother of Jesus was not rejected because of the smallness of her gift. It was the willingness of her heart that the Lord looked upon, and her love made the offering sweet. So God will accept our gift, however small, if it is the best we have, and is offered from love to Him.– *The Review and Herald, December 9, 1890.* (**CS 176.3**)

Chapter 35
Precious in God's Sight

Among the professed children of God, there are men and women who love the world, and the things of the world, and these souls are being corrupted by worldly influences. The divine is being dropped out of their nature. As instruments of unrighteousness, they are working out the purposes of the enemy. (CS 177.1)

In contrast with this class, stands the honest, industrious poor man, who is ready to help those who need help, and willing to suffer wrong rather than manifest the close, acquisitive spirit of the rich. This man esteems a clear conscience and right principles above the value of gold. He is ready to do all the good in his power. If some benevolent enterprise calls for money or for his labor, he is the first to respond, and often he goes far beyond his real ability, denying himself some needed good in order to carry out his benevolent purpose. (CS 177.2)

This man may boast of but little earthly treasure; he may be looked upon as deficient in judgment and wisdom; his influence may not be esteemed of special worth; but in the sight of God he is precious. He may be thought to have little perception, but he manifests a wisdom that is as far above that of the calculating, acquisitive mind as the divine is above the human; for is he not laying up for himself a treasure in the heavens, uncorrupted, undefiled, and that fadeth not away?– *The Review and Herald, December 19, 1899.* (CS 177.3)

As Fragrant Incense

Experience shows that a spirit of benevolence is more frequently found among those of limited means than among the more wealthy. Many who greatly desire riches would be ruined by their possession. When such persons are entrusted with talents of means, they too often hoard or waste the Lord's money, until the Master says to them individually, "Thou shalt be no longer steward." They dishonestly use that which is another's as though it were their own. God will not entrust them with eternal riches.... (CS 177.4)

The poor man's gift, the fruit of self-denial, to extend the precious light of truth, is as fragrant incense before God. Every act of self-sacrifice for the good of others will strengthen the spirit of beneficence in the giver's heart, allying him more closely to the Redeemer of the world, who was rich, yet for our sakes became poor, that we through His poverty might be rich. (CS 178.1)

The smallest sum given cheerfully as the result of self-denial is of more value in the sight of God than the offerings of those who could give thousands and yet feel no lack. The poor widow who cast two mites into the treasury of the Lord, showed love, faith, and benevolence.... God's blessing upon that sincere offering has made it the source of great results. (CS 178.2)

The widow's mite has been like a tiny stream flowing down through the ages, widening and deepening in its course, and contributing in a thousand directions to the extension of the truth and the relief of the needy. The influence of that small gift has acted and reacted upon thousands of hearts in every age and in every country. As the result, unnumbered gifts have flowed into the treasury of the Lord from the liberal, self-denying poor. And again, her example has stimulated to good works thousands of ease-loving, selfish, and doubting ones, and their gifts also have gone to swell the value of her offering.– *The Signs of the Times, November 15, 1910.* (CS 178.3)

The Givers Rewarded Though Gifts Are Misappropriated

Families in poverty, who had experienced the sanctifying influence of the truth, and who therefore prized it, and felt grateful to God for it, have thought that they could and should deprive themselves of even the necessaries of life, in order to bring in their offerings to the treasury of the Lord. Some have deprived themselves of articles of clothing which they really needed to make them comfortable. Others have sold their only cow, and have dedicated to God the means thus received. In the sincerity of their souls, with many tears of gratitude because it was their privilege to do this for the cause of God, they have bowed before the Lord with their offering, and have invoked His blessing upon it as they sent it forth, praying that it might be the means of bringing the knowledge of the truth to souls in darkness. (**CS 179.1**)

The means thus dedicated has not always been appropriated as the self-sacrificing donors designed. Covetous, selfish men, having no spirit of self-denial or self-sacrifice themselves, have handled unfaithfully means thus brought into the treasury; and they have robbed the treasury of God by receiving means which they had not justly earned. Their unconsecrated, reckless management has squandered and scattered means that had been consecrated to God with prayers and tears.... (**CS 179.2**)

Even though the means thus consecrated be misapplied, so that it does not accomplish the object which the donor had in view,–the glory of God and the salvation of souls,–those who made the sacrifice in sincerity of soul, with an eye single to the glory of God, will not lose their reward.– *Testimonies for the Church 2:518, 519.* (**CS 179.3**)

As Estimated in the Heavenly Balances

In the balances of the sanctuary, the gifts of the poor, made from love to Christ, are not estimated according to the amount given, but according to the love which prompts the sacrifice. The promises of Jesus will as surely be realized by the liberal poor man, who has but little to offer, but who gives that little freely, as by the wealthy man who gives of his abundance. The poor man makes a sacrifice of his little, which he really feels. He really denies himself of some things that he needs for his own comfort, while the wealthy man gives of his abundance, and feels no want, denies himself nothing that he really needs. Therefore there is a sacredness in the poor man's offering that is not found in the rich man's gift; for the rich give of their abundance. God's providence has arranged the entire plan of systematic benevolence for the benefit of man. His providence never stands still. If God's servants follow His opening providence, all will be active workers.– *Testimonies for the Church 3:398, 399.* (**CS 180.1**)

For Further Study

No Incense More Fragrant Than Gifts of poor, *Testimonies for the Church 7:215, 216*

Sacrifices of the Poor for the Cause, *Testimonies for the Church 5:733, 734*

Not to Leave Sacrificing to Those Better Off, *Testimonies for the Church 1:115, 177; Testimonies for the Church 9:245, 246*

Not to Put Their Last Means Into Institutions, *Testimonies for the Church 1:639*

Poor to Practice Simplicity and Economy, *The Ministry of Healing, 196, 207*

Talents Given to the Poor to Be Used, *Testimonies for the Church 2:245-247*

Poor to Help Themselves as Far as Possible, *Testimonies for the Church 1:272; Testimonies for the Church 2:30-37; Testimonies for the Church 6:277, 278*

Liberality Will Not Bring to Want, *Patriarchs and Prophets, 527, 533*

Poor in Israel Not to Come Empty-handed, *Testimonies for the Church 1:220*

Section 7
The Wealth of the Gentiles

Chapter 36
Favors to Be Received as Well as Imparted

Just as long as we are in this world, and the Spirit of God is striving with the world, we are to receive as well as to impart favors. We are to give to the world the light of truth as presented in the Sacred Scriptures, and we are to receive from the world that which God moves upon them to do in behalf of His cause. The Lord still moves upon the hearts of kings and rulers in behalf of His people, and it becomes those who are so deeply interested in the religious liberty question not to cut off any favors, or withdraw themselves from the help that God has moved men to give, for the advancement of His cause. (CS 183.1)

We find examples in the word of God concerning this very matter. Cyrus, king of Persia, made a proclamation throughout all his kingdom, and put it into writing, saying: "Thus saith Cyrus king of Persia, The Lord God of heaven hath given me all the kingdoms of the earth; and He hath charged me to build Him a house at Jerusalem, which is in Judah. Who is there among you of all His people? his God be with him, and let him go up to Jerusalem, which is in Judah, and build the house of the Lord God of Israel." A second commandment was issued by Darius for the building of the house of the Lord, and is recorded in the sixth chapter of Ezra. (CS 183.2)

The Lord God of Israel has placed His goods in the hands of unbelievers, but they are to be used in favor of doing the works that must be done for a fallen world. The agents through whom these gifts come, may open up avenues through which the truth may go. They may have no sympathy with the work, and no faith in Christ, and no practice in His words; but their gifts are not to be refused on that account.... (CS 183.3)

I have repeatedly been shown that we might receive far more favors than we do in many ways if we would approach men in wisdom, acquaint them with our work, and give them an opportunity of doing those things which it is our privilege to induce them to do for the advancement of the work of God.– *Testimonies to Ministers and Gospel Workers, 202, 203.* (CS 184.1)

Example of Nehemiah

Nehemiah did not depend upon uncertainty. The means that he lacked he solicited from those who were able to bestow. And the Lord is still willing to move upon the hearts of those in possession of His goods, in behalf of the cause of truth. Those who labor for Him are to avail themselves of the help that He prompts men to give. These gifts may open ways by which the light of truth shall go to many benighted lands. The donors may have no faith in Christ, no acquaintance with His word; but their gifts are not on this account to be refused.– *Prophets and Kings, 634.* (CS 184.2)

God's work is now to advance rapidly, and if His people will respond to His call, He will make the possessors of property willing to donate of their means, and thus make it possible for His work to be accomplished in the earth. "Faith is the substance of things hoped for, the evidence of things not seen." *Hebrews 11:1.* Faith in the word of God will place His people in the possession of property which will enable them to work the large cities that are waiting for the message of truth.– *Testimonies for the Church 9:272, 273.* (CS 184.3)

Receiving Gifts From Outside

You inquire with respect to the propriety of receiving gifts from Gentiles or the heathen. The question is not strange; but I would ask you, Who is it that owns our world? Who are the real owners of houses and lands? Is it not God? He has an abundance in our world which He has placed in the hands of men, by which the hungry might be supplied with food, the naked with clothing, the homeless with homes. The Lord would move upon worldly men, even idolaters, to give of their abundance for the support of the work, if we would approach them wisely, and give them an opportunity of doing those things which it is their privilege to do. What they would give we should be privileged to receive. **(CS 185.1)**

We should become acquainted with men in high places, and by exercising the wisdom of the serpent, and the harmlessness of the dove, we might obtain advantage from them, for God would move upon their minds to do many things in behalf of His people. If proper persons would set before those who have means and influence, the needs of the work of God in a proper light, these men might do much to advance the cause of God in our world. We have put away from us privileges and advantages that we might have had the benefit of, because we chose to stand independent of the world. But we need not sacrifice one principle of truth while taking advantage of every opportunity to advance the cause of God.– *Testimonies to Ministers and Gospel Workers, 197, 198.* **(CS 185.2)**

Chapter 37
God Preparing the Way

If the needs of the Lord's work were set forth in a proper light before those who have means and influence, these men might do much to advance the cause of present truth. God's people have lost many privileges of which they could have taken advantage, had they not chosen to stand independent of the world. (CS 186.1)

In the providence of God, we are daily brought into connection with the unconverted. By His own right hand God is preparing the way before us, in order that His work may progress rapidly. As colaborers with Him, we have a sacred work to do. We are to have travail of soul for those who are in high places; we are to extend to them the gracious invitation to come to the marriage feast. (CS 186.2)

Although now almost wholly in the possession of wicked men, all the world, with its riches and treasures, belongs to God. "The earth is the Lord's, and the fullness thereof." ... O that Christians might realize more and still more fully that it is their privilege and their duty, while cherishing right principles, to take advantage of every heaven-sent opportunity for advancing God's kingdom in this world!– *Stewardship Series, No. 1, 14, 15* (An Appeal to Ministers and Church Officers Regarding the Soliciting of Gifts for Our Foreign Mission Work). (CS 186.3)

Impressed by the Spirit to Give

Medical missionaries who labor in evangelistic lines are doing a work of as high an order as are their ministerial fellow workers. The efforts put forth by these workers are not to be limited to the poorer classes. The higher classes have been strangely neglected. In the higher walks of life will be found many who will respond to the truth, because it is consistent, because it bears the stamp of the high character of the gospel. Not a few of the men of ability thus won to the cause will enter energetically into the Lord's work. (CS 186.4)

The Lord calls upon those who are in positions of trust, those to whom He has entrusted His precious gifts, to use their talents of intellect and means in His service. Our workers should present before these men a plain statement of our plan of labor, telling them what we need in order to help the poor and needy and to establish this work on a firm basis. Some of these will be impressed by the Holy Spirit to invest the Lord's means in a way that will advance His cause. They will fulfill His purpose by helping to create centers of influence in the large cities.– *Testimonies for the Church 7:112.* (CS 187.1)

Calling Upon Rich Men

There is a world to be warned, and we have been very delicate about calling upon rich men, either church members or worldlings, to aid us in the work. We would that all professed Christians stood with us. We would that their souls might be drawn out in liberality in aiding us in building up the kingdom of God in our world. We should call upon great and good men to help us in our Christian-endeavor work. They should be invited to second our efforts in seeking to save that which is lost.– *The Origin and Development of the Thanksgiving Plan, 5* (written February 28, 1900). (CS 187.2)

God Will Open the Way

Times are growing hard, and money is difficult to obtain; but God will open the way for us from sources outside our own people. I cannot see how anyone can take exceptions to the receiving of gifts from those not of our faith. They can only do so by taking extreme views, and by creating issues which they are not authorized to do. This is God's world, and if God could move upon human agents so that the land which has been in the hands of the enemy, may be brought into our hands, so that the message may be proclaimed in regions beyond, shall men block up the way with their narrow notions? Such conscientiousness as this is anything but healthful. The Holy Spirit does not lead men to pursue such a course.– *Testimonies to Ministers and Gospel Workers, 210.* (**CS 187.3**)

A Means of Conversion

Why not ask the Gentiles for assistance? I have received instruction that there are men and women in the world who have sympathetic hearts, and who will be touched with compassion as the needs of suffering humanity are presented before them.... (**CS 188.1**)

There are men in the world who will give of their means for schools and for sanitariums. The matter has been presented to me in this light. Our work is to be aggressive. The money is the Lord's, and if the wealthy are approached in the right way, the Lord will touch their hearts, and impress them to give of their means. God's money is in the hands of these men, and some of them will heed the request for help. (**CS 188.2**)

Talk this over, and do all in your power to secure gifts. We are not to feel that it would not be the thing to ask men of the world for means; for it is just the thing to do. This plan was opened before me as a way of coming in touch with wealthy men of the world. Through this means not a few will become interested, and may hear and believe the truth for this time.– *Stewardship Series, No. 1, 15, 16.* (**CS 188.3**)

Chapter 38
The Harvest Ingathering Work

In following any plan that may be set in operation for carrying to others a knowledge of present truth, and of the marvelous providences connected with the advancing cause, let us first consecrate ourselves fully to Him whose name we wish to exalt. Let us also pray earnestly in behalf of those whom we expect to visit, by living faith bringing them, one by one, into the presence of God. (CS 189.1)

The Lord knows the thoughts and purposes of man, and how easily He can melt us! How His Spirit, like a fire, can subdue the flinty heart! How He can fill the soul with love and tenderness! How He can give us the graces of His Holy Spirit, and fit us to go in and out, in laboring for souls! The power of overcoming grace should be felt throughout the church today; and it may be felt, if we take heed to the counsels of Christ to His followers. As we learn to adorn the doctrine of Christ our Saviour we shall surely see of the salvation of God. (CS 189.2)

To all who are about to take up special missionary work with the paper prepared for use in the Harvest Ingathering campaign, I would say: Be diligent in your efforts; live under the guidance of the Holy Spirit. Add daily to your Christian experience. Let those who have special aptitude, work for unbelievers in the high places as well as in the low places of life. Search diligently for perishing souls. Oh, think of the yearning desire Christ has to bring to His fold again those who have gone astray! (CS 189.3)

Watch for souls as they that must give an account. In your church and neighborhood missionary work, let your light shine forth in such clear, steady rays that no man can stand up in the judgment, and say, "Why did you not tell me about this truth? Why did you not care for my soul?" (CS 189.4)

Then let us be diligent in the distribution of literature that has been carefully prepared for use among those not of our faith. Let us make the most of every opportunity to arrest the attention of unbelievers. Let us put literature into every hand that will receive it. Let us consecrate ourselves to the proclamation of the message, "Prepare ye the way of the Lord, make straight in the desert a highway for our God!" Divine and human instrumentalities are to unite for the accomplishment of one great object. Now is the day of our responsibility. "The Spirit and the bride say, Come. And let him that heareth say, Come. And let him that is athirst come. And whosoever will, let him take the water of life freely.– *Manuscript 2, 1914.* (CS 190.1)

Fruit of This Twofold Effort

In the providence of God, those who are bearing the burden of His work have been endeavoring to put new life into old methods of labor, and also to invent new plans and new methods of awakening the interest of church members in a united effort to reach the world. One of the new plans for reaching unbelievers is the Harvest Ingathering campaign for missions. In many places, during the past few years, this has proved a success, bringing blessing to many, and increasing the flow of means into the mission treasury. As those not of our faith have been made acquainted with the progress of the third angel's message in heathen lands, their sympathies have been aroused, and some have sought to learn more of the truth that has such power to transform hearts and lives. Men and women of all classes have been reached, and the name of God has been glorified. (CS 190.2)

In years past, I have spoken in favor of the plan of presenting our mission work and its progress before our friends and neighbors, and have referred to the example of Nehemiah. And now I desire to urge our brethren and sisters to study anew the experience of this man of prayer and faith and sound judgment, who made bold to ask his friend, King Artaxerxes, for help with which to advance the interests of God's cause. Let all understand that in presenting the needs of our work, believers can reflect light to others, only as they, like Nehemiah of old, draw nigh to God, and live in close connection with the Giver of all light. Our own souls must be firmly grounded in a knowledge of the truth, if we would win others from error to truth. We need now to search the Scriptures diligently, that, as we become acquainted with unbelievers, we may hold up before them Christ as the anointed, the crucified, the risen Saviour, witnessed to by prophets, testified of by believers, and through whose name we receive the forgiveness of our sins.– *Manuscript 2, 1914.* **(CS 191.1)**

For Further Study

Nehemiah and the Persian King, *Prophets and Kings, 628-634*

Opportunities to Secure Properties at Far Less Than Their Cash Value, *Testimonies for the Church 7:102*

Many Among Wealthy, After Responding to Appeal for Means, Will Surrender Themselves to Christ, *Testimonies for the Church 6:258*

Many Rich Converted That They May assist Cause, *Testimonies for the Church 1:174*

Many Men of Wealth Susceptible to Gospel, and Will Give of Their Entrusted Means, *Testimonies for the Church 8:114-116*

Harvest Ingathering, *Christian Service, 167-177*

Section 8

The True Motives for Acceptable Giving

Chapter 39

The True Motive in All Service

In the days of Christ the Pharisees were continually trying to earn the favor of Heaven, in order to secure the worldly honor and prosperity which they regarded as the reward of virtue. At the same time they paraded their acts of charity before the people in order to attract their attention, and gain a reputation for sanctity. (CS 195.1)

Jesus rebuked their ostentation, declaring that God does not recognize such service, and that the flattery and admiration of the people, which they so eagerly sought, was the only reward they would ever receive. (CS 195.2)

"When thou doest alms," He said, "let not thy left hand know what thy right hand doeth; that thine alms may be in secret; and thy Father, which seeth in secret, Himself shall reward thee openly." (CS 195.3)

In these words Jesus did not teach that acts of kindness should always be kept secret. Paul the apostle, writing by the Holy Spirit, did not conceal the generous self-sacrifice of the Macedonian Christians, but told of the grace that Christ had wrought in them, and thus others were imbued with the same spirit. He also wrote to the church at Corinth and said, "Your zeal hath stirred up very many." (CS 195.4)

Christ's own words make His meaning plain,-that in acts of charity the aim should not be to secure praise and honor from men. Real godliness never prompts an effort at display. Those who desire words of praise and flattery, and feed upon them as a sweet morsel, are Christians in name only. (CS 195.5)

By their good works, Christ's followers are to bring glory, not to themselves, but to Him through whose grace and power they have wrought. It is through the Holy Spirit that every good work is accomplished, and the Spirit is given to glorify, not the receiver, but the Giver. When the light of Christ is shining in the soul, the lips will be filled with praise and thanksgiving to God. Your prayers, your performance of duty, your benevolence, your self-denial, will not be the theme of your thought or conversation. Jesus will be magnified, self will be hidden, and Christ will appear as all in all. (CS 195.6)

We are to give in sincerity, not to make a show of our good deeds, but from pity and love to the suffering ones. Sincerity of purpose, real kindness of heart, is the motive that Heaven values. The soul that is sincere in its love, wholehearted in its devotion, God regards as more precious than the golden wedge of Ophir.... We are not to think of reward, but of service.– *Thoughts From the Mount of Blessing, 120, 121.* (CS 196.1)

Motive for Giving Is Chronicled

I was shown that the recording angel makes a faithful record of every offering dedicated to God, and put into the treasury, and also of the final result of the means thus bestowed. The eye of God takes cognizance of every farthing devoted to His cause, and of the willingness or reluctance of the giver. The motive in giving is also chronicled. Those self-sacrificing, consecrated ones who render back to God the things that are His, as He requires of them, will be rewarded according to their works.– *Testimonies for the Church 2:518, 519.* (CS 196.2)

Higher Motives Than Sympathy

The moral darkness of a ruined world pleads to Christian men and women to put forth individual effort, to give of their means and of their influence, that they may be assimilated to the image of Him who, though He possessed infinite riches, yet for our sakes became poor. The Spirit of God cannot abide with those to whom He has sent the message of His truth, but who need to be urged before they can have any sense of their duty to be coworkers with Christ. The apostle enforces the duty of giving from higher grounds than merely human sympathy, because the feelings are moved. He enforces the principle that we should labor unselfishly with an eye single to the glory of God.– *Testimonies for the Church 3:391.* (**CS 196.3**)

Love the Principle of Action

Love must be the principle of action. Love is the underlying principle of God's government in heaven and earth, and it must be the foundation of the Christian's character. This alone can make and keep him steadfast. This alone can enable him to withstand trial and temptation. (**CS 197.1**)

And love will be revealed in sacrifice. The plan of redemption was laid in sacrifice,–a sacrifice so broad and deep and high that it is immeasurable. Christ gave all for us, and those who receive Christ will be ready to sacrifice all for the sake of their Redeemer. The thought of His honor and glory will come before anything else. (**CS 197.2**)

If we love Jesus, we shall love to live for Him, to present our thank offerings to Him, to labor for Him. The very labor will be light. For His sake we shall covet pain and toil and sacrifice. We shall sympathize with His longing for the salvation of men. We shall feel the same tender craving for souls that He has felt. (**CS 197.3**)

This is the religion of Christ. Anything short of it is a deception. No mere theory of truth or profession of discipleship will save any soul. We do not belong to Christ unless we are His wholly. It is by halfheartedness in the Christian life that men become feeble in purpose and changeable in desire. The effort to serve both self and Christ makes one a stony-ground hearer, and he will not endure when the test comes upon him.– *Christ's Object Lessons, 49, 50.* (**CS 197.4**)

Chapter 40
Freewill Offerings

All that we do is to be done willingly. We are to bring our offerings with joy and gratitude, saying as we present them, Of Thine own we freely give Thee. The most costly service we can render is but meager compared to the gift of God to our world. Christ is a gift every day. God gave Him to the world, and He graciously takes the gifts entrusted to His human agents for the advancement of His work in the world. Thus we show that we recognize and acknowledge that every thing belongs to God, absolutely and entirely.- *Manuscript 124, 1898.* (CS 198.1)

The offering from the heart that loves, God delights to honor, giving it highest efficiency in service for Him. If we have given our hearts to Jesus, we also shall bring our gifts to Him. Our gold and silver, our most precious earthly possessions, our highest mental and spiritual endowments, will be freely devoted to Him who loved us, and gave Himself for us.- *The Desire of Ages, 65.* (CS 198.2)

Thank and Trespass Offerings

Come to the Lord with hearts overflowing with thankfulness for past and present mercies, and manifest your appreciation of God's bounties by bringing to Him your thank offerings, your freewill offerings, and your trespass offerings.- *The Review and Herald, January 4, 1881.* (CS 198.3)

Grudging Gift a Mockery to God

God has made men His almoners, copartners with Himself in the great work of advancing His kingdom on the earth; but they may pursue the course pursued by the unfaithful servant, and by so doing lose the most precious privileges ever granted to men. For thousands of years God has worked through human agencies, but at His will He can drop out the selfish, the money-loving, and the covetous. He is not dependent upon our means, and He will not be restricted by the human agent. He can carry on His own work though we act no part in it. But who among us would be pleased to have the Lord do this? (CS 198.4)

It were better not to give at all than to give grudgingly; for if we impart of our means when we have not the spirit to give freely, we mock God. Let us bear in mind that we are dealing with One upon whom we depend for every blessing. One who reads every thought of the heart, every purpose of the mind.- *The Review and Herald, May 15, 1900.* (CS 199.1)

The Cheerful Giver Accepted

"But this I say, He which soweth sparingly shall reap also sparingly; and he which soweth bountifully shall reap also bountifully. Every man according as he purposeth in his heart, so let him give; not grudgingly, or of necessity: for God loveth a cheerful giver." If we act in the spirit of this counsel, we may invite the Divine One to audit the accounts of our temporal matters. We may feel that we are only giving offerings from that which is our Lord's entrusted gift. (CS 199.2)

All our offerings should be presented with cheerfulness; for they come from the fund which the Lord has seen fit to place in our hands for the purpose of carrying forward His work in the world, in order that the banner of truth may be unfurled in the highways and byways of the earth. If all who profess the truth would give to the Lord His own in tithes and gifts and offerings, there would be meat in the house of the Lord. The cause of benevolence would no longer be dependent on the uncertain gifts of impulse, and vary according to the changing feelings of men. God's claims would be welcomed, and His cause would be considered as justly entitled to a portion of the funds entrusted to our hands. (CS 199.3)

How much more eager will every faithful steward be to enlarge the proportion of gifts to be placed in the Lord's treasure house, than to decrease his offering one jot or tittle. Whom is he serving? For whom is he preparing an offering?–For the One upon whom he is dependent for every good thing which he enjoys. Then let not one of us who is receiving the grace of Christ, give occasion for the angels to be ashamed of us, and for Jesus to be ashamed to call us brethren. (CS 200.1)

Shall ingratitude be cultivated, and made manifest by our niggardly practices in giving to the cause of God?–No, no! Let us surrender ourselves a living sacrifice, and give our all to Jesus. It is His; we are His purchased possession. Those who are recipients of His grace, who contemplate the cross of Calvary, will not question concerning the proportion to be given, but will feel that the richest offering is all too meager, all disproportionate to the great gift of the only-begotten Son of the infinite God. Through self-denial, the poorest will find ways of obtaining something to give back to God.– *The Review and Herald, July 14, 1896.* (CS 200.2)

Chapter 41
Popular Methods of Appeal

We see the churches of our day encouraging feasting, gluttony, and dissipation, by the suppers, fairs, dances, and festivals gotten up for the purpose of gathering means into the church treasury. Here is a method invented by carnal minds to secure means without sacrificing. (CS 201.1)

Such an example makes an impression upon the minds of youth. They notice that lotteries and fairs and games are sanctioned by the church, and they think there is something fascinating in this way of obtaining means. A youth is surrounded by temptations. He enters the bowling alley, the gambling saloon, to see the sport. He sees the money taken by the one who wins. This looks enticing. It seems an easier way of obtaining money than by earnest work, which requires persevering energy and strict economy. He imagines there can be no harm in this; for similar games have been resorted to in order to obtain means for the benefit of the church. Then why should he not help himself in this way? (CS 201.2)

He has a little means, which he ventures to invest, thinking it may bring in quite a sum. Whether he gains or loses, he is in the downward road to ruin. But it was the example of the church that led him into the false path. (CS 201.3)

Lame and Diseased Offerings

Let us stand clear of all these church corruptions, dissipations, and festivals, which have a demoralizing influence upon young and old. We have no right to throw over them the cloak of sanctity because the means is to be used for church purposes. Such offerings are lame and diseased, and bear the curse of God. They are the price of souls. The pulpit may defend festivals, dancing, lotteries, fairs, and luxurious feasts, to obtain means for church purposes; but let us participate in none of these things; for if we do, God's displeasure will be upon us. We do not propose to appeal to the lust of the appetite or resort to carnal amusements as an inducement to Christ's professed followers to give of the means which God has entrusted to them. If they do not give willingly, for the love of Christ, the offering will in no case be acceptable to God. (CS 201.4)

Characters Wrecked

Death, clad in the livery of heaven, lurks in the pathway of the young. Sin is gilded over by church sanctity. These various forms of amusement in the churches of our day have ruined thousands who, but for them, might have remained upright and become the followers of Christ. Wrecks of character have been made by these fashionable church festivals and theatrical performances, and thousands more will be destroyed; yet people will not be aware of the danger, nor of the fearful influences exerted. Many young men and women have lost their souls through these corrupting influences.– *The Review and Herald, November 21, 1878.* (CS 202.1)

Giving for Selfish Considerations

In professedly Christian gatherings, Satan throws a religious garment over delusive pleasures and unholy revelings to give them the appearance of sanctity, and the consciences of many are quieted because means are raised to defray church expenses. Men refuse to give for the love of God; but for the love of pleasure, and the indulgence of appetite for selfish considerations, they will part with their money. (CS 202.2)

Is it because there is not power in the lessons of Christ upon benevolence, and in His example, and the grace of God upon the heart to lead men to glorify God with their substance, that such a course must be resorted to in order to sustain the church? The injury sustained to the physical, mental, and moral health in these scenes of amusement and gluttony is not small. And the day of final reckoning will show souls lost through the influence of these scenes of gaiety and folly. (CS 203.1)

It is a deplorable fact that sacred and eternal considerations do not have that power to open the hearts of the professed followers of Christ to make freewill offerings to sustain the gospel, as the tempting bribes of feasting and general merriment. It is a sad reality that these inducements will prevail when sacred and eternal things will have no force to influence the heart to engage in works of benevolence. (CS 203.2)

Moses Did Not Institute Lotteries

The plan of Moses in the wilderness to raise means was highly successful. There was no compulsion necessary. Moses made no grand feast. He did not invite the people to scenes of gaiety, dancing, and general amusement. Neither did he institute lotteries or anything of this profane order to obtain means to erect the tabernacle of God in the wilderness. God commanded Moses to invite the children of Israel to bring the offerings. Moses was to accept gifts of every man that gave willingly from his heart. These freewill offerings came in so great abundance that Moses proclaimed it was enough. They must cease their presents; for they had given abundantly, more than they could use. (CS 203.3)

Satan's temptations succeed with the professed followers of Christ on the point of indulgence of pleasure and appetite. Clothed as an angel of light, he will quote Scripture to justify the temptations he places before men to indulge the appetite, and in worldly pleasures which suit the carnal heart. The professed followers of Christ are weak in moral power, and are fascinated with the bribe which Satan has presented before them, and he gains the victory. (CS 204.1)

How does God look upon churches that are sustained by such means? Christ cannot accept these offerings, because they were not given through their love and devotion to Him, but through their idolatry of self. But what many would not do for the love of Christ, they will do for the love of delicate luxuries to gratify the appetite, and for love of worldly amusements to please the carnal heart.– *The Review and Herald, October 13, 1874.* (CS 204.2)

Repeating the Sin of Nadab and Abihu

Professed Christians reject the Lord's plan of raising means for His work; and to what do they resort to supply the lack? God sees the wickedness of the methods they adopt. Places of worship are defiled by all manner of idolatrous dissipation, that a little money may be won from selfish pleasure lovers to pay church debts or to sustain the work of the church. Many of these persons would not of their own accord pay one shilling for religious purposes. Where, in God's directions for the support of His work, do we find any mention of bazaars, concerts, fancy fairs, and similar entertainments? Must the Lord's cause be dependent upon the very things He has forbidden in His word–upon those things that turn the mind away from God, from sobriety, from piety and holiness? (CS 204.3)

And what impression is made upon the minds of unbelievers? The holy standard of the word of God is lowered into the dust. Contempt is cast upon God and upon the Christian name. The most corrupt principles are strengthened by this un-Scriptural way of raising means. And this is as Satan would have it. Men are repeating the sin of Nadab and Abihu. They are using common instead of sacred fire in the service of God. The Lord accepts no such offerings. (CS 205.1)

All these methods for bringing money into His treasury are an abomination to Him. It is a spurious devotion that prompts all such devising. O what blindness, what infatuation, is upon many who claim to be Christians! Church members are doing as did the inhabitants of the world in the days of Noah, when the imagination of their hearts was only evil continually. All who fear God will abhor such practices as a misrepresentation of the religion of Jesus Christ.– *The Review and Herald December 8,*

1896. (**CS 205.2**)

Liberality With No Depth of Principle

The minister may be the special favorite of some wealthy man, and he may be very liberal with him; this gratifies the minister, and he in turn lavishes praise upon the benevolence of his donor. His name may be exalted by appearing in print, and yet that liberal donor may be entirely unworthy of the credit given him. (**CS 205.3**)

His liberality did not arise from a deep, living principle to do good with his means, to advance the cause of God because he appreciated it, but from some selfish motive, a desire to be thought liberal. He may have given from impulse, and his liberality have no depth of principle. He may have been moved upon by listening to stirring truth, which for the time being loosed his purse strings; yet, after all, his liberality has no deeper motive. He gives by spasms; his purse opens spasmodically, and closes just as securely, spasmodically. He deserves no commendation, for he is in every sense of the word a stingy man; and unless thoroughly converted, purse and all, will hear the withering denunciation, "Go to, now, ye rich men, weep and howl for your miseries that shall come upon you. Your riches are corrupted, and your garments are moth-eaten." (**CS 205.4**)

Such will awake at last from a horrible self-deception. Those who praised their spasmodic liberalities, helped Satan to deceive them, and make them think that they were very liberal, very sacrificing, when they know not the first principles of liberality or self-sacrifice.– *Testimonies for the Church 1:475, 476.* (**CS 206.1**)

For Further Study

Willing Obedience and Pure Love to Bind Every Offering on the Altar, *Testimonies for the Church 5:269, 270*

Small Offering Given in Cheerfulness Is Greatly Blessed, *Testimonies for the Church 7:295*

No Virtue in Giving More With Grudging Heart, *Testimonies for the Church 5:285*

None Compelled to Sacrifice, Must Be a Freewill Offering, *Early Writings, 50, 51*

Those Who Give Must Esteem It a Privilege to Do So, *Testimonies for the Church 1:177*

Anciently Offerings Must Be Without Blemish, the Best, and Given Freely, *Testimonies for the Church 1:221*

Selfishness the Reason for No Freewill Offerings, *Testimonies for the Church 1:225*

Responsibility for Large or Small Gift an Individual One, *Testimonies for the Church 1:237, 238*

Freewill and Thank Offerings Brought to Convocations, *Testimonies for the Church 2:573, 576*

Freewill Offerings Enrich Not God but the Giver, *Testimonies for the Church 2:653*

No Heart-stirring Appeals Needed When Heart Is Filled With Grateful Love, *Testimonies for the Church 3:396, 413*

Section 9
The Pursuit of Earthly Treasure

Chapter 42
The Peril of Covetousness

Many of the people of God are stupefied by the spirit of the world, and are denying their faith by their works. They cultivate a love for money, for houses and lands, until it absorbs the powers of mind and being, and shuts out love for the Creator and for souls for whom Christ died. The god of this world has blinded their eyes; their eternal interests are made secondary; and brain, bone, and muscle are taxed to the utmost to increase their worldly possessions. And all this accumulation of cares and burdens is borne in direct violation of the injunction of Christ, who said, "Lay not up for yourselves treasures upon earth, where moth and rust doth corrupt, and where thieves break through and steal." (CS 209.1)

They forget that He said also, "Lay up for yourselves treasures in heaven;" that in so doing they are working for their own interest. The treasure laid up in heaven is safe; no thief can approach nor moth corrupt it. But their treasure is upon the earth, and their affections are upon their treasure. (CS 209.2)

Christ's Victory

In the wilderness, Christ met the great leading temptations that would assail man. There, singlehanded, He encountered the wily, subtle foe, and overcame him. The first great temptation was upon appetite; the second, presumption; the third, love of the world. The thrones and kingdoms of the world, and the glory of them, were offered to Christ. Satan came with worldly honor, wealth, and the pleasures of life, and presented them in the most attractive light to allure and deceive. "All these things," said he to Christ, "will I give Thee, if Thou wilt fall down and worship me." Yet Christ repelled the wily foe, and came off victor. (CS 209.3)

Man will never be tried by temptations as powerful as those which assailed Christ; yet Satan has better success in approaching him. "All this money, this gain, this land, this power, these honors and riches, will I give thee"—for what? The condition is seldom as plainly stated as it was to Christ,—"If Thou wilt fall down and worship me." He is content to require that integrity shall be yielded, conscience blunted. Through devotion to worldly interests he receives all the homage he asks. The door is left open for him to enter as he pleases, with his evil train of impatience, love of self, pride, avarice, and dishonesty. Man is charmed, and treacherously allured on to ruin. (CS 210.1)

The example of Christ is before us. He overcame Satan, showing us how we also may overcome. Christ resisted Satan with Scripture. He might have had recourse to His own divine power, and used His own words; but He said, "It is written, Man shall not live by bread alone, but by every word that proceedeth out of the mouth of God." If the Sacred Scriptures were studied and followed, the Christian would be fortified to meet the wily foe; but the word of God is neglected, and disaster and defeat follow. (CS 210.2)

The Rich Young Ruler

A young man came to Christ, and said, "Good Master, what good thing shall I do, that I may have eternal life?" Jesus bade him keep the commandments. He replied, "All these things have I kept from my youth up: what lack I yet?" Jesus looked with love upon the young man, and faithfully pointed out to him his deficiency in keeping the divine law. He did not love his neighbor as himself. His selfish love of riches was a defect, which, if not remedied, would debar him from heaven. "If thou wilt be perfect, go and sell that thou hast, and give to the poor, and thou shalt have treasure in heaven: and come and follow Me." (CS 210.3)

Christ would have the young man understand that He required nothing of him more than to follow the example that He Himself, the Lord of heaven, had set. He left His riches and glory, and became poor, that man, through His poverty, might be made rich; and for the sake of these riches, He requires man to yield earthly wealth, honor, and pleasure. He knows that while the affections are upon the world, they will be withdrawn from God; therefore He said to the young man, "Go and sell that thou hast, and give to the poor, and thou shalt have treasure in heaven: and come and follow Me." How did he receive the words of Christ? Was he rejoiced that he could secure the heavenly treasure? Oh, no! "He went away sorrowful: for he had great possessions." To him riches were honor and power; and the great amount of his treasure made such a disposal of it seem almost an impossibility. (CS 211.1)

This world-loving man desired heaven; but he wanted to retain his wealth, and he renounced immortal life for the love of money and power. Oh, what a miserable exchange! Yet many who profess to be keeping all the commandments of God are doing the same thing. (CS 211.2)

Here is the danger of riches to the avaricious man; the more he gains the harder it is for him to be generous. To diminish his wealth is like parting with his life; and he turns from the attractions of the immortal reward, in order to retain and increase his earthly possessions. Had he kept the commandments, his worldly possessions would not have been so great. How could he, while plotting and striving for self, love God with all his heart, and with all his mind, and with all his strength, and his neighbor as himself? Had he distributed to the necessities of the poor as their wants demanded, he would have been far happier, and would have had greater heavenly treasure, and less of earth upon which to place his affections.... (CS 211.3)

Accountable to God

Said Paul, "I am debtor both to the Greeks, and to the barbarians; both to the wise, and to the unwise." God had revealed His truth to Paul, and in so doing had made him a debtor to those who were in darkness to enlighten them. But many do not realize their accountability to God. They are handling their Lord's talents; they have powers of mind, that, if employed in the right direction, would make them coworkers with Christ and His angels. Many souls might be saved through their efforts, to shine as stars in the crown of their rejoicing. But they are indifferent to all this. Satan has sought, through the attractions of this world, to enchain them and paralyze their moral powers, and he has succeeded only too well. (CS 212.1)

The Future Destiny at Stake

How can houses and lands compare in value with precious souls for whom Christ died? Through your instrumentality, dear brethren and sisters, these souls may be saved with you in the kingdom of glory; but you cannot take with you there the smallest portion of your earthly treasure. Acquire what you may, preserve it with all the jealous care you are capable of exercising, and yet the mandate may go forth from the Lord, and in a few hours a fire which no skill can quench, may destroy the accumulations of your entire life, and lay them a mass of smoldering ruins. You may devote all your talent and energy to laying up treasures on earth; but what will they advantage you when your life closes or Jesus makes His appearance? Just as much as you have been exalted here by worldly honors and riches to the neglect of spiritual life, just so much lower will you sink in moral worth before the tribunal of the great Judge. "What shall it profit a man, if he shall gain the whole world, and lose his own soul?" (CS 212.2)

The wrath of God will fall upon those who have served mammon instead of their Creator. But those who live for God and heaven, pointing out the way of life to others, will find that the path of the just is as the shining light, that shineth more and more unto the perfect day. And they will hear by and by the welcome invitation, "Well done, thou good and faithful servant; enter thou into the joy of thy Lord." The joy of Christ was that of seeing souls saved in His glorious kingdom; and for this joy He "endured the cross, despising the shame." But soon "He shall see of the travail of His soul, and shall be satisfied." How happy will those be, who, having shared in His work, are permitted to share in His joy!– *The Review and Herald, June 23, 1885.* (CS 213.1)

The Bewitching Power of Satan

It is the purpose of Satan to make the world very attractive. He has a bewitching power which he exercises to allure the affections of even the professed followers of Christ. There are many professedly Christian men who will make any sacrifice in order to gain riches, and the more successful they are in obtaining the object of their desires, the less they care for the precious truth and its advancement in the world. They lose their love for God, and act like men who are insane. The more they are prospered in material wealth, the less they invest in the cause of God. (CS 213.2)

The works of those who have an insane love for riches, make it evident that it is impossible to serve two masters, God and mammon. They show to the world that money is their god. They yield their homage to its power, and to all intents and purposes they serve the world. The love of money becomes a ruling power, and for its sake they violate the law of God. They may profess the religion of Christ, but they do not love its principles, or heed its admonitions. They give their best strength to serve the world, and they bow to mammon. (CS 214.1)

It is alarming that so many are deluded by Satan. He excites the imagination with brilliant prospects of worldly gain, and men become infatuated, and think that before them is a prospect of perfect happiness. They are lured on by the hope of obtaining honor and riches and position. Satan says to the soul, "All this will I give thee, all this power and wealth with which you may do good to your fellow men;" but when the object for which they seek is gained, they find themselves with no connection with the self-denying Redeemer; they are not partakers of the divine nature. They hold to earthly treasures, and despise the requirements of self-denial, self-sacrifice, and humiliation for the truth's sake. They have no desire to part with the dear earthly treasure upon which their heart is set.

They have exchanged masters, and accepted the service of mammon instead of the service of Christ. Satan has secured to himself the worship of these deceived souls through the love of worldly treasure. (CS 214.2)

It is often found that the change from godliness to worldliness has been made so imperceptibly by the wily insinuations of the evil one, that the deceived soul is not aware that he has parted company with Christ, and is His servant only in name.– *The Review and Herald, September 23, 1890.* (CS 214.3)

Departure From the Self-Sacrifice of the Pioneers

There was a time when there were but few who listened to and embraced the truth, and they had not much of this world's goods. Then it was necessary for some to sell their houses and lands, and obtain cheaper, while their means were freely lent to the Lord to publish the truth, and otherwise aid in advancing the cause of God. These self-sacrificing ones endured privations; but if they endure unto the end, great will be their reward. (CS 215.1)

God has been moving upon many hearts. The truth for which a few sacrificed so much has triumphed, and multitudes have laid hold of it. In the providence of God, those who have means have been brought into the truth, that, as the work increases, the wants of His cause may be met. God does not now call for the houses His people need to live in; but if those who have an abundance do not hear His voice, cut loose from the world, and sacrifice for God, He will pass them by, and will call for those who are willing to do anything for Jesus, even to sell their homes to meet the wants of the cause. God will have freewill offerings. Those who give must esteem it a privilege to do so.– *The Review and Herald, September 16, 1884.* (CS 215.2)

God's people are on trial before the heavenly universe; but the scantiness of their gifts and offerings, and the feebleness of their efforts in God's service, mark them as unfaithful. If the little that is now accomplished were the best they could do, they would not be under condemnation; but with their resources they could do much more. They know, and the world knows, that they have to a large degree lost the spirit of self-denial and cross bearing.– *Testimonies for the Church 6:445, 446.* (**CS 215.3**)

Everyone Tested

To Matthew in his wealth, and to Andrew and Peter in their poverty, the same test was brought; the same consecration was made by each. At the moment of success, when the nets were filled with fish, and the impulses of the old life were strongest, Jesus asked the disciples at the sea to leave all for the work of the gospel. So every soul is tested as to whether the desire for temporal good or for fellowship with Christ is strongest.

(**CS 216.1**)

Principle is always exacting. No man can succeed in the service of God unless his whole heart is in the work, and he counts all things but loss for the excellency of the knowledge of Christ. No man who makes any reserve can be the disciple of Christ, much less can be His colaborer. When men appreciate the great salvation, the self-sacrifice seen in Christ's life will be seen in theirs. Wherever He leads the way, they will rejoice to follow.– *The Desire of Ages, 273.* (**CS 216.2**)

Chapter 43
Trying to Serve God and Mammon

There is danger of losing all in the pursuit of worldly gain; for in the feverish eagerness for earthly treasure, higher interests are forgotten. The care and perplexity that are involved in laying up treasures upon the earth, leave no time nor desire to estimate the value of eternal riches.... "Where your treasure is, there will your heart be also." Your thoughts, your plans, your motives, will have an earthly mold, and your soul will be defiled with covetousness and selfishness. "What shall it profit a man, if he shall gain the whole world, and lose his own soul?" ... (CS 217.1)

The heart of man may be the abode of the Holy Spirit. The peace of Christ, which passeth understanding, may rest in your soul; and the transforming power of His grace may work in your life, and fit you for the courts of glory. But if brain and nerve and muscle are all employed in the service of self, you are not making God and heaven the first consideration of your life. It is impossible to be weaving the graces of Christ into your character while you are putting all your energies on the side of the world. You may be successful in heaping up treasure on the earth, for the glory of self; but "where your treasure is, there will your heart be also." Eternal considerations will be made of secondary importance. You may take part in the outward forms of worship; but your service will be an abomination to the God of heaven. You cannot serve God and mammon. You will either yield your heart and put your will on the side of God, or you will give your energies to the service of the world. God will accept no halfhearted service.– *The Review and Herald, September 1, 1910.* (CS 217.2)

Enduring Substance or Passing Shadow

Christ calls upon the members of His church to cherish the true, genuine hope of the gospel. He points them upward, distinctly assuring them that the riches that endure are above, not below. Their hope is in heaven, not on the earth. "Seek ye first the kingdom of God, and His righteousness," He says; "and all these things"–all that is essential for your good–"shall be added unto you." (CS 218.1)

With many, the things of this world obscure the glorious view of the eternal weight of glory that awaits the saints of the Most High. They cannot distinguish the true, the real, the enduring substance, from the false, the counterfeit, the passing shadow. Christ urges them to remove from before their eyes that which is obscuring their view of eternal realities. He insists upon the removal of that which is causing them to mistake phantoms for realities, and realities for phantoms. God entreats His people to give the strength of body, mind, and soul to the service that He expects them to perform. He calls upon them to be able to say for themselves that the gains and advantages of this life are not worthy to be compared with the riches that are reserved for the diligent, rational seeker for eternal life.– *The Review and Herald, June 23, 1904.* (CS 218.2)

Engrossed in Pursuit of Wealth

The enemy is just as perseveringly at work now as he was before the flood. By the use of various enterprises and inventions, he is diligently working to keep the minds of men engrossed in the things of this world. He is employing all his ingenuity to lead men to act foolishly, to keep them absorbed in commercial enterprises, and thus to imperil their hope of eternal life. He devises the inventions that imperil human life. Under his leadership, men carry through that which he devises. They become so absorbed in the pursuit of wealth and worldly power that they give no heed to a "Thus saith the Lord." (**CS 218.3**)

Satan exults as he sees that he is successful in keeping minds from a consideration of the solemn, important matters that have to do with eternal life. He seeks to crowd the thought of God out of the mind, and to put worldliness and commercialism in its place. He desires to keep the world in darkness. It is his studied purpose to lead men to forget God and heaven, to bring all the souls that he can under his own jurisdiction. And to this end he brings forward enterprises and inventions that will so occupy men's attention that they will have no time to think of heavenly things. (**CS 219.1**)

The people of God must now awake and do their neglected work. Into our planning for this work, we must put all the powers of the mind. We should spare no effort to present the truth as it is in Jesus, so simply and yet so forcibly that minds will be strongly impressed. We must plan to work in a way that will consume as little means as possible; for the work must extend into the regions beyond.– *The Review and Herald, December 15, 1910.* (**CS 219.2**)

A Lesson From Judas

Judas had valuable qualities, but there were some traits in his character that would have to be cut away before he could be saved. He must be born again, not of corruptible seed, but of incorruptible. His great hereditary and cultivated tendency to evil was covetousness. And by practice this became a habit which he carried into all his trading. His economical habits developed a parsimonious spirit, and became a fatal snare. Gain was his measurement of a correct religious experience, and all true righteousness became subordinate to this. Christlike principles of uprightness and justice had no room in his life practices.... (**CS 219.3**)

Knowing that he was being corrupted by covetousness, Christ gave him the privilege of hearing many precious lessons. He heard Christ laying down the principles which all must possess who would enter His kingdom. He was given every opportunity to receive Christ as his personal Saviour, but he refused this gift. He would not yield his way and will to Christ. He did not practice that which was contrary to his own inclinations; therefore his strong avaricious spirit was not corrected. While he continued a disciple in outward form, and while in the very presence of Christ, he appropriated to himself means that belonged to the Lord's treasury.... (**CS 220.1**)

Judas might have been benefited by these lessons, had he possessed a desire to be right at heart; but his acquisitiveness overcame him, and the love of money became a ruling power. Through indulgence, he permitted this trait in his character to grow and take so deep a root that it crowded out the good seed of truth sown in his heart.– *The Review and Herald, October 5, 1897.* (**CS 220.2**)

Blinded by Love of the World

The cause of God is to hold the first place in our plans and affections. There is need of bearing a straight message concerning the indulgence of self while the cause of God is in need of means. Some are so cold and backslidden that they do not realize that they are setting their affections on earthly treasure, which is soon to be swept away forever. The love of the world is binding them about, like a thick garment; and unless they change their course, they will not know how precious it is to practice self-denial for Christ's sake. All our idols, our love of the world, must be expelled from the heart. (**CS 220.3**)

There are ministers and faithful friends who see the danger that surrounds these self-bound souls, and who faithfully present to them the error of their course, but instead of taking admonitions in the spirit in which they are given, and profiting thereby, those reproved rise up against the ones who deal with them faithfully. (**CS 221.1**)

O, that they might arouse from their spiritual lethargy, and now acquaint themselves with God! The world is blinding their eyes from seeing Him who is invisible. They are unable to discern the most precious things that are of eternal interest, but view the truth of God in so dim a light that it seems of little value to them. The merest atom concerning their temporal interests assumes magnified proportions, while the things concerning eternity are dropped out of their reckoning.– *The Review and Herald, October 31, 1893.* **(CS 221.2)**

True Generosity Destroyed

Men who are in comparative poverty are usually the ones who do the most to sustain the cause of God. They are generous with their little. They have strengthened their generous impulses by continual liberalities. When their expenditures pressed close upon the income, their passion for earthly riches had no room or chance to strengthen. **(CS 221.3)**

But many, when they begin to gather earthly riches, commence to calculate how long it will be before they can be in possession of a certain sum. In their anxiety to amass wealth for themselves, they fail to become rich toward God. Their benevolence does not keep pace with their accumulation. As their passion for riches increases, their affections are bound up with their treasure. The increase of their property strengthens the eager desire for more, until some consider that their giving to the Lord a tenth is a severe and unjust tax. Inspiration has said, "If riches increase, set not your heart upon them." Many have said, "If I were as rich as such a one, I would multiply my gifts to the treasury of God. I would do nothing else with my wealth but use it for the advancement of the cause of God." God has tested some of these by giving them riches; but with the riches came the fiercer temptation, and their benevolence was far less than in the days of their poverty. A grasping desire for greater riches absorbed their minds and hearts, and they committed idolatry.– *Testimonies for the Church 3:403.* **(CS 221.4)**

Some, when in poverty, are generous with their little; but as they acquire property, they become penurious. The reason they have so little faith, is because they do not keep moving forward as they prosper, and give to the cause of God even at a sacrifice.– *Testimonies for the Church 4:77.* **(CS 222.1)**

Chapter 44
Vain Professors

The Scriptures speak of the large class of professors who are not doers. Many who claim to believe in God deny Him by their works. Their worship of money, houses, and lands marks them as idolaters and apostates. All selfishness is covetousness, and is, therefore, idolatry. Many who have placed their names on the church roll, as believers in God and the Bible, are worshiping the goods the Lord has entrusted to them that they may be His almoners. They may not literally bow down before their earthly treasure, but nevertheless it is their god. They are worshipers of mammon. To the things of this world they offer the homage which belongs to the Creator. He who sees and knows all things records the falsity of their profession. (**CS 223.1**)

From the soul temple of a worldly Christian, God is excluded, in order that worldly policy may have abundant room. Money is his god. It belongs to Jehovah, but he to whom it is entrusted refuses to let it flow forth in deeds of benevolence. Did he appropriate it in accordance with God's design, the incense of his good works would ascend to heaven, and from thousands of converted souls would be heard songs of praise and thanksgiving. (**CS 223.2**)

To advance God's kingdom, to arouse those dead in trespasses and sins, to speak to sinners of the healing balm of the Saviour's love,–it is for this that our money should be used. But too often it is used for self-glorification. Instead of being the means of bringing souls to a knowledge of God and Christ, thus calling forth praise and gratitude to the Giver of all good, earthly possessions have been the means of eclipsing the glory of God and obscuring the view of heaven. By the wrong use of money the world has been filled with evil practices. The door of the mind has been closed against the Redeemer. (**CS 223.3**)

God declares, "The gold and the silver is Mine." He keeps a strict account with every son and daughter of Adam, that He may know how they are appropriating His means. Worldly men and worldly women may say, "But I am not a Christian. I do not profess to serve God." But does this make them any less guilty for burying His means, His resources, in worldly enterprises, to advance their selfish interests? (**CS 224.1**)

I speak to you who know not God, who may read these lines; for in His providence they may be brought to your notice. What are you doing with your Lord's goods? What are you doing with the physical and mental powers He has given you? Are you able of yourself to keep the human machinery in motion? Did God speak but one word to say that you must die, you would at once be still in death. Day by day, hour by hour, minute by minute, God works by His infinite power to keep you alive. It is He who supplies the breath which keeps life in your body. Did God neglect man as man neglects God, what would become of the race? (**CS 224.2**)

The great Medical Missionary has an interest in the work of His hands. He presents before men the peril of closing the door of the heart against the Saviour, saying, "Turn ye, turn ye; for why will ye die?"– *The Review and Herald, May 23, 1907.* (**CS 224.3**)

A Title to the Heavenly Possessions

The day is coming when "a man shall cast his idols of silver, and his idols of gold, which made each one for himself to worship, to the moles and to the bats; to go into the clefts of the rocks, and into the tops of the ragged rocks, for fear of the Lord, and for the glory of His majesty." The riches of the world will not avail in the day of wrath; but faith and obedience will bring the victory. (CS 224.4)

We shall act out all the faith we have. We must educate ourselves to talk faith, and prepare for the future life. What earnest efforts men make to obtain a lawful title to their land. They must have deeds that will stand the test of law. The possessor is never satisfied unless he is confident that there is no flaw in his title. O that men were as earnest to obtain a title to their heavenly possessions that would stand the test of law! The apostle exhorts the follower of Christ to give diligence to make his calling and election sure. There must be no error, no flaw in your claim to immortality. Says the Saviour, "Blessed are they that do His commandments, that they may have right to the tree of life, and may enter in through the gates into the city."– *The Review and Herald, April 30, 1889.* (CS 225.1)

Eternal Riches Slighted

The Lord looks with pity on those who allow themselves to be burdened with household cares and business perplexities. They are cumbered with much serving, and neglect the one thing essential. "Seek ye first the kingdom of God, and His righteousness," the Saviour says; "and all these things shall be added unto you." That is, Look away from this world to the eternal. Put forth your most earnest endeavors to obtain those things upon which God places value, and which Christ gave His precious life that you might secure. His sacrifice has thrown open wide to you the gates of heavenly commerce. Lay up your treasure beside the throne of God, by doing with His entrusted capital the work that He desires done in the winning of souls to a knowledge of the truth. This will secure you eternal riches.... (CS 225.2)

When we think of the great gift of heaven for the redemption of a sinful world, and then consider the offerings that we can make, we shrink from drawing a comparison. The demands that might be made upon a whole universe could not compare with that one gift. Immeasurable love was expressed when One equal with the Father came to pay the price for the souls of men, and bring to them eternal life. Shall those who profess the name of Christ see no attraction in the world's Redeemer, be indifferent to the possession of truth and righteousness, and turn from the heavenly treasure to the earthly? (CS 226.1)

"And this is the condemnation, that light is come into the world, and men loved darkness rather than light, because their deeds were evil. But everyone that doeth evil hateth the light, neither cometh to the light, lest his deeds should be reproved. But he that doeth truth cometh to the light, that his deeds may be made manifest, that they are wrought in God." (CS 226.2)

This gospel message is one of the most precious passages in the New Testament. When it is accepted, it yields in the lives of the receiver good deeds whose value is far above that of diamonds and gold. It has power to bring gladness and consolation into the earthly life, and to bestow eternal life upon the believer. O that we might have our understanding so enlightened by grace that we could take in its full meaning! The Father is saying to us, I will bestow upon you a treasure more precious than any earthly possession, a treasure that will make you rich and blessed forever.– *The Review and Herald, March 5, 1908.* (CS 226.3)

How Inconsistent! How Worthless!

Christ declares, "He that will come after Me, let him deny himself, and take up his cross, and follow Me." Those who have on the wedding garment, the robe of Christ's righteousness, will not question whether they should lift the cross, and follow in the footsteps of the Saviour. Willingly and cheerfully they will obey His commands. Souls are perishing out of Christ. How inconsistent, then, is all striving after position and wealth. How feeble are the motives which Satan may present, which selfishness and ambition can furnish, in comparison with the lessons which Christ has given in His word! How worthless the reward the world offers beside that offered by our heavenly Father!– *The Review and Herald, September 19, 1899.* (CS 227.1)

God Will Provide

While men should see that no bounty of providence is needlessly wasted, a parsimonious, acquisitive spirit will have to be overcome. This disposition will lead to overreaching and unjust dealing, which is an abhorrence in the sight of God. Christians should not allow themselves to be troubled with anxious care as to the necessities of life. If men love and obey God, and do their part, God will provide for all their wants. Although your living may have to be obtained by the sweat of your brow, you are not to distrust God; for in the great plan of His providence, He will supply your need from day to day. This lesson of Christ's is a rebuke to the anxious thoughts, the perplexities and doubts, of the faithless heart. No man can add one cubit to his stature, no matter how solicitous he may be to do so. It is no less unreasonable to be troubled about the morrow and its needs. Do your duty, and trust in God; for He knows of what things you have need.– *The Review and Herald, September 18, 1888.* (**CS 227.2**)

For Further Study

Love of the World, *Testimonies for the Church* 3:477-482

Worldliness in the Church, *Testimonies for the Church* 2:196-199

Vision of the Two Crowns, *Testimonies for the Church* 1:347-352

Deceptive Thought of Acquiring Riches to Help God's Cause, *Testimonies for the Church* 1:476, 477

Deceitfulness of Riches (a personal experience), *Testimonies for the Church* 2:275-283

The More Men Love Earthly Riches, the Farther They Depart From God, *Testimonies for the Church* 3:478

Through Love of Riches, Satan Secures Worship of Himself, *Testimonies for the Church* 3:479

Becoming Rich in Worldly Things, but Not Toward God, *Testimonies for the Church* 2:196

Alarming That So Many Are Deceived by Satan, *Testimonies for the Church* 3:479

The Pursuit of Wealth a Species of Insanity, *Testimonies for the Church* 5:261

Conversation Reveals Where the Treasure Is, *Testimonies for the Church* 2:59

Acquiring Riches by Dishonest Means, *Testimonies for the Church* 4:489-491

Angels Amazed at Selfishness of Christians, *Testimonies for the Church* 4:475

Deceitfulness of Riches, *Testimonies for the Church* 1:476-478

Immoderate Labor in Pursuit of Wealth, *Testimonies for the Church* 1:176

Many Girt With Selfishness as With Iron Bands, *Testimonies for the Church* 2:197

One Reason Why as a People We Are Sickly, *Testimonies for the Church* 2:198

Prosperity Is Blinding the Eyes, Deceiving the Soul, *Testimonies for the Church* 2:183, 184

Cares of Life Affect One as Drink Does the Drunkard, *Testimonies for the Church* 5:258, 259

The Close and Covetous Should Be Alarmed for Themselves, *Testimonies for the Church* 1:194

Greatest Danger in Accumulation of Property, *Testimonies for the Church* 1:492

Secular Business Necessary, but Not to Be All-absorbing, *Testimonies for the Church* 5:459

Ambition for Riches and Honor Among Church Members, *Testimonies for the Church* 5:456

Satan's Strategy to Defeat the Church, *Early Writings,* 266-269

Early Cautions From the First Number of Testimonies for the Church, *Testimonies for the Church* 1:114, 115

Manifestation of Lack of Faith in God's Care, *Testimonies for the Church* 2:656-658

Section 10
The Lure of Speculation

Chapter 45
Grasping for Riches

The people of God, who have been blessed with great light in regard to the truth for this time, should not forget that they are to be waiting and watching for the coming of their Lord in the clouds of heaven. Let them not forget that they are to put off the works of darkness, and put on the armor of light. Let no man set up his idols of gold, or silver, or lands, and give the service of his heart to this world, and to its interests. There is a mania for speculating in land, pervading both city and country. The old safe, healthful paths to competence are losing popularity. The idea of accumulating substantial means by the moderate gains of industry and frugality, is an idea that is scorned by many, as no longer suited to this progressive age. (CS 231.1)

The desire to engage in speculation, in buying up country and city lots, or anything that promises sudden and exorbitant gains, has reached a fever heat; and mind, and thought, and labor are all directed toward securing all that is possible of the treasures of earth in the shortest possible time. Some of our youth bid fair to be hastened on to ruin, because of this feverish grasping for riches. This desire for gain opens the door of the heart to the temptations of the enemy. And the temptations that come are of such an alluring nature, that there are some who cannot resist them.... (CS 231.2)

The Spirit of Gain Getting

The spirit of gain getting, of making haste to be rich, of this all-absorbing worldliness, is painfully contradictory to our faith and doctrines. Should the Lord most high be pleased to impart His Holy Spirit, and seek to revive His work, how many would be hungering for the heavenly manna, and thirsting for the waters of life? ... (CS 231.3)

I see there is danger of some of our brethren saying, as did the foolish rich man, "Soul, thou hast much goods laid up for many years; take thine ease, eat, drink, and be merry." Many are forgetting that they are God's servants, and are saying, "Tomorrow shall be as this day and much more abundant." God is looking on your every business transaction. Be on your guard. It is time that deep, earnest thought should be given to laying up treasure in heaven, where neither moth nor rust doth corrupt, not thieves break through and steal.– *Special Testimonies, Series B, No. 17a, 4, 5* ["The Unwise Use of Money and the Spirit of Speculation"]. (CS 232.1)

The Infatuation of New Enterprises

If a new patent passes through the country, men who profess to believe the truth find a way to raise means to invest in the enterprise. God is acquainted with every heart. Every selfish motive is known to Him, and He suffers circumstances to arise to try the hearts of His professed people, to prove them and develop character. In some instances the Lord will suffer men to go on, and meet with an entire failure. His hand is against them to disappoint their hopes and scatter what they possess. (CS 232.2)

Those who really feel an interest in the cause of God, and are willing to venture something for its advancement, will find it a sure and safe investment. Some will have a hundredfold in this life, and in the world to come life everlasting. But all will not receive their hundredfold in this life, because they cannot bear it. If entrusted with much, they would become unwise stewards. The Lord withholds it for their good; but their treasure in heaven will be secure. How much better is such an investment as this! (CS 232.3)

Drunk with Anticipated Gains

The desire that some of our brethren possess to earn means fast, leads them to engage in a new enterprise and invest means, but often their expectations of making money are not realized. They sink that which they could have spent in God's cause. There is an infatuation in these new enterprises. And notwithstanding these things have been acted over so many times, and they have before them the example of others who have made investments and have met with an utter failure, yet many are slow to learn. Satan allures them on, and makes them drunk with anticipated gains. (CS 233.1)

When their hopes are blasted, they suffer many discouragements in consequence of their unwise adventures. If means is lost, the person looks upon it as a misfortune to himself,–as his loss. But he must remember that it is the means of another which he is handling, that he is only a steward, and God is displeased with the unwise management of that means which could have been used to advance the cause of present truth. At the reckoning day the unfaithful steward must give an account of his stewardship.– *Testimonies for the Church 1:225, 226.* (CS 233.2)

More Attractive Than Persevering Labor

The enemy of souls is very anxious to hinder the completion of the special work for this time by bringing in some erroneous transaction. He will bring it under the garb of great liberality; and if those pursuing this course have apparent success for a time, others will follow. And the very truths that are testing our people for this time, and which, if clearly understood, would cut off such a course of action, lose their force. (CS 233.3)

Some will strike out into flattering speculative money-making schemes, and others will quickly catch the spirit of speculation. It is just what they want, and they will engage in lines of speculation that take the mind off from the sacred preparation that is essential for their souls in order for them to be prepared to meet the trials which will come in these last days. (CS 234.1)

The enemy of souls has his plans carefully laid, and he will try in every possible way to carry them to success. Something after this order, [Reference is here made to a plan for land and mine speculation to be promoted among Seventh-day Adventists, with a large part of the anticipated gains dedicated to the Lord's work.–Compiler.] a plan that promises to be as gracious and successful as this, has been started a good many times among our people. But when the time came that they expected great success, it proved to be an entire failure. That confused the minds of the people. They had gotten into speculation, and they liked that plan better than hard work and going right on as we have done usually, laboring perseveringly and trusting in the Lord.... (CS 234.2)

Diverting Minds from the Truth

Every movement of this order, which comes in to excite the desire to get riches quickly by speculation, takes the minds of the people away from the most solemn truths that ever were given to mortals. There may be encouraging prospects for a time, but the end of the matter is failure. The Lord endorses no such movements. If this work is sanctioned, many would be attracted by these speculative schemes that could not in any other way be led away from the work of presenting the solemn truths that must be given to the people at this time.– *Special Testimonies, Series B, No. 17a, 15-19.* (CS 234.3)

A Snare of Satan

Many times when the Lord has opened the way for brethren to handle their means to advance His cause, the agents of Satan have presented some enterprise by which they were positive the brethren could double their means. They take the bait; their money is invested, and the cause, and frequently themselves, never receive a dollar. (CS 235.1)

Brethren, remember the cause, and when you have means at your command lay up for yourselves a good foundation against the time to come, that you may lay hold on eternal life. Jesus for your sakes became poor, that you through His poverty might be made rich in heavenly treasure. What will you give for Jesus, who has given all for you?– *Testimonies for the Church*

5:154, 155. (**CS 235.2**)

Chapter 46
The Temptation to Speculate

Satan has destroyed many souls by leading them to place themselves in the way of temptation. He comes to them as he came to Christ, tempting them to love the world. He tells them that they may invest with profit in this or that enterprise, and in good faith they follow his dictation. (CS 236.1)

Soon they are tempted to swerve from their integrity in order to make as good bargains for themselves as possible. Their course may be perfectly lawful, according to the world's standard of right, and yet not bear the test of the law of God. Their motives are called in question by their brethren, and they are suspected of overreaching to serve themselves, and thus is sacrificed that precious influence which should have been sacredly guarded for the benefit of the cause of God. The business which might be a financial success in the hands of a sharper who will sell his integrity for worldly gain, would be entirely inappropriate for a follower of Christ. (CS 236.2)

All such speculations are attended with unseen trials and difficulties, and are a fearful ordeal for those who engage in them. Circumstances often occur which naturally cause reflections to be cast upon the motives of these brethren; but although some things may look decidedly wrong, these should not always be considered a true test of character. Yet they often prove to be the turning point in one's experience and destiny. The character becomes transformed by the force of circumstances under which the individual has placed himself. (CS 236.3)

A Dangerous Experiment

I was shown that it is a dangerous experiment for our people to engage in speculation. They thereby place themselves on the enemy's ground, subject to great temptations, disappointments, trials, and losses. Then comes a feverish unrest, a longing desire to obtain means more rapidly than present circumstances will admit. Their surroundings are accordingly changed, in hope of making more money. But frequently their expectations are not realized, and they become discouraged and go backward rather than forward. This has been the case with some in–. They are backsliding from God. (CS 237.1)

Had the Lord prospered some of our dear brethren in their speculations, it would have proved their eternal ruin. God loves His people, and He loves those who have been unfortunate. If they will learn the lessons which He intends to teach them, their defeat will in the end prove a precious victory. The love of the world has crowded out the love of Christ. When the rubbish is cleared away from the door of the heart, and it is thrown open in response to the invitation of Christ, He will come in and take possession of the soul temple.– *Testimonies for the Church 4:616-618.* (CS 237.2)

Deceiving Enchantments and Bribes

Now, in probationary time, we are all on test and trial. Satan is working with his deceiving enchantments and bribes, and some will think that by their schemes they have made a wonderful speculation. But lo, as they believe that they are rising securely, and are carrying themselves loftily in their selfishness, they learn that God can scatter faster than they can gather.– *Special Testimonies, Series B, No. 17a, 6.* (CS 237.3)

Misleading Prospects

Many have conscientiously loaned their money to our institutions, that it may be used to do a good work for the Master. But Satan sets in operation schemes that will produce in the minds of our brethren a great desire to try their fortunes, as in a lottery. One and still another are flattered by strong representations of financial gain if they will only invest their money in lands; and they take their means out of our institutions, and bury it in the earth, where the Lord's cause is not benefited. (**CS 238.1**)

Then if one is successful, he is so elated over the fact that he has gained a few hundred dollars, that he decides to keep on getting money if he can. He continues to invest in real estate or in mines. The device of Satan is successful; in the place of increased funds flowing into the treasury, there is withdrawal of means from our institutions, in order that the owners may try their fortunes in the mining business or in land speculation. The spirit of greed is fostered, and the naturally penurious man begrudges every dollar that is called for to be used in the advancement of the cause of God in the earth.– *Special Testimonies, Series B, No. 17a, 8.* (**CS 238.2**)

Speculation by Ministers

We are nearing the close of time. We want not only to teach present truth in the pulpit, but to live it out of the pulpit. Examine closely the foundation of your hope of salvation. While you stand in the position of a herald of truth, a watchman upon the walls of Zion, you cannot have your interest interwoven with mining or real-estate business, and at the same time do effectually the sacred work committed to your hands. Where the souls of men are at stake, where eternal things are involved, the interest cannot safely be divided. (**CS 238.3**)

This is especially so in your case. While engaged in this business, you have not been cultivating heartfelt piety. You have had a feverish desire to obtain means. You have talked to many about the financial advantages to be gained by investing in lands in–. Again and again you have been engaged in picturing the advantages of these enterprises; and this while you were an ordained minister of Christ, pledged to give your soul, body, and spirit to the work of the salvation of souls. At the same time you were receiving money from the treasury to support

yourself and your family. Your talk was calculated to draw the attention and money of our people away from our institutions and from the business of promoting the Redeemer's kingdom on the earth. Its tendency was to beget in them a desire to invest their means where you assured them that it would be doubled in a short time, and to flatter them with the prospect that they could help the cause a great deal more by so doing.... (**CS 239.1**)

To Avoid Worldly Entanglements

Especially should the minister keep himself from every worldly entanglement, and bind himself to the Source of all power, that he may represent correctly what it means to be a Christian. He should cut loose from everything that would in any way divert his mind from God and the great work for this time. Christ expects him, as His employed servant, to be like Himself in mind, in thought, in word, in action. He expects every man who opens the Scriptures to others, to work carefully and intelligently, not exercising his powers unwisely, in a way to injure or overtask them, but so that he may be fitted to do good work for the Lord.– *Testimonies for the Church 5:530, 531.* (**CS 239.2**)

Speculating in Land Near Our Institutions

I was instructed to bear a testimony to our brethren, telling them that they must guard themselves against unfair speculation in connection with the purchase and sale of land near the school property. Every transaction in buying and selling must be characterized by strictest integrity. Selfishness must not be indulged. The principles for which our school shall stand, and which are to be taught the students as part of their education, are to be cultivated and revealed by those who closely connect themselves with the school interest. They must not, by efforts for personal gain, counterwork the principles of Christian education for which this school is to be established. (**CS 240.1**)

Day by day we are making our record for time and for eternity. Let every action be just and square, in selling as in buying. Let nothing of an overreaching character be brought in, for that would discourage our brethren and displease God. Large sacrifices have been made by the people in our churches in order that this property might be secured for our school. Let not those who secure advantages for themselves take unfair advantage of their brethren who may need to settle near the school. Some who have the spirit of speculation should be discouraged from coming to–, because they would not be a blessing to the school, but a hindrance. (**CS 240.2**)

Let us remember that we are standing in review before God, and that every unfair action to serve self is recorded against us in the books of heaven. O, I entreat our brethren to put away the spirit of commercialism. I pray that none may gather about the school whose chief purpose is to advantage self. Let all seek to excel in spiritual things, that the ambitious spirit may be changed to a spirit of unselfishness. This change must be wrought in us if we would be wholly approved of God.– *Letter 72, 1909.* (**CS 240.3**)

The Lure of Lotteries

Then there is some lottery business connected with it, and one young man that goes there, obtains a gold watch. What then? The watch may be genuine gold, it may be no fraud, but ah, there is a fraud back of that, and that is the snare. If he has gained this once, he will want to try it again. Oh, I would rather, if it had been a son of mine, have him lying in his coffin than sporting that gold watch. Then, here are other boys. He shows his watch to them, and then there is an itching with them to try their luck in just the same way, and so they will attempt this matter themselves. Then another will attempt it, and another; and so the influence extends from one to another; and the devil knows just how to play his game.– *Manuscript 1, 1890.* (**CS 241.1**)

Chapter 47
Unwise Investments

A few weeks ago, while I was attending the camp meeting at San Jose [1905], some of our brethren presented before me what they considered wonderful opportunities to invest means in mining and railroad stock, that would bring large returns. They seemed confident of success, and spoke of the good they would do with the profits they expected to receive. (CS 242.1)

Others were present, and seemed interested to see how I would receive their proposition. I told them that such investments were very uncertain. They could not be sure that these enterprises would succeed. I spoke to them of the everlasting reward that is assured to those who lay up their treasures in heaven; but in these uncertain ventures, I begged them, for Christ's sake, to stop right where they were. (CS 242.2)

In the night season I was instructed to tell God's people that it is not according to His will that those who believe in His near coming should invest their means in mining stock. This would be burying our Lord's talent in the earth. I will read a copy of a letter I wrote to one of the brethren I have mentioned: (CS 242.3)

"San Jose, California,

July 2, 1905.

"Dear Brother,

"You have presented before me a proposition to invest in mining stock. You feel confident that such an investment would prove successful, and you think that in this way you will be able greatly to help the cause of God. (CS 242.4)

"The Lord has given me instruction that at the meetings I would attend I would find men encouraging our people to invest their money to work mines. I am bidden to say that this is a device of the enemy to consume or to tie up means that is greatly needed to carry on the work of God. It is a snare of the last days, to involve God's people in loss of their Lord's entrusted capital, that should be used wisely in the work of winning souls. Because so much money is invested in these very uncertain enterprises, the work of God is sadly crippled for lack of the talent that will win souls to Christ.... (CS 243.1)

"Last night in vision, I was raising my voice in warning against worldly speculations. I said, 'I invite you to take shares in the greatest mine that has ever been worked.' (CS 243.2)

"'The kingdom of heaven is like unto a treasure hid in a field; the which when a man hath found, he hideth, and for joy thereof goeth and selleth all that he hath, and buyeth that field.'... (CS 243.3)

"If we will invest in God's mining stock, the return is sure. He says, 'Hearken diligently unto Me, and eat ye that which is good, and let your soul delight itself in fatness.'... (CS 243.4)

"Again, the kingdom of heaven is like unto a merchantman, seeking goodly pearls: who, when he had found one pearl of great price, went and sold all that he had, and bought it.' (CS 243.5)

"My brother, will you make an investment to secure the heavenly pearl of great price? ... This is mining stock, in which you may invest without running a risk of disappointment. But, my dear friend, we have not a dollar of the Lord's money to invest in mining enterprises in this world." (CS 243.6)

I am exceedingly sorry that any of our people have made the mistake of burying their God-given capital in mining stock, thinking thereby to increase their revenue. The prospect may seem flattering, but many will be sadly disappointed. (CS 244.1)

I recall the case of a brother who was once interested in the work and cause of God. Some years ago, when I was in Australia, this brother wrote to me, saying that he had purchased a mine from which he expected to receive great profits. He said that he would give me a portion of what he would receive. Occasionally he would write to me, saying: "Now the prospects are good. Soon we shall receive returns." But the returns did not materialize; and after sinking many thousands of dollars, his ventures proved to be an entire loss. (**CS 244.2**)

This is one of many similar cases that have come to my attention. Many have expressed to me their sorrow that they had ever encouraged anyone to invest their means in mining stock. If there is one here who has received money from a brother or sister for any such investment, it is his duty to return it, if the one who gave it so desires. (**CS 244.3**)

I warn you to be careful what you do with your Lord's goods. By placing it in God's treasury you may ensure for yourselves a revenue from the inexhaustible treasures of His kingdom. (**CS 244.4**)

The people of God have been too easily satisfied with mere surface truths. We should search diligently for the deep, eternal, far-reaching truths of God's word. Having found them, we shall joyfully sell all, that we may buy the field.– *Special Testimonies, Series B, No. 17a, 8-13.* (**CS 244.5**)

For Further Study

Some Must Learn by Experience to Let Speculative Enterprises Alone, *Testimonies for the Church 1:304, 305*

A Trap for the Poor, *Testimonies for the Church 1:480, 481*

Many Outgeneraled by Satan, With No Seeming Possibility of Failure, *Testimonies for the Church 2:664, 665*

Especially Should Ministers Keep Themselves Free, *Testimonies for the Church 2:622, 626; The Acts of the Apostles, 366; Gospel Workers, 340-342*

Speculation Is a Dangerous Experiment, *Testimonies for the Church 4:616, 617*

Speculation and Business Enterprises With Unbelievers a Hindrance, *Testimonies for the Church 9:19*

Land and Mining Speculation, *Gospel Workers, 341*

Aftermath of Regret, Remorse, and Self-Reproach, *Testimonies for the Church 1:455*

Purses of God's People Drained, Means Transferred to Enemy's Ranks, *Testimonies for the Church 1:551*

Section 11
The Tyranny of Debt

Chapter 48
Living Within the Income

Many, very many, have not so educated themselves that they can keep their expenditures within the limit of their income. They do not learn to adapt themselves to circumstances, and they borrow and borrow again and again, and become overwhelmed in debt, and consequently they become discouraged and disheartened. (CS 249.1)

Many do not remember the cause of God, and carelessly expend money in holiday amusements, in dress and folly, and when there is a call made for the advancement of the work in home and foreign missions, they have nothing to give, or even have overdrawn their account. Thus they rob God in tithes and offerings, and through their selfish indulgence they lay the soul open to fierce temptations, and fall into the wiles of Satan. (CS 249.2)

We should be on our guard, and not allow ourselves to spend money upon that which is unnecessary, and simply for display. We should not permit ourselves to indulge tastes that lead us to pattern after the customs of the world, and rob the treasury of the Lord.– *The Review and Herald, December 19, 1893.* (CS 249.3)

Industry and Economy in the Family

I was shown that you, my brother and sister, have much to learn. You have not lived within your means. You have not learned to economize. If you earn high wages, you do not know how to make it go as far as possible. You consult taste or appetite instead of prudence. At times you expend money for a quality of food in which your brethren cannot afford to indulge. Dollars slip from your pocket very easily.... (CS 249.4)

It is as wrong for you to fail to use your strength to the best advantage, as it is for a rich man to covetously retain his riches because it is agreeable to do so. You do not make the exertion that you should to support your family. You can and do work if work is conveniently prepared to hand; but you do not exert yourself to set yourself to work, feeling that it is a duty to use your time and strength to the very best advantage, and in the fear of God. (CS 250.1)

You have been in a business which would at times yield you large profits at once. After you have earned means, you have not studied to economize in reference to a time when means could not be earned so easily, but have expended much for imaginary wants. Had you and your wife understood it to be a duty that God enjoined upon you, to deny your taste and your desires, and make provision for the future, instead of living merely for the present, you could now have had a competency, and your family have had the comforts of life. You have a lesson to learn which you should not be backward in learning. It is to make a little go the longest way.... (CS 250.2)

Jesus wrought a miracle, and fed five thousand, and then He taught an important lesson of economy: "Gather up the fragments that remain, that nothing be lost." Duties, important duties, rest upon you. "Owe no man anything." Were you infirm, were you unable to labor, then your brethren would be in duty bound to help you. As it is, all you needed from your brethren when you changed your location, was a start. If you felt as ambitious as you should, and you and your wife would agree to live within your means, you could be free from embarrassment. You will have to labor for small wages as well as for large. Industry and economy would have placed your family, ere this, in a much more favorable condition.– *Testimonies for the Church 2:431-436.* (CS 250.3)

Economy From Principle

Those whose hands are open to respond to the calls for means to sustain the cause of God and to relieve the suffering and the needy, are not the ones who are found loose and lax and dilatory in their business management. They are always careful to keep their outgoes within their income. They are economical from principle; they feel it their duty to save, that they may have something to give.– *Testimonies for the Church 4:573.* (**CS 251.1**)

The First Lesson–Self-Denial

I have seen poor families struggling with debt, and yet the children were not trained to deny themselves in order to aid their parents. In one family where I visited, the daughters expressed a desire for an expensive piano. Gladly would the parents have gratified this wish, but they were embarrassed with debt. The daughters knew this, and had they been taught to practice self-denial, they would not have given their parents the pain of denying their wishes; but although they were told that it would be impossible to gratify their desires, the matter did not end there. The wish was expressed again and again, thus continually adding to the heavy burden of the parents. (**CS 251.2**)

On another visit I saw the coveted musical instrument in the house, and knew that some hundreds of dollars had been added to the burden of debt. I hardly know whom to blame most, the indulgent parents or the selfish children. Both are guilty before God. This one case will illustrate many. These young persons, although they profess to be Christians, have never taken the cross of Christ; for the very first lesson to be learned of Christ is the lesson of self-denial. Said our Saviour, "If any man will come after Me, let him deny himself, and take up his cross, and follow Me." In no way can we become disciples of Christ, except by complying with this condition.– *The Signs of the Times, March 31, 1887.* (**CS 251.3**)

Chapter 49
Bringing Reproach Upon God's Cause

The religion you profess makes it as much your duty to employ your time during the six working days, as to attend church on the Sabbath. You are not diligent in business. You let hours, days, and even weeks pass without accomplishing anything. The very best sermon you could preach to the world would be to show a decided reformation in your life, and provide for your own family. Says the apostle, "If any provide not for his own, and specially for those of his own house, he hath denied the faith, and is worse than an infidel." (CS 253.1)

You bring a reproach upon the cause by locating in a place where you indulge indolence for a time, and then are obliged to run in debt for provision for your family. These, your honest debts, you are not always particular to pay, but, instead, move to another place. This is defrauding your neighbor. The world has a right to expect strict integrity in those who profess to be Bible Christians. By one man's indifference in regard to paying his just dues, all our people are in danger of being regarded as unreliable. (CS 253.2)

"Whatsoever ye would that men should do to you, do ye even so to them." This refers to those who labor with their hands as well as to those who have gifts to bestow. God has given you strength and skill, but you have not used them. Your strength is sufficient to abundantly support your family. Rise in the morning, even while the stars are shining, if need be. Lay your plans to do something, and then accomplish it. Redeem every pledge, unless sickness lays you prostrate. Better deny yourself food and sleep than be guilty of keeping from others their just dues.– *Testimonies for the Church 5:179, 180.* (CS 253.3)

What the Eighth Commandment Requires

The eighth commandment condemns manstealing and slave dealing, and forbids wars of conquest. It condemns theft and robbery. It demands strict integrity in the minutest details of the affairs of life. It forbids overreaching in trade, and requires the payment of just debts or wages. It declares that every attempt to advantage oneself by the ignorance, weakness, or misfortune of another, is registered as fraud in the books of heaven.– *Patriarchs and Prophets, 309.* (CS 254.1)

One of Satan's Nets for Souls

All must practice economy. No worker should manage his affairs in a way to incur debt.... When one voluntarily becomes involved in debt, he is entangling himself in one of Satan's nets which he sets for souls.– *Christian Education, 67.* (CS 254.2)

Weakens Faith, Tends to Discouragement

Dear Brother,

I am sorry that you are situated as you are, under the pressure of debt. I know of quite a number, who, like yourself, are troubled and distressed over their financial condition.... (CS 254.3)

The Lord does not take pleasure in your distress. He wants to bestow upon you the consolations of His Holy Spirit, that you may be a free man, abiding in His light and in His love. He has lessons for you to learn, and He would have you move quick in learning them. You ought not to allow yourself to become financially embarrassed; for the fact that you are in debt weakens your faith and tends to discourage you;

and even the thought of it makes you nearly wild. You need to cut down your expenses, and strive to supply this deficiency in your character. You can and should make determined efforts to bring under control your disposition to spend means beyond your income.– *Letter 48, 1888.* (CS 254.4)

A Demoralizing Practice

The practice of borrowing money to relieve some pressing necessity, and making no calculation for canceling the indebtedness, however common, is demoralizing. The Lord would have all who believe the truth converted from these self-deceiving practices. They should choose rather to suffer want than to commit a dishonest act. No soul can resort to prevarication or dishonesty in handling the Lord's goods, and stand guiltless before God. All who do this deny Christ in action, while they profess to keep and teach the commandments of God. They do not maintain the principles of God's law. If those who see the truth do not change in character corresponding to the sanctifying influence of the truth, they will be a savor of death unto death. They will misrepresent the truth, bring a reproach upon it, and dishonor Christ, who is truth.– *Manuscript 168, 1898.* (CS 255.1)

Chapter 50
A Call to Prayer or Change of Occupation

Dear Brother and Sister,

I feel tender sympathy for you, and I am praying that you may see matters in a correct light. You must see that one should not manage his affairs in a way that will incur debt.... (CS 256.1)

When a man sees that he is not successful, why does he not betake himself to prayer, or change his work? There are stormy times before us, and the Lord will accept all who can cooperate with Him. Practice self-denial and self-sacrifice. Consider every movement carefully and prayerfully. Walk softly before the Lord. We must preserve a devotedness to God, and make straight paths for our feet, lest the lame be turned out of the way.– *Letter 63, 1897.* (CS 256.2)

Counsel to a Colporteur

In your letter you complain of the yoke of debt. But there is no excuse for your being in debt.... Your freedom in borrowing, with no reason to suppose that you will be in a position to repay it, is doing great injustice to others, robbing them of their little all, and bringing reproach upon the cause of God. If you realized what you were doing at the time of your action, you would stop. You would see the sinfulness of robbing men, believers or unbelievers, and bringing them into strait places in order to relieve your present necessities. (CS 256.3)

This case of yours, Brother -----, is not a small affair. In the course you have pursued, you will leave upon the track of other canvassers a blighting influence, difficult for you to efface. You will have closed the door to other persons who would canvass, and do the work honestly, but who will be regarded as untrustworthy. To those who really need to have some indulgence and favors in the line of trust, because of the

wrong course some canvassers have pursued, they dare not venture. And with the experience they have had, in the loss from the treasury of hundreds of pounds, why should they not be afraid to repose confidence in men who so manage as to draw from the treasury, and leave them minus the means they so greatly need to sustain the work of God for this time?– *Letter 36, 1897.* (CS 256.4)

Freedom Through Self-Denial

Be determined never to incur another debt. Deny yourself a thousand things rather than run in debt. This has been the curse of your life, getting into debt. Avoid it as you would the smallpox. (CS 257.1)

Make a solemn covenant with God that by His blessing you will pay your debts and then owe no man anything if you live on porridge and bread. It is so easy in preparing your table to throw out of your pocket twenty-five cents for extras. Take care of the pennies, and the dollars will take care of themselves. It is the mites here and the mites there that are spent for this, that, and the other, that soon run up into dollars. Deny self at least while you are walled in with debts.... Do not falter, be discouraged, or turn back. Deny your taste, deny the indulgence of appetite, save your pence and pay your debts. Work them off as fast as possible. When you can stand forth a free man again, owing no man anything, you will have achieved a great victory.– *Letter 4, 1877.* (CS 257.2)

Personal Debt Not to Hinder Liberality

Some have not come up and united in the plan of systematic benevolence, excusing themselves because they were not free from debt. They plead that they must first "owe no man anything." But the fact that they are in debt does not excuse them. I saw that they should render to Caesar the things that are Caesar's, and to God the things that are God's. Some feel conscientious to "owe no man anything," and think that God can require nothing of them until their debts are all paid. Here they deceive themselves. They fail to render to God the things that are His. Everyone must bring to the Lord a suitable offering. Those who are in debt should take the amount of their debts from what they possess, and give a proportion of the remainder.– *Testimonies for the Church 1:220.* **(CS 258.1)**

Chapter 51
Lifting Debts on Church Buildings

I rejoice with you in the prospect of clearing the church buildings from debt. How much might have been saved if extra efforts had been made every year to do this. There is no necessity for our meetinghouses to continue year after year in debt. If every member of the church will do his duty, practicing self-denial and self-sacrifice, for the Lord Jesus, whose purchased possession he is, that His church may be free from debt, he will do honor to God. (CS 259.1)

The Lord's great centers, His own instrumentalities, should be free from all debt. Every year many pounds [Written from Australia.] are being swallowed up by the interest paid on debts. If this money was all appropriated to settle the principal, the debt would not be eating, eating, and ever eating. It is a poor, wretched policy to go into debt. If the money that is needed to build could be first accumulated, by strenuous efforts, and the church dedicated free from debt, how much better it would be. O, shall we not make it a rule when building a house for the Lord, to put forth earnest, persevering efforts, that it may be dedicated to Him free from debt.... (CS 259.2)

The Lord has shown me that debts need not be left on our meetinghouses in Australia or New Zealand. A debt in every case means a neglect of God's special, sacred things; for selfish, common things are made first and all-absorbing.... The very highest honor is to be shown to God's tabernacle. Every other consideration should be second to this. Our ideas must be elevated, ennobled, and sanctified. Worldliness and covetousness have been indulged by parents for their children and for relatives and friends. Money has been appropriated when and where it could not honor God, where it has done positive harm. Gifts have been liberally bestowed on children and relatives and friends, while the gifts that have been made to that which the Lord honors, have been stinted and limited in value and in recurrence.... (CS 259.3)

Self-Denial and the Church Mortgage

The test question for every Christian to ask himself is, Have I, in my innermost soul, a love for Jesus? Do I love His tabernacle?... Is my love for God and my Redeemer strong enough to lead me to deny self? When temptations come to indulge in pleasure and selfish enjoyment, shall I not say, No, I will not spend one shilling or even sixpence for my own gratification while the house of God is under mortgage, or bearing the pressure of debt? (CS 260.1)

Should not Christ have our first and highest consideration? Should He not demand this token of our respect and loyalty? These very things underlie our heart life, in the home circle, and in the church life. If the heart, the soul, the strength, the life, is surrendered wholly to God, if the affection is given wholly to Him, you will make God supreme in all your service. The result will be that you will have a sense of what it means to be a partner with Jesus Christ in the sacred firm. The building erected for the worship of God will not be left crippled with debt. It will appear almost like a denial of your faith to allow such a thing.– *Letter 52, 1897.* (CS 260.2)

Church Debts Dishonoring to God

It is dishonoring to God for our churches to be burdened with debt. This state of things need not exist. It shows wrong management from beginning to end, and it is a dishonor to the God of heaven. Read and study prayerfully the fourth chapter of Zechariah. Then read the first chapter of Haggai, and see if this representation does not apply to you. While you have thought much of your own selves, of your own selfish interests, you have either neglected to arise and build, or have built on hired money, and have not made donations to free the church buildings from debt. Will you consider what it is your duty to do? Year after year passes by, and very little sacrifice is made to lessen the debt. The interest swallows up the means that should be used to pay off the principal. (CS 261.1)

Why the Debts Remain

Slothful servants is the charge that God makes of those in the churches. His will is not done when sacred things are left to remain in a withered, neglected condition. Self-sacrifice, self-denial in every church would change the order of things. "The silver is Mine, and the gold is Mine, saith the Lord of hosts." When that gold and silver is used for selfish purposes, to gratify ambition or pride or selfish indulgence, as has been done, God is dishonored. (CS 261.2)

Can those who are representative men be so sound asleep that they do not comprehend that the state of things that exists is a result of neglect on their part? When the people chosen by God embellish their own houses, and invest God's money in ... various things for selfish gratification, knowing that the very means thus used should be used to keep the house of God in the very best condition, that no means may be taken from the treasury to defray running expenses, they cannot be blessed. (CS 261.3)

I have a message from the Lord. The churches must awaken from their torpor, and think of these things. "The silver is Mine, and the gold is Mine, saith the Lord of hosts." Are we as families appropriating the Lord's silver and gold to selfish purposes, and doing nothing to lighten the debt on His house? The churches are burdened with debt, not because it is impossible for them to be freed, but because of selfish indulgence on the part of the members. By this neglect God is dishonored, and if He binds about your resources, be not blind as to the cause. When you place the Lord first, and realize that the Lord's house is dishonored by debt, God will bless you.– *Manuscript 116, 1897.* (CS 262.1)

Need for Counsel and Cooperation

Dear Brother,

You will need in every move you make to know that you are moving in that way that you will not follow your own judgment, but the united advice of your brethren. You have failed in this work, working too much independently.... You can borrow money. But have you taken your brethren right along with you in your building plans? Have you yoked up with them, and they with you? ... One man's mind and judgment is not to be allowed to become an efficiency in any case where the building of a church is concerned. It takes every member of the church who can carry responsibilities, and the minister is not the man to lift this work alone.... This is a lesson you must learn, to seek the mind and judgment of your brethren, and not advance without their advice, counsel, and cooperation.– *Letter 49, 1900.* (CS 262.2)

An Inexcusable Laxness

The lax way which many churches have of incurring debts, and keeping in debt, was presented before me. In some cases a continual debt is upon the house of God, and continual interest to be paid. These things should not and need not be. If there is that wisdom, and tact, and zeal manifested for the Master that God requires of every one of His servants, there will be a change in these things. The debts will be lifted. Self-denial and self-sacrifice will work wonders in advancing the spirituality of the church. Let every church member do something. Let the necessity of each acting a part be most strenuously impressed upon the worshipers. (CS 263.1)

The----college and church need not be loaded with debt as it is. This shows unwise stewardship. God calls for self-sacrifice. He calls for offerings from those who can give, and even the poorer members can do their little. And when there is a will to do, God will open the way. But the Lord is not pleased with the management. He does not design that His cause shall be trammeled with debt. (CS 263.2)

Self-denial will enable those who have done

nothing in the past to do something tangible, and show that they believe the teachings of the word, that they believe the truth for this time. All, both old and young, parents and children, are to show their faith by their works. Faith is made perfect by works. We are in the very closing scenes of this earth's history; yet there are but few who realize this because the world has come in between God and the soul.– *Letter 81, 1897.* (CS 263.3)

Building the Church and School at Avondale

There are times when much is to be gained by a united, prompt, and persistent effort. The time for opening our school had been appointed; but our brethren throughout the colonies were looking for a postponement. They had waited long for the school to open, and were discouraged. There was much work yet to be done on the buildings, and our funds were exhausted. Therefore the builders said that the work could not be done at the appointed time. But we said there must be no delay. The school must be opened at the time named. So we laid the matter before the church, and called for volunteers. Thirty men and women offered themselves for the work; and although it was hard for them to spare the time, a strong company continued at the work day after day till the buildings were completed, cleaned, and furnished, ready to be used at the day set for opening the school. (CS 263.4)

When the time came for this meetinghouse to be built, there was another test of faith and loyalty. We had a council to consider what should be done. The way seemed hedged about with difficulties. Some said: "Enclose a small building, and when money shall come in,

enlarge; for we cannot possibly complete at this time such a house as we desire." Others said, "Wait till we have money with which to build a commodious house." This we thought to do; but the word of the Lord came to me in the night season, "Arise, and build without delay." (CS 264.1)

We then decided that we would take hold of the work, and walk out by faith to make a beginning. The very next night there came from South Africa a draft for two hundred pounds. This was a gift from Brother and Sister Lindsay, of Cape Town, to help us in building the meetinghouse. Our faith had been tested, we had decided to begin the work, and now the Lord put into our hands this large gift with which to begin. (CS 264.2)

With this encouragement the work was begun in earnest. The school board gave the land and one hundred pounds. Two hundred pounds was received from the union conference, and the members of the church gave what they could. Friends outside of the church helped, and the builders gave a part of their time, which was as good as money. (CS 265.1)

Thus the work was completed, and we have this beautiful house, capable of seating four hundred people. We thank the Lord for this house in which to worship Him. He understands all the strait places through which we were brought. When difficulties arose, Elder Haskell, who was superintending the work, would call the workmen together, and they would pray earnestly for God's blessing upon themselves and the work. The Lord heard prayer, and the house was completed in seven weeks.– *The Review and Herald, November 1, 1898.* (CS 265.2)

Chapter 52
Avoiding Institutional Debts

God does not want His work to be continually embarrassed with debt. When it seems desirable to add to the buildings or other facilities of an institution, beware of going beyond your means. Better to defer the improvements until Providence shall open the way for them to be made without contracting heavy debts and having to pay interest. (CS 266.1)

The publishing houses have been made places of deposit by our people, and have thus been enabled to furnish means to support branches of the work in different fields, and have aided in carrying other enterprises. This is well. None too much has been done in these lines. The Lord sees it all. But, from the light He has given me, every effort should be made to stand free from debt. (CS 266.2)

In the Publishing House

The publishing work was founded in self-denial, and should be conducted upon strictly economical principles. The question of finance can be managed, if, when there is a pressure for means, the workers will consent to a reduction in wages. This was the principle the Lord revealed to me to be brought into our institutions. When money is scarce, we should be willing to restrict our wants. (CS 266.3)

Let the proper estimate be placed upon the publications, and then let all in our publishing houses study to economize in every possible way, even though considerable inconvenience is thus caused. Watch the little outgoes. Stop every leak. It is the little losses that tell heavily in the end. Gather up the fragments; let nothing be lost. Waste not the minutes in talking; wasted minutes mar the hours. Persevering diligence, working in faith, will always be crowned with success. (CS 266.4)

Some think it beneath their dignity to look after small things. They think it the evidence of a narrow mind and a niggardly spirit. But small leaks have sunk many a ship. Nothing that would serve the purpose of any should be allowed to waste. A lack of economy will surely bring debt upon our institutions. Although much money may be received, it will be lost in the little wastes of every branch of the work. Economy is not stinginess. (CS 267.1)

Every man or woman employed in the publishing house should be a faithful sentinel, watching that nothing be wasted. All should guard against supposed wants that require an expenditure of means. Some men live better on four hundred dollars a year than others do on eight hundred. Just so it is with our institutions; some persons can manage them with far less capital than others can. God desires all the workers to practice economy, and especially to be faithful accountants.– *Testimonies for the Church 7:206, 207.* (CS 267.2)

Saving Expense Through Careful Sanitarium Management

Those connected with our institutions need to study how to save expense, so that the institutions shall not become involved in debt. Wisdom must be shown in the matter of purchasing. Money must be made to go as far as possible. By careful management, many dollars may be saved. (CS 267.3)

Expenditures should not be made unless they are warranted by the means in hand. There are those connected with our institutions who incur debts that might be avoided. Perhaps unnecessary expense is entailed to beautify the building. Money is often used to gratify taste and inclination. (CS 267.4)

Every Worker to be a Producer

Let everyone now strive with courage and activity to save rather than to spend. Say to those who are willing to consume without producing, It is my duty to economize in every line. I cannot encourage extravagance. I cannot let means go out of my hands to purchase that which is not needed. (CS 268.1)

From the highest to the lowest, God's workmen are to study to economize. Let each one say to himself, I am to restrain in myself any inclination to spend means unnecessarily. Let those who work in God's service be producers as well as consumers. Look at the greatness of the work, and restrain the unchristian inclination to spend money for self-gratification. Count the cost of the thing you desire to buy. (CS 268.2)

This is an excellent opportunity for everyone to stand in his lot and in his place. Let each one try to produce something. Those in God's work should be willing to help wherever help is needed. They should make their expenditures as few as possible; for necessities will arise where every dollar will be needed to carry forward the Lord's work. (CS 268.3)

The employment of helpers, for indoor and outdoor work, is a matter that needs careful consideration. The managers of our institutions are to be careful and prudent. They should not engage large numbers of helpers unless it is a positive necessity. In this matter mistakes are often made. (CS 268.4)

Employees a Part of the Firm

The helpers in our institutions should act as though they were a part of the firm. They should not think that they must work only for a certain number of hours each day. When emergencies arise, and extra help is needed, they should respond willingly and cheerfully. They should feel an intense interest in the success of the institution for which they are working. Thus others are encouraged to work interestedly and conscientiously. (CS 268.5)

Christ said, "Gather up the fragments, that nothing be lost." Let those who act any part in our institutions heed this instruction. Let them take care that there is no waste in the spiritual and temporal supplies which the Lord provides. Economy is to be learned by the educators and taught to the helpers. And by precept and example parents should teach their children the science of making a small amount go as far as possible. Many poor families are poor because they spend their money as soon as they receive it. (CS 269.1)

The one who occupies the position of cook in a sanitarium should be trained to habits of economy. He should realize that no food is to be wasted. (CS 269.2)

"Not Slothful in Business"

The word of inspiration tells us that we are to be "not slothful in business; fervent in spirit; serving the Lord." Let all who are connected with our sanitariums take hold of their work interestedly and earnestly. If helpers have not learned the science of being quick, let them begin at once to train themselves in this line, or else consent that their wages shall be proportionate to the amount of work done. Every day nurses and helpers should become more efficient, more all-round and helpful. They can individually help themselves to reach a higher and still higher standard as the Lord's helping hand. Let those who are naturally slow train themselves day by day to do their work more quickly, and at the same time carefully.... (CS 269.3)

Those who receive pay for their labor should put in good time. They should be producers as well as consumers. As they obtain an education in these lines, they will become more and more able to do perfectly the work assigned to them. They will be ready to take hold of the work in any place.– *Letter 87, 1901.* (CS 270.1)

Economy in School Management

Economy must be practiced in every line to keep afloat, and not be drowned with debts; but there is to be an increase in the sum paid for tuition. This was presented to me while in Europe, and has been presented since to you and our schools. And the problem, "How shall our schools keep out of debt?" will always remain a problem until there are wiser calculations. Charge higher rates for students' educational advantages, and then let persons have the management in cooking who know how to save and economize. Let the best talent be secured, even if good, reasonable wages have to be paid. The binding about the edges is essential. When these precautions are attended to, you will not have increasing debts in your schools.... (**CS 270.2**)

The Students to Cooperate

Some will say, "We shall have fewer students." This may be; but those that you do have will appreciate their time, and see the necessity of diligent work to qualify them for the positions they must fill. If the Lord is kept ever before the students as the One to whom they should look for counsel, like Daniel, they will receive of Him knowledge and wisdom. All will then become channels of light. Lay the matter before the students themselves. Inquire who of them will practice self-denial and make sacrifice to cancel the debt already incurred. With some students only the willing mind is needed. (**CS 270.3**)

God help the managers of our schools never to allow the outgo to exceed the income, if the school has to be closed. There has not been the talent that is needed in the management of our schools financially. These things God will require of the managers. Every needless, expensive habit is to be laid aside, every unnecessary indulgence cut away. When the principles so manifestly indicated by the word of God to all schools, are taken hold of as earnestly as they should be, the debts will not accumulate.– *Letter 137, 1898.* (**CS 271.1**)

Guarding School Finance

Especially should the president of a school look carefully after the finances of the institution. He should understand the underlying principles of bookkeeping. He is faithfully to report the use of all monies passing through his hands for the use of the school. The funds of the school are not to be overdrawn, but every effort is to be made to increase the usefulness of the school. Those entrusted with the financial management of our educational institutions, must allow no carelessness in the expenditure of means. Everything connected with the finances of our schools should be perfectly straight. The Lord's way must be strictly followed, though this may not be in harmony with the ways of man.... (**CS 271.2**)

If you are tempted to appropriate the money coming into the school, in ways that bring no special benefit to the school, your standard of principle needs to be carefully criticized, that the time may not come when you will have to be criticized and found wanting. Who is your bookkeeper? Who is your treasurer? Who is your business manager? Are they careful and competent? Look to this. It is possible for money to be misappropriated, without anyone's understanding clearly how it came about; and it is possible for a school to be losing continually because of unwise expenditures. Those in charge may feel this loss keenly, and yet suppose they have done their best. But why do they permit debts to accumulate? Let those in charge of a school find out each month the true financial standing of the school.– *Manuscript 65, 1906.* (**CS 271.3**)

Shun Debt as Leprosy

Economy should be exercised in everything connected with the school. Those who come to the school generally leave homes that are unadorned, where they have been accustomed to eat simple food without a number of courses. They are accustomed to plain, hearty food at noon. It would be better for all to have only a simple evening meal. There must be a strict regard to economy or a heavy debt will be incurred. Keep within bounds. Shun the incurring of debt as you would shun leprosy.– *Letter 60, 1896.* (**CS 272.1**)

Chapter 53
Failing to Count the Cost

There are men who do not move wisely. They are anxious to make a large appearance. They think that outward display will give them influence. In their work, they do not first sit down and count the cost, to see whether they are able to finish what they have begun. Thus they show their weakness. They show that they have much to learn in regard to the necessity of moving carefully and guardedly. In their self-confidence they make many mistakes. Thus some have received harm from which they will never recover. (CS 273.1)

This has been the case with several who have felt competent to establish and conduct sanitariums. Failure comes to them, and when they find themselves involved in debt, they ask the Medical Missionary Association to take over the unsuccessful institution and to assume its liabilities.... It does harm to the Medical Missionary Association to take over so many bankrupt sanitariums. Let those who have conducted these sanitariums and who have walked in false paths, begin to think sensibly. Let not failure be written upon them. This spoils the courage of good men. (CS 273.2)

Men who might have done well if they had consecrated themselves to God, if they had been willing to work in a humble way, enlarging their business slowly, and refusing to go into debt, have made a failure because they have not worked on right lines. And after getting into difficulty, they have sold out, as men incompetent to manage. They desired relief from financial pressure, and did not stop to think of the after-results. (CS 273.3)

Those who help such ones out of difficulty are tempted to bind them with such strong cords in the shape of pledges that ever after they feel that they are bondslaves. They seldom outgrow the reputation of poor management and failure. (CS 273.4)

To those who thus become involved in debt, I am instructed to say: Do not give up if you are moving in right lines. Work with all your power to relieve the situation yourselves. Do not throw an embarrassed institution upon an association that is already heavily burdened with debt. It is best for every sanitarium to stand in its own responsibility. (CS 274.1)

Those who have charge of our sanitariums should move guardedly. There are times when they will see little increase. Let them act with wisdom and tact and adaptability. Let them study and practice the instruction Christ gave in regard to building a tower. Forethought is of far more value than afterthought–when a neglect of wise calculation and careful management is plainly seen to result in failure. Managers who are slack, who do not know how to manage, should be separated from the work. Secure the services of men and women who know how to bind about the edges, so that the work shall not ravel out. (CS 274.2)

Let all who are connected with our institutions humble themselves before God. Let them ask God to help them to plan so wisely and economically that the institutions will take firm root and will bear fruit to God's glory. Depend not on men. Look to Jesus. Continue instant in prayer and watch unto prayer with thanksgiving. Be sure that you have a close connection with Christ.– *Letter 199, 1901.* (CS 274.3)

Debt Through Overbuilding

Brother -----, it is not wisdom to become involved in debt. You are a wise man, and do not need this reminder. A debt is a yoke,–a binding, galling yoke. It would not be wisdom to purchase another place near -----. You have been pressed almost beyond measure in the effort to build and equip the ----- Sanitarium. It would have been wiser to make the building smaller. I have always thought that it would be best to cut down the building plans still more than they were cut down, and then, when means came in, and if more room was needed, the building could have been enlarged. It would cost much less to furnish a smaller building,– *Letter 158, 1902.* (CS 274.4)

Entrapped Through Miscalculation

If we walk in the counsel of the Lord, we shall have opportunity to purchase for sanitarium purposes, at a reasonable rate, properties on which there already are buildings that can be utilized, and where the grounds are already ornamented by ornamental trees. Many such places have been presented to me. I have been instructed that the liberal offers made on these places should be carefully considered.... (CS 275.1)

It may sometimes be necessary, however, to select a site on which no improvements have been made and no buildings erected. In such a case, we must be careful not to select a place which will of necessity require a large outlay of means for improvements. Through lack of experience, and miscalculation, we may be entrapped into the incurring of large debts, because the buildings and improvements cost two or three times as much as was estimated.– *Manuscript 114, 1902.* (CS 275.2)

Counting on Money Only in Prospect

The president and the business manager are to work unitedly together. The business manager is to see that the expenditure does not exceed the income. He is to know what there is to depend on, so that the work here shall not be burdened with debt as it is in Battle Creek. The condition of things there need never have existed. It is the result of men not being under God's rule. When men are under God's rule, the work moves harmoniously; but when men of strong temperament, who are not controlled by God, are placed in responsible positions in the work, the cause is imperiled; for their strong temperaments lead them to use money which is only in prospect.– *Manuscript 106, 1899.* (CS 275.3)

Premature Enterprises Without Wide Counsel

Special talent is required to start a sanitarium and place it in running order, even though the enterprise be a private one. Before starting out in such an enterprise, our brethren should ask the advice of wise counselors. ----- must be worked; but it must be worked in the right way. Were enterprises started that would prove a disappointment, were the one who had taken the responsibility of the work upon himself, to fail in his enterprise, it would be very difficult to overcome the impression thus made against the truth. (CS 276.1)

Whoever has in view the starting of a sanitarium should consult those of his brethren who carry the burden of the work in fields nigh and afar off. We cannot afford to have any impression made by our medical work in the cities other than that God is our leader and our defense.... (CS 276.2)

To our brethren everywhere I am instructed to say, Let the enterprises already started in needy fields be considered before new enterprises are begun, else a large burden of debt will be brought upon our people.– *Letter 5, 1905.* (CS 276.3)

Chapter 54
Moving Forward in Faith

To make no move that calls for the investment of means unless we have the money in hand to complete the contemplated work, should not always be considered the wisest plan. In the upbuilding of His work, the Lord does not always make everything plain before His servants. He sometimes tries the confidence of His people by having them move forward in faith. Often He brings them into strait and trying places, bidding them go forward when their feet seem to be touching the waters of the Red Sea. It is at such times, when the prayers of His servants ascend to Him in earnest faith, that He opens the way before them, and brings them out into a large place. (CS 277.1)

The Lord wants His people in these days to believe that He will do as great things for them as He did for the children of Israel in their journey from Egypt to Canaan. We are to have an educated faith that will not hesitate to follow His instructions in the most difficult experiences. "Go forward" is the command of God to His people. (CS 277.2)

Faith and cheerful obedience are needed to bring the Lord's designs to pass. When He points out the necessity of establishing the work in places where it will have influence, the people are to walk and work by faith. By their godly conversation, their humility, their prayers and earnest efforts, they should strive to bring the people to appreciate the good work that the Lord has established among them. It was the Lord's purpose that the Loma Linda Sanitarium should become the property of our people, and He brought it about at a time when the rivers of difficulty were full and overflowing their banks. (CS 277.3)

The working of private interests for the gaining of personal ends is one thing. In this, men may follow their own judgment. But the carrying forward of the Lord's work in the earth is entirely another matter. When He designates that a certain property should be secured for the advancement of His cause and the building up of His work, whether it be for sanitarium or school work, or for any other branch, He will make the doing of that work possible, if those who have experience will show their faith and trust in His purposes, and will move forward promptly to secure the advantages He points out. While we are not to seek to wrest property from any man, yet when advantages are offered, we should be wide awake to see the advantage, that we may make plans for the upbuilding of the work. And when we have done this, we should exert every energy to secure the freewill offerings of God's people for the support of these new plants.– *Testimonies for the Church 9:271, 272*. (CS 278.1)

Danger in Extreme Position

It is right to borrow money to carry forward a work that we know God desires to have accomplished. We should not wait in inconvenience, and make the work much harder, because we do not wish to borrow money. Mistakes have been made in incurring debt to do that which could well have waited till a future time. But there is danger of going to the other extreme. We are not to place ourselves in a position that will endanger health and make our work wearing. We are to act sensibly. We must do the work that needs to be done, even if we have to borrow money and pay interest.– *Letter 111, 1903*. (CS 278.2)

Guard Against Mistakes on Both Sides

The question now before us is, Shall we try to secure the places that seem desirable in price and location, when we cannot tell where our money is coming from? Brethren ------, ------, and others are opposed to the increasing of debts. But I am not prepared to say that we should not, under any circumstances, purchase land to which the Lord seems to have directed our minds, when there is no hindrance but the question of ready money, and which property, in the providence of God, we could soon pay for. We have to guard against mistakes on both sides.– *Letter 167, 1902.* (**CS 279.1**)

A Brake on Wheels of Progress

The idea that a sanitarium should not be established unless it could be started free from debt, has put the brake upon the wheels of progress. In building meetinghouses we have had to borrow money, in order that something might be done at once. We have been obliged to do this, in order to fulfill the directions of God. Persons deeply interested in the progress of the work have borrowed money and paid interest on it, to help establish schools and sanitariums and to build meetinghouses. The institutions thus established and the churches built have been the means of winning many to the truth. Thus the tithe has been increased, and workers have been added to the Lord's forces.– *Letter 211, 1904.* (**CS 279.2**)

Loss Through Lack of Faith

God would have the standard lifted higher and still higher. The church cannot abridge her task without denying her Master. Meetinghouses must be built in many places. Is it economy to fail to provide in our cities places of worship where the Redeemer may meet with His people? Let us not give the impression that we find it too great an expense to provide properly for the reception of the heavenly Guest. (**CS 279.3**)

In laying plans for building, we need the wisdom of God. We should not needlessly incur debt, but I would say that in every case all the money required to complete a building need not be in hand before the work is begun. We must often move forward by faith, working as expeditiously as possible. It is through a lack of faith that we fail of receiving the fulfillment of God's promises. We must work and pray and believe. We are to move forward steadily and earnestly, trusting in the Lord, and saying, "We will not fail nor become discouraged."– *The Review and Herald, September 7, 1905.* (**CS 280.1**)

Chapter 55
Words From a Divine Counselor

In a vision of the night a short time ago, I was in council meetings. At these meetings words were spoken that savored of the human more than of the divine. The medical work in ----- was under consideration. Plans were proposed which, unless modified, would bind about the work and fail of relieving the situation. The General Conference was asked to pledge itself to raise a sum of no less than twenty thousand dollars, or to become responsible for that amount, to establish a sanitarium in -----. Because Elder ----- refused to consent to place this additional obligation upon the General Conference, he was severely reflected upon by some. But, under the existing circumstances, he felt that he was forbidden by the Lord to lay this burden upon the Conference. I honor Elder -----'s judgment on this question.... (CS 281.1)

But to return to the council meeting: Once more the One who has long been our Counselor, was present, to give us the word of the Lord. He said: "The Lord would not be glorified by your placing a yoke of debt upon the General Conference. In a special manner He has wrought to break from the necks of His people the binding yokes of debt which they have worn so long. The Conference must not again tread the same path that they have trodden." ... (CS 281.2)

Some have not yet learned the lesson that Christ taught in regard to building a tower. "Which of you," He inquired, "intending to build a tower, sitteth not down first, and counteth the cost, whether he have sufficient to finish it? Lest haply, after he hath laid the foundation, and is not able to finish it, all that behold it begin to mock him, saying, This man began to build, and was not able to finish." This warning has been disregarded. (CS 281.3)

When men in positions of responsibility are in such a hurry to establish some new institution that is untimely, the showing made is not only against the interests of the Lord's cause, but against the interests of the men who in human wisdom have tried to advance too rapidly. God is not glorified by those who attempt to go faster than He leads. Perplexity, embarrassment, and distress are the result. The Lord does not desire His representatives to repeat these mistakes; for the past record of such movements does not glorify Him.– *Manuscript 144, 1902.* (CS 282.1)

Let Not Mistakes of the Past Be Repeated

A kind of frenzy has taken hold of the minds of some, leading them to do that which would absorb means without any prospect of afterward producing means. Had this money been used in the way the Lord signified it should be, workers would have been raised up and prepared to do the work that must be done before the coming of the Lord. The misappropriation of means shows the need of the Lord's warning that His work must not be bound about by human projects, that it must be done in a way that will strengthen His cause. (CS 282.2)

By working on wrong plans, men have brought debts upon the cause. Let not this be repeated. Let those at the head of the work move cautiously, refusing to bury the cause of God in debt. Let no one move recklessly, heedlessly, thinking, without knowing, that all will be well.– *Testimonies for the Church 7:283, 284.* (CS 282.3)

Lift the Debts

God designs that we shall learn lessons from the failures of the past. It is not pleasing to Him to have debts rest upon His institutions. We have reached the time when we must give character to the work by refusing to erect large and costly buildings. (CS 283.1)

We are not to copy the mistakes of the past, and become more and more involved in debt. We are rather to endeavor to clear off the indebtedness that still remains on our institutions. Our churches can help in this matter if they will. Those members to whom the Lord has given means can invest their money in the cause without interest or at a low rate of interest, and by their freewill offerings they can help to support the work. The Lord asks you to return cheerfully to Him a portion of the goods He has lent you, and thus become His almoners.– *The Review and Herald, August 13, 1908.* (**CS 283.2**)

In Time of Reformation Means Will Come

When there is a seeking of the Lord and a confession of sin, when the needed reformation takes place, united zeal and earnestness will be shown in restoring what has been withheld. The Lord will manifest His pardoning love, and means will come to cancel the debts on our institutions.– *Testimonies for the Church 8:89.* (**CS 283.3**)

For Further Study

School Management and Finance, *Testimonies for the Church 6:206-218*

Debt on the Danish Sanitarium, *Testimonies for the Church 6:463-467*

Relief of the Schools, *Testimonies for the Church 6:468-478*

Consideration in Buildings, *Testimonies for the Church 7:90-94*

Advantages of a Humble Beginning, *Testimonies for the Church 1:558, 559*

Relief Plan for Liquidating Institutional Debts, *Testimonies for the Church 9:71, 75, 79, 80, 88; Fundamentals of Christian Education, 520-524*

Shun as Disease, *Testimonies for the Church 6:211*

Shun as Leprosy, *Testimonies for the Church 6:217*

Guard Against as With Barbed-Wire Fence, *Testimonies for the Church 7:236*

A Blot of Debt a Dark Shadow, *Testimonies for the Church 6:217, 216*

Promptness in Paying Dues for Missionary Literature, *Testimonies for the Church 2:628*

Lifting Church Debts, *Testimonies for the Church 6:103*

Section 12

Saving to Give

Chapter 56
Left to the Honor of Men

The only plan which the gospel has marked out for sustaining the work of God is one that leaves the support of His cause to the honor of men. With an eye single to the glory of God, men are to give to God the proportion which He has required. Viewing the cross of Calvary, looking upon the world's Redeemer, who for our sake became poor, that we through His poverty might be made rich, we shall feel that we are not to lay up for ourselves treasures on the earth, but to lay up treasures in the bank of heaven, which will never suspend payment nor fail. The Lord has given Jesus to our world, and the question is, What can we give back to God in gifts and offerings to show our appreciation of His love? "Freely ye have received, freely give." (CS 287.1)

How much more eager will every faithful steward be to enlarge the proportion of gifts to be placed in the Lord's treasure house, than to decrease his offering one jot or tittle. Whom is he serving? For whom is he preparing an offering?–For the One upon whom he is dependent for every good thing which he enjoys. Then let not one of us who is receiving the grace of Christ, give occasion for the angels to be ashamed of us, and for Jesus to be ashamed to call us brethren. (CS 287.2)

Shall ingratitude be cultivated, and made manifest by our niggardly practices in giving to the cause of God?–No, no! Let us surrender ourselves a living sacrifice, and give our all to Jesus. It is His; we are His purchased possession. Those who are recipients of His grace, who contemplate the cross of Calvary, will not question concerning the proportion to be given, but will feel that the richest offering is all too meager, all disproportionate to the great gift of the only-begotten Son of the infinite God. Through self-denial, the poorest will find ways of obtaining something to give back to God.

(CS 287.3)

Stewardship of Time

Time is money, and many are wasting precious time which might be used in useful labor, working with their hands the thing that is good. The Lord will never say, "Well done, thou good and faithful servant," to the man who has not taxed the physical powers which have been lent him of God as precious talents by which to gather means, wherewith the needy may be supplied, and offerings may be made to God. (CS 288.1)

The rich are not to feel that they can be content in giving of their money merely. They have talents of ability, and they are to study to show themselves approved unto God, to be earnest spiritual agents in educating and training their children for fields of usefulness. Parents and children are not to regard themselves as their own, and feel that they can dispose of their time and property as shall please themselves. They are God's purchased possession, and the Lord calls for the profit of their physical powers, which are to be employed in bringing a revenue to the treasury of the Lord. (CS 288.2)

Self-Denial and the Cross

Were the thousand channels of selfishness cut off that now exist, and the means directed in the right channel, there would be a large revenue flowing into the treasury. Many purchase idols with money that should go to the house of God. No one can practice real benevolence without practicing genuine self-denial. Self-denial and the cross lie directly in the path of every Christian who is truly following Christ. Jesus says: "If any man will come after Me, let him deny himself, and take up his cross daily, and follow Me." Will every soul consider the fact that

Christian discipleship includes self-denial, self-sacrifice, even to the laying down of life itself, if need be, for the sake of Him who has given His life for the life of the world? (CS 288.3)

Christians who view Christ upon the cross, are bound by their obligation to God because of the infinite gift of His Son, to withhold nothing which they possess, however dear it may be to them. If they possess anything that can be employed to draw any soul, no matter how rich, or no matter how poor, to the Lamb of God who taketh away the sins of the world, they are to use it freely for this purpose. The Lord employs human agents to be coworkers with Him in the salvation of sinners. (CS 289.1)

All heaven is actively engaged in furnishing facilities by which to extend the knowledge of the truth to all peoples, nations, and tongues. If those who profess to have been truly converted, do not let their light shine forth to others, they are neglecting the doing of the words of Christ. (CS 289.2)

We need not tax ourselves with rehearsing how much has been given to the cause of God, but rather let us consider how much has been kept back from His treasury to be devoted to the indulgence of self in pleasure seeking and self-gratification. We need not reckon up how many agents have been sent forth, but rather recount how many have closed the eyes of their understanding, so that they might not see their duty and minister to others according to their several ability. (CS 289.3)

How many might now be employed were there means in the treasury to sustain them in the work! How many facilities might be used in extending the work of God as His providence opens the way! Hundreds could be employed in the field in doing good in various branches, but they are not there. Why?–Selfishness keeps them at home; they love ease, and so remain away from the vineyard of the Lord. Some would go into regions beyond, but they have not the means to take them; for others have left undone that which they ought to have done. These are some of the reasons why a few workers have to go loaded down as a cart beneath sheaves, while others take no burden.– *The Review and Herald, July 14, 1896.* (CS 289.4)

The Dollar That Might Save a Soul

The Lord has made provision that all may be reached by the message of truth, but the means placed in the hands of His stewards for this very purpose has been selfishly devoted to their own gratification. (CS 290.1)

How much has been thoughtlessly wasted by our youth, spent for self-indulgence and display, for that which they would have been just as happy without. Every dollar which we possess is the Lord's. Instead of spending means for needless things, we should invest it in answering the calls of missionary work. (CS 290.2)

As new fields are opened, the calls for means are constantly increasing. If ever we needed to exercise economy, it is now. All who labor in the cause should realize the importance of closely following the Saviour's example of self-denial and economy. They should see in the means that they handle a trust which God has committed to them, and they should feel under obligation to exercise tact and financial ability in the use of their Lord's money. Every penny should be carefully treasured. A cent seems like a trifle, but a hundred cents make a dollar, and rightly spent may be the means of saving a soul from death. If all the means which has been wasted by our own people in self-gratification had been devoted to the cause of God, there would be no empty treasuries, and missions could be established in all parts of the world. (CS 290.3)

Let the members of the church now put away their pride and lay off their ornaments. Each should keep a missionary box at hand, and drop into it every penny he is tempted to waste in self-indulgence. But something more must be done than merely to dispense with superfluities. Self-denial must be practiced. Some of our comfortable and desirable things must be sacrificed. The preachers must sharpen up their message, not merely assailing self-indulgence, and pride in dress, but presenting Jesus, His life of self-denial and sacrifice. Let love, piety, and faith be cherished in the heart, and the precious fruits will appear in the life.– *Historical Sketches of the Foreign Missions of the Seventh-day*

Adventists, 293. (**CS 291.1**)

Chapter 57
Words to the Youth

Much might be said to the young people regarding their privilege to help the cause of God by learning lessons of economy and self-denial. Many think that they must indulge in this pleasure and that, and in order to do this, they accustom themselves to live up to the full extent of their income. God wants us to do better in this respect. We sin against ourselves when we are satisfied with enough to eat and drink and wear. God has something higher than this before us. When we are willing to put away our selfish desires, and give the powers of heart and mind to the work of the cause of God, heavenly agencies will cooperate with us, making us a blessing to humanity. (CS 292.1)

Even though he may be poor, the youth who is industrious and economical can save a little for the cause of God. When I was only twelve years old, I knew what it was to economize. With my sister I learned a trade, and although we would earn only twenty-five cents a day, from this sum we were able to save a little to give to missions. We saved little by little until we had thirty dollars. Then when the message of the Lord's soon coming came to us, with a call for men and means, we felt it a privilege to hand over the thirty dollars to father, asking him to invest it in tracts and pamphlets to send the message to those who were in darkness. (CS 292.2)

It is the duty of all who touch the work of God to learn economy in the use of time and money. Those who indulge in idleness reveal that they attach little importance to the glorious truths committed to us. They need to be educated in habits of industry, and to learn to work with an eye single to the glory of God. (CS 292.3)

Deny Self and Improve Talent

Those who have not good judgment in the use of time and money, should advise with those who have had experience. With the money that we had earned at our trade, my sister and I provided ourselves with clothes. We would hand our money to mother, saying, "Buy, so that after we have paid for our clothes, there will be something left to give for missionary work." And she would do this, thus encouraging in us a missionary spirit. (CS 293.1)

The giving that is the fruit of self-denial, is a wonderful help to the giver. It imparts an education that enables us more fully to comprehend the work of Him who went about doing good, relieving the suffering, and supplying the needs of the destitute. The Saviour lived not to please Himself. In His life there was no trace of selfishness.– *Youth's Instructor, September 10, 1907.* (CS 293.2)

Children May Learn Self-Denial

While parents are making sacrifices for the sake of advancing the cause of God, they should teach their children also to take part in this work. The children may learn to show their love for Christ by denying themselves needless trifles, for the purchase of which much money slips through their fingers. In every family this work should be done. It requires tact and method, but it will be the best education the children can receive. And if all the little children would present their offerings to the Lord, their gifts would be as little rivulets, which, when united and set flowing, would swell into a river. (CS 293.3)

The Lord looks with pleasure upon the little children who deny themselves that they may make an offering to Him. He was pleased with the widow who put her two mites into the treasury, because she gave with a willing heart. The Saviour thought her sacrifice in giving all that she had of more value than the large gifts of the rich men, who made no sacrifice in order to give. And He is glad when the little ones are willing to deny self that they may become laborers together with Him who loved them, and took them in His arms and blessed them.– *The Review and Herald, December 25, 1900.* (CS 293.4)

Keep Account of Income and Outgoes

In the study of figures the work should be made practical. Let every youth and every child be taught, not merely to solve imaginary problems, but to keep an accurate account of his own income and outgoes. Let him learn the right use of money by using it. Whether supplied by their parents or by their own earnings, let boys and girls learn to select and purchase their own clothing, their books, and other necessities; and by keeping an account of their expenses they will learn, as they could learn in no other way, the value and the use of money. (CS 294.1)

This training will help them to distinguish true economy from niggardliness on the one hand and prodigality on the other. Rightly directed, it will encourage habits of benevolence. It will aid the youth in learning to give, not from the mere impulse of the moment, as their feelings are stirred, but regularly and systematically.– *Education 238, 239.* (CS 294.2)

Following Satan's Suggestions

How the enemy has wrought to place temporal things above spiritual! Many families who have but little to spare for God's cause, will yet spend money freely to purchase rich furniture or fashionable clothing. How much is spent for the table, and often for that which is only a hurtful indulgence; how much for presents that benefit no one! (CS 294.3)

Many spend considerable sums for photographs to give to their friends. Picture taking is carried to extravagant lengths, and encourages a species of idolatry. How much more pleasing to God it would be if all this means were invested in publications which would direct souls to Christ and the precious truths for this time! The money wasted on needless things would supply many a table with reading matter on present truth, which would prove a savor of life unto life. (CS 295.1)

Satan's suggestions are carried out in many, many things. Our birthday anniversaries and Christmas and Thanksgiving festivals are too often devoted to selfish gratification, when the mind should be directed to the mercy and loving-kindness of God. God is displeased that His goodness, His constant care, His unceasing love, are not brought to mind on these anniversary occasions. (CS 295.2)

If all the money that is used extravagantly, for needless things, were placed in the treasury of God, we should see men and women and youth giving themselves to Jesus, and doing their part to cooperate with Christ and angels. The richest blessing of God would come into our churches, and many souls would be converted to the truth.– *The Review and Herald, December 23, 1890.* (CS 295.3)

Birthdays and Holidays

Parents are to bring up and educate and train their children in habits of self-control and self-denial. They are ever to keep before them their obligation to obey the word of God and to live for the purpose of serving Jesus. They are to educate their children that there is need of living in accordance with simple habits in their daily life, and to avoid expensive dress, expensive diet, expensive houses, and expensive furniture. The terms upon which eternal life will be ours are set forth in these words, "Thou shalt love the Lord thy God with all thy heart; ... and thy neighbor as thyself." (CS 295.4)

Parents have not taught their children the precepts of the law as God has commanded them. They have educated them in selfish habits. They have taught them to regard their birthdays and holidays as occasions when they expect to receive gifts, and to follow the habits and customs of the world. These occasions, which should serve to increase the knowledge of God and to awaken thankfulness of heart for His mercy and love in preserving their lives for another year, are turned into occasions for self-pleasing, for the gratification and glorification of the children. They have been kept by the power of God through every moment of their life, and yet parents do not teach their children to think of this, and to express thanksgiving for His mercy toward them. (**CS 296.1**)

If children and youth had been properly instructed in this age of the world, what honor, what praise and thanksgiving, would flow from their lips to God! What a revenue of small gifts would be brought from the hands of the little ones to be put into His treasury as thank offerings! God would be remembered instead of forgotten. (**CS 296.2**)

Not only on birthdays should parents and children remember the mercies of the Lord in a special way, but Christmas and New Year's should also be seasons when every household should remember their Creator and Redeemer. Instead of bestowing gifts and offerings in such abundance on human objects, reverence, honor, and gratitude should be rendered to God, and gifts and offerings should be caused to flow in the divine channel. Would not the Lord be pleased with such a remembrance of Him? O how God has been forgotten on these occasions! ... (**CS 296.3**)

When you have a holiday, make it a pleasant and happy day for your children, and make it also a pleasant day for the poor and the afflicted. Do not let the day pass without bringing thanksgiving and thank offerings to Jesus. Let parents and children now make earnest effort to redeem the time, and to remedy their past neglect. Let them follow a different course of action from that which the world follows. (**CS 297.1**)

There are many things which can be devised with taste and cost far less than the unnecessary presents that are so frequently bestowed upon our children and relatives, and thus courtesy can be shown, and happiness brought into the home. You can teach your children a lesson while you explain to them the reason why you have made a change in the value of their presents, telling them that you are convinced that you have hitherto considered their pleasure more than the glory of God. Tell them that you have thought more of your own pleasure and of their gratification and of keeping in harmony with the customs and traditions of the world, in making presents to those who did not need them, than you have of advancing the cause of God. (**CS 297.2**)

Like the wise men of old, you may offer to God your best gifts, and show by your offerings to Him that you appreciate His Gift to a sinful world. Set your children's thoughts running in a new, unselfish channel, by inciting them to present offerings to God for the gift of His only-begotten Son.– *The Review and Herald, November 13, 1894.* (**CS 297.3**)

Chapter 58
A Plea for Economy

There should be no extravagance in building fine homes, in buying costly furniture, in indulging in worldly dress, or in providing luxurious food; but in everything let us think of the souls for whom Christ has died. Let selfishness and pride die. Let none continue to expend means to multiply pictures to be sent to their friends. Let us save every dollar that can be saved, that the matchless charms of Christ may be presented before the souls of the perishing. (CS 298.1)

Satan will suggest many ways in which you may expend money. But if it is spent for self-gratification,–for unnecessary things, no matter how trifling their cost,–it is not spent for the glory of God. Let us look well to this matter, and see if we are denying ourselves as we should. Are we making sacrifices, that we may send the light of truth to the lost? ... (CS 298.2)

There should be but one interest in the church; one desire should control all, and that is the desire to conform to the image of Christ. Each one should strive to do for Jesus all that it is possible for him to do, by personal effort, by gifts, by sacrifices. There should be meat in the house of the Lord, and that means a full treasury, that responses may be made to Macedonian cries coming from every land. How pitiful it is that we are obliged to say to these who cry for help, "We cannot send you men or money. We have an empty treasury." (CS 298.3)

Let all the pennies, dimes, and dollars that are lost to the cause through selfish love of pleasure, through desire to meet the world's standard, through love of ease, be turned into the channel that flows to God's treasury. It is the rills flowing into one that finally make the river. Let us be conscientious Christians, be laborers together with God.... (CS 298.4)

New fields of work must be opened, souls are to be added to the faith, new names will appear on the church records,–names that will appear in the immortal records in heaven. O that we might realize what might be done with the money expended for the gratification of self!– *The Review and Herald, January 27, 1891.* (CS 299.1)

A Partner in God's Firm

The cause of God is ever demanding. Industry is therefore required on the part of all, high and low, rich and poor, in order that due returns may be made to God, that there may be "meat" in His house, and that the servants whom He has called to do the work of communicating the truth to a perishing world may be supported. (CS 299.2)

Not only does God require the tithe, but He requires that all we have be used to His glory. There must be no spendthrift habits; it is God's property that we are handling. Not one dollar or one shilling is our own. The squandering of money in luxuries deprives the poor of the means necessary to supply them with food and clothing. That which is spent for the gratification of pride in dress, in buildings, in furniture, and in decorations, would relieve the distress of many wretched, suffering families. God's stewards are to minister to the needy. This is the fruit of pure and undefiled religion. The Lord condemns men for their selfish indulgence while their fellow beings are suffering for the want of food and clothing.... (CS 299.3)

The Lord calls upon every one of His children to let heaven's light–the light of His own unselfish love– shine out amid the darkness of this degenerate age. If He sees you acknowledge Him as the possessor of yourself and all your possessions, if He sees you use your entrusted means as a faithful steward, He will register your name in the books of heaven as a laborer together with Him, a partner in His great firm, to work in behalf of your fellow men. And joy will be yours in the final day, as it is seen that the means wisely used in helping others has caused through you thanksgiving to God.– *The Review and Herald, December 8, 1896.* (CS 299.4)

The Care of the Mites

I wish I could impress on every mind the grievous sinfulness of wasting the Lord's money on fancied wants. The expenditure of sums that look small may start a train of circumstances that will reach into eternity. When the judgment shall sit, and the books are opened, the losing side will be presented to your view–the good that you might have done with the accumulated mites and the larger sums that were used for wholly selfish purposes.... (CS 300.1)

Jesus does not require of man any real sacrifice; for whatever we are asked to surrender is only that which we are better off without. We are only letting go the lesser, the more worthless, for the greater, the more valuable. Every earthly, temporal consideration must be subordinate to the higher.– *The Review and Herald, August 11, 1891.* (CS 300.2)

Then the Message Will Go With Power

God's people should practice strict economy in their outlay of means, that they may have something to bring to Him, saying, "Of Thine own have we given Thee." Thus they are to offer God thanksgiving for the blessings received from Him. Thus, too, they are to lay up for themselves treasure beside the throne of God. (CS 300.3)

Worldlings spend upon dress large sums of money that ought to be used to feed and clothe those suffering from hunger and cold. Many for whom Christ gave His life have barely sufficient of the cheapest, most common clothing, while others spend thousands of dollars in the efforts to satisfy the never-ending demands of fashion. (CS 301.1)

The Lord has charged His people to come out from the world, and be separate. Gay or expensive clothing is not becoming to those who believe that we are living in the last days of probation. "I will therefore," the apostle Paul writes, "that men pray everywhere, lifting up holy hands, without wrath and doubting. In like manner also, that women adorn themselves in modest apparel, with shamefacedness and sobriety; not with broided hair, or gold, or pearls, or costly array; but (which becometh women professing godliness) with good works." (CS 301.2)

Even among those who profess to be children of God, there are those who spend more than is necessary upon dress. We should dress neatly and tastefully, but, my sisters, when you are buying and making your own and your children's clothing, think of the work in the Lord's vineyard that is still waiting to be done. It is right to buy good material, and have it carefully made. This is economy. But rich trimmings are not needed, and to indulge in them is to spend for self-gratification money that should be put into God's cause. (CS 301.3)

It is not your dress that makes you of value in the Lord's sight. It is the inward adorning, the graces of the Spirit, the kind word, the thoughtful consideration for others, that God values. Do without the unnecessary trimmings, and lay aside for the advancement of the cause of God the means thus saved. Learn the lesson of self-denial, and teach it to your children. All that can be saved by self-denial is needed now in the work to be done. The suffering must be relieved, the naked clothed, the hungry fed; the truth for this time must be told to those who know it not. By denying ourselves of that which is not necessary, we may have a part in the great work of God. (CS 301.4)

We are Christ's witnesses, and we are not to allow worldly interests so to absorb our time and attention that we pay no heed to the things that God has said must come first. There are higher interests at stake. "Seek ye first the kingdom of God, and His righteousness." Christ gave His all to the work that He came to do, and His word to us is, "If any man will come after Me, let him deny himself, and take up his cross, and follow Me." "So shall ye be My disciples." (CS 302.1)

Willingly and cheerfully Christ gave Himself to the carrying out of the will of God. He became obedient unto death, even the death of the cross. Shall we feel it a hardship to deny ourselves? Shall we draw back from being partakers of His sufferings? His death ought to stir every fiber of the being, making us willing to consecrate to His work all that we have and are. As we think of what He has done for us, our hearts should be filled with love. (CS 302.2)

When those who know the truth practice the self-denial enjoined in God's word, the message will go with power. The Lord will hear our prayers for the conversion of souls. God's people will let their light shine forth, and unbelievers, seeing their good works, will glorify our heavenly Father. Let us relate ourselves to God in self-sacrificing obedience.– *The Review and Herald, December 1, 1910.* (CS 302.3)

Progress Despite Poverty

There were but very few of us to carry forward the work at first, and it was very necessary for us to be of one mind in order to have the work advance with order and uniformity. When we saw the importance of being in the unity of faith, our prayers were answered, and Christ's prayer was answered that we should be one as He was one with the Father. We were as destitute of means as you are here in these kingdoms, [Written in Europe.] and we frequently went hungry, and suffered from cold for want of proper clothing. But we saw that the truth must advance, and we must have means to carry it forward. We then sought the Lord most earnestly that he would open ways that we might reach the people in the different cities and towns, and my husband and myself would have to work with our hands to get means to carry us from place to place, to open the treasures of faith to others. We could see that the Lord of heaven was preparing the way before us in the work. (CS 303.1)

My husband has worked at handling stone till the skin was worn from his fingers, and the blood started from the wounds, that he might get means to carry him from place to place to speak to the people the words of truth. This is the way the work went in the beginning, and our petitions must now ascend to the God of heaven as they did then, that He will open the way, and the truth find access to hearts. The gold and the silver are the Lord's. The cattle upon the thousand hills are His; but he wants you to move

forward in faith just as far and as fast as you can. The Lord's blessing will rest upon those who do to the very best of their ability.... (CS 303.2)

When the Scriptures were opened in the Piedmont Valleys, the truth was carried forward by those who were very poor in this world's goods. Those who had Bible truth were not allowed to bring it before the people; they could not get Bibles into families; so they went as merchants selling goods, and carried parts of the Bible with them, and when they saw that it would do, they would read from the Scriptures; and those who were hungering for truth could in this way obtain light. With bare and bleeding feet, these men traveled over the hard rocks of the mountains in order that they might reach souls, and open to them the words of life. I wish the very same spirit that animated them was in the heart of everyone who professes the truth at the present time. (CS 303.3)

We can every one of us do something, if we will only take the position that God would have us. Every move that you make to enlighten others, brings you nearer in harmony with the God of heaven. If you sit down and look at yourself and say, "I can barely support my family," you will never do anything; but if you say, "I will do something for the truth, I will see it advance, I will do what I can," God will open ways so that you can do something. You should invest in the cause of truth so that you will feel that you are a part of it. (CS 304.1)

God does not require of the man to whom He has given one talent, the interest of ten. Remember that it was the man who had one talent that wrapped it in a napkin and hid it in the earth. You should use the talent, influence, and means which God has given you that you may act a part in this work.– *The Review and Herald, July 8, 1890.* (CS 304.2)

For Further Study

Cherishing the Spirit of Sacrifice, *Testimonies for the Church 9:130, 131*

A Plea for Money Spent Needlessly, *Testimonies for the Church 9:54, 55*

Jewels and Expensive Dress, *The Ministry of Healing, 287, 288*

Section 13

The Sacredness of Vows and Pledges

Chapter 59
Promises to God Binding

God works through human instrumentalities; and whoever shall awaken the consciences of men, provoking them to good works and a real interest in the advancement of the cause of truth, does not do it of himself, but by the Spirit of God which worketh in him. Pledges made under these circumstances are of a sacred character, being the fruit of the work of the Spirit of God. When these pledges are canceled, Heaven accepts the offering, and these liberal workers are credited for so much treasure invested in the bank of heaven. Such are laying up a good foundation against the time to come, that they may lay hold on eternal life.... (CS 309.1)

A Lack of Integrity

One of the greatest sins in the Christian world of today, is dissembling and covetousness in dealing with God. There is an increasing carelessness on the part of many in regard to meeting their pledges to the various institutions and religious enterprises. Many look upon the act of pledging as though it imposed no obligation to pay. If they think that their money will bring them considerable profit by being invested in bank stock or in merchandise, or if there are individuals connected with the institution which they have pledged to help to whom they take exceptions, they feel perfectly free to use their means as they please. This lack of integrity is prevailing to quite an extent among those who profess to be keeping the commandments of God, and looking for the soon appearing of their Lord and Saviour.... (CS 309.2)

Responsibility of a Church

A church is responsible for the pledges of its individual members. If they see that there is a brother who is neglecting to fulfill his vows, they should labor with him kindly but plainly. If he is not in circumstances which render it possible for him to pay his vow, and he is a worthy member and has a willing heart, then let the church compassionately help him. Thus they can bridge over the difficulty, and receive a blessing themselves. (CS 310.1)

God would have the members of His church consider their obligations to Him as binding as their indebtedness to the merchant or the market. Let everyone review his past life and see if any unpaid, unredeemed pledges have been neglected, and then make extra exertions to pay the "uttermost farthing;" for we must all meet and abide the final issue of a tribunal where nothing will stand the test but integrity and veracity.– *Testimonies for the Church 4:473-476.* (CS 310.2)

A Reason for Adversity

Some of you have been stumbling over your pledges. The Spirit of the Lord came into the ----- meeting in answer to prayer, and while your hearts were softened under its influence, you pledged. While the streams of salvation were pouring upon your hearts, you felt that you must follow the example of Him who went about doing good, and who cheerfully gave His life to ransom man from sin and degradation. Under the heavenly, inspiring influence, you saw that selfishness and worldliness were not consistent with Christian character, and that you could not live for yourselves and be Christlike. But when the influence of His abundant love and mercy was not felt in so marked a manner in your hearts, you withdrew your offerings, and God withdrew His blessing from you. (CS 310.3)

Adversity came upon some. There was a failure in their crops, so that they could not redeem their pledges; and some were even brought into straitened circumstances. Then, of course, they could not be expected to pay. But had they not murmured and withdrawn their hearts from their pledges, God would have worked for them, and would have opened ways whereby everyone could have paid what he had promised. They did not wait in faith, trusting God to open the way so that they could redeem their pledges. (**CS 311.1**)

Some had means at their command; and had they possessed the same willing mind as when they pledged, and had they heartily rendered to God in tithes and offerings that which He had lent them for this purpose, they would have been greatly blessed. But Satan came in with his temptations, and led some to question the motives and the spirit which actuated the servant of God in presenting the call for means. Some felt that they had been deceived and defrauded. In spirit they repudiated their vows, and whatever they did afterward was with reluctance, and therefore they received no blessing.– *Testimonies for the Church 5:281, 282.* (**CS 311.2**)

Chapter 60
The Sin of Ananias

The hearts of Ananias and his wife were moved by the Holy Spirit to devote their possessions to God as their brethren had done. But after they had made the pledge, they drew back, and determined not to fulfill it. While professing to give all, they kept back part of the price. They had practiced fraud toward God, they had lied to the Holy Spirit, and their sin was visited with swift and terrible judgment. They lost not only the present life, but eternal life. (CS 312.1)

The Lord saw that this signal manifestation of His justice was needed to guard others against incurring the same guilt. It testified that men cannot deceive God, that He detects the hidden sin of the heart, and that He will not be mocked. It was designed as a warning to the young church, to lead them to examine their motives, to beware of indulging selfishness and vainglory, to beware of robbing God. (CS 312.2)

In the case of Ananias, the sin of fraud against God was speedily detected and punished. This example of God's judgment was designed to be a danger signal to all future generations. The same sin was often repeated in the afterhistory of the church, and it is committed by many in our time; but though not attended with the visible manifestation of God's displeasure, it is no less heinous in His sight now than in the apostles' time. The warning has been given, God has clearly manifested His abhorrence of this sin, and all who pursue a similar course of action may be sure that they are destroying their own souls.... (CS 312.3)

It is only when Christian motives are fully acknowledged, and the conscience is awake to duty, when divine light makes impressions upon the heart and character, that selfishness is overcome, and the mind of Christ is exemplified. The Holy Spirit, working upon human hearts and characters, will expel all tendency to covetousness, to deceptive dealing.... (CS 313.1)

On some occasions the Lord has moved decidedly upon worldly, selfish men. Their minds were illuminated by the Holy Spirit, their hearts felt its softening, subduing influence. Under a sense of the abundant mercy and grace of God, they felt it their duty to promote His cause, to build up His kingdom.... They felt a desire to have a share in the kingdom of God, and they pledged to give of their means to some of the various enterprises of the Lord's cause. That pledge was not made to man, but to God in the presence of His angels, who were moving upon the hearts of these selfish, money-loving men. (CS 313.2)

In making the pledge, they were greatly blessed; but how quickly the feelings change when they stand on common ground. As the immediate impression of the Holy Spirit becomes dim, as the mind and heart become absorbed again in worldly business, it is most difficult for them to maintain the consecration of themselves and their property to the Lord. Satan assails them with his temptation, "You were foolish to pledge that money, you need it to invest in your business, and you will meet with loss if you pay the pledge." (CS 313.3)

Now they draw back, they murmur, they complain of the Lord's message and His messengers. They say things that are not true, claiming that they pledged under excitement, that they did not fully understand the matter, the case was overstated, their feelings were moved, and this led them to make the pledge. They talked as though the precious blessing they received was the result of a deception practiced upon them by the minister to secure money. They change their minds, and feel under no obligation to pay their vows to God. There is most fearful robbery of God, and flimsy excuses are made for resisting and denying the Holy Spirit. Some plead inconvenience; they say they need their money–to do what? To bury in houses and lands, in some money-making scheme. Because the pledge was made for a religious object, they think it cannot be enforced by law, and the love of money is so strong upon them that they deceive their own souls, and presume to rob God. To many it might be said, "You treat no other friend so ill." (CS 313.4)

The number of those who commit the sin of Ananias and Sapphira is increasing. Men do not lie to man, but to God in their disregard of the pledges which His Spirit moved upon them to make. Because sentence against an evil work is not, as in the case of Ananias and Sapphira, executed speedily, the hearts of the sons of men are fully set in them to do evil, to strive against the Spirit of God. How will these men stand in the judgment? Dare you abide the final issue of this question? How will you stand in the scenes described in the Revelation? "I saw a great white throne, and Him that sat on it, from whose face the earth and the heaven fled away; and there was found no place for them. And I saw the dead, small and great, stand before God;... and they were judged every man according to their works."– *The Review and Herald, May 23, 1893.* (CS 314.1)

Chapter 61
A Contract With God

When a verbal or written pledge has been made in the presence of our brethren, to give a certain amount, they are the visible witnesses of a contract made between ourselves and God. The pledge is not made to man, but to God, and is as a written note given to a neighbor. No legal bond is more binding upon the Christian for the payment of money, than a pledge made to God. (CS 315.1)

Persons who thus pledge to their fellow men do not generally think of asking to be released from their pledges. A vow made to God, the giver of all favors, is of still greater importance; then why should we seek to be released from our vows to God? Will man consider his promise less binding because made to God? Because his vow will not be put to trial in courts of justice, is it less valid? Will a man who professes to be saved by the blood of the infinite sacrifice of Jesus Christ, "rob God"? Are not his vows and his actions weighed in the balances of justice in the heavenly courts? (CS 315.2)

Each of us has a case pending in the court of heaven. Shall our course of conduct balance the evidence against us? The case of Ananias and Sapphira was of the most aggravated character. In keeping back part of the price, they lied to the Holy Ghost. Guilt likewise rests upon every individual in proportion to like offenses. (CS 315.3)

When the hearts of men are softened by the presence of the Spirit of God, they are more susceptible to the impressions of the Holy Spirit, and resolves are made to deny self and to sacrifice for the cause of God. It is when divine light shines into the chambers of the mind with unusual clearness and power, that the feelings of the natural man are overcome, that selfishness loses its power upon the heart, and that desires are awakened to imitate the Pattern, Jesus Christ,

in practicing self-denial and benevolence. The disposition of the naturally selfish man then becomes kind and pitiful toward lost sinners, and he makes a solemn pledge to God, as did Abraham and Jacob. Heavenly angels are present on such occasions. The love of God and love for souls triumph over selfishness and love of the world. Especially is this the case when the speaker, in the Spirit and power of God, presents the plan of redemption, laid by the Majesty of heaven in the sacrifice of the cross. By the following scriptures we may see how God regards the subject of vows: (CS 315.4)

"And Moses spake unto the heads of the tribes concerning the children of Israel, saying, This is the thing which the Lord hath commanded. If a man vow a vow unto the Lord, or swear an oath to bind his soul with a bond, he shall not break his word; he shall do according to all that proceedeth out of his mouth." *Numbers 30:1, 2.* (CS 316.1)

"Suffer not thy mouth to cause thy flesh to sin; neither say thou before the angel, that it was an error; wherefore should God be angry at thy voice, and destroy the work of thine hands?" *Ecclesiastes 5:6.* (CS 316.2)

"I will go into Thy house with burnt offerings; I will pay Thee my vows, which my lips have uttered, and my mouth hath spoken, when I was in trouble." *Psalm 66:13, 14.* (CS 316.3)

It is a snare to the man who devoureth that which is holy, and after vows to make inquiry." *Proverbs 20:25.* "When thou shalt vow a vow unto the Lord thy God. thou shalt not slack to pay it; for the Lord thy God will surely require it of thee; and it would be sin in thee. But if thou shalt forbear to vow, it shall be no sin in thee. That which is gone out of thy lips thou shalt keep and perform; even a freewill offering, according as thou hast vowed unto the Lord thy God, which thou hast promised with thy mouth." *Deuteronomy 23:21-23.* (CS 316.4)

"Vow, and pay unto the Lord your God; let all that be round about Him bring presents unto Him that ought to be feared." *Psalm 76:11.* (CS 317.1)

"But ye have profaned it, in that ye say, The table of the Lord is polluted; and the fruit thereof, even his meat, is contemptible. Ye said also, Behold, what a weariness is it! and ye have snuffed at it, saith the Lord of hosts; and ye brought that which was torn, and the lame, and the sick; thus ye brought an offering: should I accept this of your hand? saith the Lord. But cursed be the deceiver, which hath in his flock a male, and voweth, and sacrificeth unto the Lord a corrupt thing; for I am a great King, saith the Lord of hosts, and My name is dreadful among the heathen." *Malachi 1:12-14.* (CS 317.2)

"When thou vowest a vow unto God, defer not to pay it; for He hath no pleasure in fools: pay that which thou hast vowed. Better is it that thou shouldst not vow, than that thou shouldst vow and not pay." *Ecclesiastes 5:4, 5. – Testimonies for the Church 4:470-472.* (CS 317.3)

Conditions for Receiving God's Promises

There have been special occasions at large gatherings, when appeals have been made to the professed followers of Christ, for the cause of God, and hearts have been stirred, and many have made pledges to sustain the work. But many of those who pledged have not dealt honorably with God. They have been negligent, and have failed to redeem their pledges to their Maker. But if man is so indifferent about his promises to God, can he expect that the Lord will fulfill a promise made on conditions that have never been kept? It is best to deal honestly with your fellow men and with God.– *The Review and Herald, December 17, 1889.* (CS 317.4)

Satan's Protest

Of the means entrusted to men, God claims a certain portion,–the tenth. He leaves all free to say whether or not they will give more than this. But when the heart is stirred by the influence of the Holy Spirit, and a vow is made to give a certain amount, the one who vows has no longer any right to the consecrated portion. Promises of this kind made to men would be looked upon as binding; are those not more binding that are made to God? Are promises tried in the court of conscience less binding than written agreements of men? (CS 318.1)

When divine light is shining into the heart with unusual clearness and power, habitual selfishness relaxes its grasp, and there is a disposition to give to the cause of God. But none need think that they will be allowed to fulfill the promises then made, without a protest on the part of Satan. He is not pleased to see the Redeemer's kingdom on earth built up. He suggests that the pledge made was too much, that it may cripple them in their efforts to acquire property or gratify the desires of their families.– *The Acts of the Apostles, 74, 75.* (CS 318.2)

Need for an Aroused Conscience

There must be an awakening among us as a people upon this matter. There are but few men who feel conscience stricken if they neglect their duty in beneficence. But few feel remorseful of soul because they are daily robbing God. (CS 318.3)

If a Christian deliberately or accidentally underpays his neighbor, or refuses to cancel an honest debt, his conscience, unless seared, will trouble him; he cannot rest although no one may know but himself. There are many neglected vows and unpaid pledges, and yet how few trouble their minds over the matter; how few feel the guilt of this violation of duty. (CS 318.4)

We must have new and deeper convictions on this subject. The conscience must be aroused, and the matter receive earnest attention: for an account must be rendered to God in the last day, and His claims must be settled.– *Testimonies for the Church 4:468* (CS 319.1)

For Further Study

Sacredness of Vows, *Testimonies for the Church 4:462-476*

Vowing and Not Paying, *Testimonies for the Church 5:281-285*

Section 14
Wills and Legacies

Chapter 62
Preparation for Death

There are aged ones among us who are nearing the close of their probation; but for the want of wide-awake men to secure to the cause of God the means in their possession, it passes into the hands of those who are serving Satan. This means was only lent them of God to be returned to Him; but in nine cases out of ten, these brethren, when passing from the stage of action, appropriate God's property in a way that cannot glorify Him, for not one dollar of it will ever flow into the Lord's treasury. In some cases these apparently good brethren have had unconsecrated advisers, who counseled from their own standpoint, and not according to the mind of God. (CS 323.1)

Property is often bequeathed to children and grandchildren only to their injury. They have no love for God or for the truth, and therefore this means, all of which is the Lord's, passes into Satan's ranks, to be controlled by him. Satan is much more vigilant, keen-sighted, and skillful in devising ways to secure means to himself than our brethren are to secure the Lord's own to His cause. (CS 323.2)

Some wills are made in so loose a manner that they will not stand the test of the law, and thus thousands of dollars have been lost to the cause. Our brethren should feel that a responsibility rests upon them, as faithful servants in the cause of God, to exercise their intellect in regard to this matter, and secure to the Lord His own. (CS 323.3)

Many manifest a needless delicacy on this point. They feel that they are stepping upon forbidden ground when they introduce the subject of property to the aged or to invalids in order to learn what disposition they design to make of it. But this duty is just as sacred as the duty to preach the word to save souls. Here is a man with God's money or property in his hands.

He is about to change his stewardship. Will he place the means which God has lent him to be used in His cause, in the hands of wicked men, just because they are his relatives? Should not Christian men feel interested and anxious for that man's future good as well as for the interest of God's cause, that he shall make a right disposition of his Lord's money, the talents lent him for wise improvement? Will his brethren stand by, and see him losing his hold on this life, and at the same time robbing the treasury of God? This would be a fearful loss to himself and to the cause; for, by placing his talent of means in the hands of those who have no regard for the truth of God, he would, to all intents and purposes, be wrapping it in a napkin and hiding it in the earth. (CS 323.4)

A Better Way

The Lord would have His followers dispense their means while they can do it themselves. Some may inquire, "Must we actually dispossess ourselves of everything which we call our own?" We may not be required to do this now; but we must be willing to do so for Christ's sake. We must acknowledge that our possessions are absolutely His, by using of them freely whenever means is needed to advance His cause. Some close their ears to the calls made for money to be used in sending missionaries to foreign countries, and in publishing the truth and scattering it like autumn leaves all over the world. (CS 324.1)

Such excuse their covetousness by informing you that they have made arrangements to be charitable at death. They have considered the cause of God in their wills. Therefore they live a life of avarice, robbing God in tithes and in offerings, and in their wills return to God but a small portion of that which

He has lent them, while a very large proportion is appropriated to relatives who have no interest in the truth. This is the worst kind of robbery. They rob God of His just dues, not only all through life, but also at death. (**CS 324.2**)

A Fearful Risk

It is utter folly to defer to make a preparation for the future life until nearly the last hour of the present life. It is also a great mistake to defer to answer the claims of God for liberality to His cause until the time comes when you are to shift your stewardship upon others. Those to whom you entrust your talents of means may not do as well with them as you have done. How dare rich men run so great risks? Those who wait till death before they make a disposition of their property, surrender it to death rather than to God. In so doing, many are acting directly contrary to the plan of God plainly stated in His word. If they would do good, they must seize the present golden moments, and labor with all their might, as if fearful that they may lose the favorable opportunity. (**CS 325.1**)

Those who neglect known duty by not answering to God's claims upon them in this life, and who soothe their consciences by calculating on making their bequests at death, will receive no words of commendation from the Master, nor will they receive a reward. They practiced no self-denial, but selfishly retained their means as long as they could, yielding it up only when death claimed them. (**CS 325.2**)

That which many propose to defer until they are about to die, if they were Christians indeed they would do while they have a strong hold on life. They would devote themselves and their property to God, and, while acting as His stewards, they would have the satisfaction of doing their duty. By becoming their own executors, they could meet the claims of God themselves, instead of shifting the responsibility upon others. (**CS 325.3**)

We should regard ourselves as stewards of the Lord's property, and God as the supreme proprietor, to whom we are to render His own when He shall require it. When He shall come to receive His own with usury, the covetous will see that instead of multiplying the talents entrusted

to them, they have brought upon themselves the doom pronounced upon the unprofitable servant. (**CS 326.1**)

Living Benevolence or Dying Legacies

The Lord designs that the death of His servants shall be regarded as a loss, because of the influence for good which they exerted and the many willing offerings which they bestowed to replenish the treasury of God. Dying legacies are a miserable substitute for living benevolence. The servants of God should be making their wills every day, in good works and liberal offerings to God. They should not allow the amount given to God to be disproportionately small when compared with that appropriated to their own use. In making their wills daily, they will remember those objects and friends that hold the largest place in their affections. (**CS 326.2**)

Their best friend is Jesus. He did not withhold His own life from them, but for their sakes became poor, that through His poverty they might be made rich. He deserves the whole heart, the property, all that they have and are. But many professed Christians put off the claims of Jesus in life, and insult Him by giving Him a mere pittance at death. (**CS 326.3**)

Let all of this class remember that this robbery of God is not an impulsive action, but a well-considered plan which they preface by saying, "Being in sound mind." After having defrauded the cause of God through life, they perpetuate the fraud after death. And this is with the full consent of all the powers of the mind. Such a will many are content to cherish for a dying pillow. Their will is a part of their preparation for death, and is prepared so that their possessions shall not disturb their dying hours. Can these dwell with pleasure upon the requirement that will be made of them to give an account of their stewardship? (**CS 327.1**)

We must all be rich in good works in this life, if we would secure the future, immortal life. When the judgment shall sit, and the books shall be opened, every man will be rewarded according to his works. Many names are enrolled on the church book that have robbery recorded against them in the ledger of heaven. And unless these repent, and work for the Master with disinterested benevolence, they will certainly share in the doom of the unfaithful steward. (CS 327.2)

Losses Due to Lack of Will

It often happens that an active businessman is cut down without a moment's warning, and on examination his business is found to be in a most perplexing condition. In the effort to settle his estate, the lawyers' fees eat up a large share, if not all, of the property, while his wife and children and the cause of Christ are robbed. Those who are faithful stewards of the Lord's means will know just how their business stands, and, like wise men, they will be prepared for any emergency. Should their probation close suddenly, they would not leave such great perplexity upon those who are called to settle their estate. (CS 327.3)

Many are not exercised upon the subject of making their wills while they are in apparent health. But this precaution should be taken by our brethren. They should know their financial standing, and should not allow their business to become entangled. They should arrange their property in such a manner that they may leave it at any time. (CS 328.1)

Wills should be made in a manner to stand the test of law. After they are drawn, they may remain for years, and do no harm, if donations continue to be made from time to time as the cause has need. Death will not come one day sooner, brethren, because you have made your will. In disposing of your property by will to your relatives, be sure that you do not forget God's cause. You are His agents, holding His property; and His claims should have your first consideration. Your wife and children, of course, should not be left destitute; provision should be made for them if they are needy. But do not, simply because it is customary, bring into your will a long line of relatives who are not needy. (CS 328.2)

A Call for Reform

Let it ever be kept in mind that the present selfish system of disposing of property is not God's plan, but man's device. Christians should be reformers, and break up this present system, giving an entirely new aspect to the formation of wills. Let the idea be ever present that it is the Lord's property which you are handling. The will of God in this matter is law. (CS 328.3)

If man had made you the executor of his property, would you not closely study the will of the testator, that the smallest amount might not be misapplied? Your heavenly Friend has entrusted you with property, and given you His will as to how it should be used. If this will is studied with an unselfish heart, that which belongs to God will not be misapplied. The Lord's cause has been shamefully neglected, when He has provided men with sufficient means to meet every emergency, if they only had grateful, obedient hearts. (CS 328.4)

Those who make their wills should not feel that when this is done they have no further duty, but they should be constantly at work using the talents entrusted to them, for the upbuilding of the Lord's cause. God has devised plans that all may work intelligently in the distribution of their means. He does not propose to sustain His work by miracles. He has a few faithful stewards, who are economizing and using their means to advance His cause. Instead of self-denial and benevolence being an exception, they should be the rule. The growing necessities of the cause of God require means. Calls are constantly coming in from men in our own and foreign countries for messengers to come to them with light and truth. This will necessitate more laborers and more means to support them.– *Testimonies for the Church 4:478-483.* (CS 329.1)

How to Make Your Property Secure

Would you make your property secure? Place it in the hand that bears the nailprint of the crucifixion. Retain it in your possession, and it will be to your eternal loss. Give it to God, and from that moment it bears His inscription. It is sealed with His immutability. Would you enjoy your substance? Then use it for the blessing of the suffering.– *Testimonies for the Church 9:51.* (CS 329.2)

Chapter 63
Stewardship a Personal Responsibility

Parents should exercise the right that God has given them. He entrusted to them the talents He would have them use to His glory. The children were not to become responsible for the talents of the father. While they have sound minds and good judgment, parents should, with prayerful consideration, and with the help of proper counselors who have experience in the truth and a knowledge of the divine will, make disposition of their property. (CS 330.1)

If they have children who are afflicted or are struggling in poverty, and who will make a judicious use of means, they should be considered. But if they have unbelieving children who have abundance of this world, and who are serving the world, they commit a sin against the Master who has made them His stewards, by placing means in their hands merely because they are their children. God's claims are not to be lightly regarded. (CS 330.2)

And it should be distinctly understood that because parents have made their will, this will not prevent them from giving means to the cause of God while they live. This they should do. They should have the satisfaction here, and the reward hereafter, of disposing of their surplus means while they live. They should do their part to advance the cause of God. They should use the means lent them by the Master to carry on the work which needs to be done in His vineyard. (CS 330.3)

The love of money lies at the root of nearly all the crimes committed in the world. Fathers who selfishly retain their means to enrich their children, and who do not see the wants of the cause of God and relieve them, make a terrible mistake. The children whom they think to bless with their means are cursed with it. (CS 330.4)

Inherited Riches Often a Snare

Money left to children frequently becomes a root of bitterness. They often quarrel over the property left them, and in case of a will, are seldom all satisfied with the disposition made by the father. And instead of the means left exciting gratitude and reverence for his memory, it creates dissatisfaction, murmuring, envy, and disrespect. Brothers and sisters who were at peace with one another are sometimes made at variance, and family dissensions are often the result of inherited means. Riches are desirable only as a means of supplying present wants, and of doing good to others. But inherited riches oftener become a snare to the possessor than a blessing. Parents should not seek to have their children encounter the temptations to which they expose them in leaving them means which they themselves have made no effort to earn. (CS 331.1)

Transferring Property to Children

I was shown that some children professing to believe the truth, would, in an indirect manner, influence the father to keep his means for his children, instead of appropriating it to the cause of God while he lives. Those who have influenced their father to shift his stewardship upon them, little know what they are doing. They are gathering upon themselves double responsibility, that of balancing the father's mind so that he did not fulfill the purpose of God in the disposition of the means lent him of God to be used to His glory, and the additional responsibility of becoming stewards of means that should have been put out to the exchangers by the father, that the Master could have received His own with usury. (CS 331.2)

Many parents make a great mistake in

placing their property out of their hands into the hands of their children while they are themselves responsible for the use or abuse of the talents lent them of God. Neither parents nor children are made happier by this transfer of property. And the parents, if they live a few years even, generally regret this action on their part. Parental love in their children is not increased by this course. The children do not feel increased gratitude and obligation to their parents for their liberality. A curse seems to lay at the root of the matter, which only crops out in selfishness on the part of the children, and unhappiness and miserable feelings of cramped dependence on the part of the parents. **(CS 332.1)**

If parents, while they live, would assist their children to help themselves, it would be better than to leave them a large amount at death.

Children who are left to rely principally upon their own exertions, make better men and women, and are better fitted for practical life, than those children who have depended upon their father's estate. The children left to depend upon their own resources generally prize their abilities, improve their privileges, and cultivate and direct their faculties to accomplish a purpose in life. They frequently develop characters of industry, frugality, and moral worth, which lie at the foundation of success in the Christian life. Those children for whom parents do the most, frequently feel under the least obligation toward them.– *Testimonies for the Church 3:121-123.* **(CS 332.2)**

Chapter 64
Shifting Responsibility to Others

Those Sabbathkeeping brethren who shift the responsibility of their stewardship into the hands of their wives, while they themselves are capable of managing the same, are unwise, and in the transfer displease God. The stewardship of the husband cannot be transferred to the wife. Yet this is sometimes attempted, to the great injury of both. (CS 333.1)

A believing husband has sometimes transferred his property to his unbelieving companion, hoping thereby to gratify her, disarm her opposition, and finally induce her to believe the truth. But this is no more nor less than an attempt to purchase peace, or to hire the wife to believe the truth. The means which God has lent to advance His cause the husband transfers to one who has no sympathy for the truth; what account will such a steward render when the great Master requires His own with usury? (CS 333.2)

Believing parents have frequently transferred their property to their unbelieving children, thus putting it out of their power to render to God the things that are His. By so doing, they lay off that responsibility which God has laid upon them, and place in the enemy's ranks means which God has entrusted to them to be returned to Him by being invested in His cause when He shall require it of them. (CS 333.3)

It is not God's order that parents who are capable of managing their own business, should give up the control of their property, even to children who are of the same faith. These seldom possess as much devotion to the cause as they should, and they have not been schooled in adversity and affliction, so as to place a high estimate upon the eternal treasure, and less upon the earthly. The means placed in the hands of such is the greatest evil. It is a temptation to them to place their affections upon the earthly, and trust to property, and feel that they need but little besides. When means which they have not acquired by their own exertion, comes into their possession, they seldom use it wisely. (CS 333.4)

The husband who transfers his property to his wife, opens for her a wide door of temptation, whether she is a believer or an unbeliever. If she is a believer, and naturally penurious, inclined to selfishness and acquisitiveness, the battle will be much harder for her with her husband's stewardship and her own to manage. In order to be saved, she must overcome all those peculiar, evil traits, and imitate the character of her divine Lord, seeking opportunity to do others good, loving others as Christ has loved us. She should cultivate the precious gift of love possessed so largely by our Saviour. His life was characterized by noble, disinterested benevolence. His whole life was not marred by one selfish act. (CS 334.1)

Whatever the motives of the husband, he has placed a terrible stumbling block in his wife's way, to hinder her in the work of overcoming. And if the transfer be made to the children, the same evil results may follow. God reads his motives. If he is selfish, and has made the transfer to conceal his covetousness, and excuse himself from doing anything to advance the cause, the curse of Heaven will surely follow. (CS 334.2)

God reads the purposes and intents of the hearts, and tries the motives of the children of men. His signal, visible displeasure may not be manifested as in the case of Ananias and Sapphira, yet in the end the punishment will in no case be lighter than that which was inflicted upon them. In trying to deceive men, they were lying to God. "The soul that sinneth, it shall die." ... (CS 334.3)

Those who flatter themselves that they can

shift their responsibility upon wife or children, are deceived by the enemy. A transfer of property will not lessen their responsibility. They are accountable for the means which Heaven has entrusted to their care, and in no way can they excuse themselves from this responsibility, until they are released by rendering back to God that which He has committed to them.– *Testimonies for the Church 1:528-530.* **(CS 335.1)**

For Further Study

Wills a Subject of Dissension Among Children, *Testimonies for the Church 4:484*

Seeking Legal Advice in Making of Wills, That They May Stand Test, *Testimonies for the Church 3:117*

Shifting Stewardship Upon Children by Legacies, *Testimonies for the Church 3:118-120*

A Division of Property Among Children Did Not Increase Their Affection, *Testimonies for the Church 3:129*

Section 15

The Reward of Faithful Stewardship

Chapter 65

The Place of Reward as a Motive in Service

Repeatedly the Saviour says, "Many that are first shall be last; and the last shall be first." Jesus would have those who are engaged in His service, not eager for rewards, nor feel that they must receive compensation for all that they do. The Lord would have our minds run in a different channel; for He sees not as man sees. He does not judge by appearances, but estimates a man by the sincerity of his heart. (CS 339.1)

Those who have brought into their service the spirit of true sacrifice, of self-abasement, are the ones who will stand first at last. The laborers who were first hired, represented those who have an envious, self-righteous spirit, and claim that, for their services, preference should be given to them rather than to others. The householder said to the one who questioned his right to give more to others than to him, "Friend, I do thee no wrong: didst not thou agree with me for a penny?" I have kept my part of the agreement. (CS 339.2)

In a subordinate sense we should all have respect unto the recompense of the reward. But while we appreciate the promise of blessing, we should have perfect confidence in Jesus Christ, believing that He will do right, and give us reward according as our works have been. The gift of God is eternal life, but Jesus would have us not so anxious concerning rewards, as that we may do the will of God because it is right to do it, irrespective of all gain. (CS 339.3)

Paul kept in view the crown of life to be given him, and not only to be given to him, but to all who love His appearing. It was the victory gained through faith in Jesus Christ that made the crown so desirable. He ever exalted Jesus. All boasting of talent, of victory in ourselves, is out of place. "Let not the wise man glory in his wisdom, neither let the mighty man glory in his might, let not the rich man glory in his riches:

but let him that glorieth glory in this, that he understandeth and knoweth Me, that I am the Lord which exercise loving-kindness, judgment, and righteousness, in the earth: for in these things I delight, saith the Lord." (CS 339.4)

Those who will receive the most abundant reward will be those who have mingled with their activity and zeal, gracious, tender pity for the poor, the orphan, the oppressed, and the afflicted. But those who pass by on the other side, who are too busy to give attention to the purchase of the blood of Christ, who are full of doing the great things, will find themselves least and last. (CS 340.1)

Men act out the true character of the heart. There are about us those who have a meek and lowly spirit, the spirit of Christ, who do many little things to help those around them, and who think nothing of it; they will be astonished at last to find that Christ has noticed the kind word spoken to the disheartened, and taken account of the smallest gift given for the relief of the poor, that cost the giver some self-denial. The Lord measures the spirit, and rewards accordingly, and the pure, humble, childlike spirit of love makes the offering precious in His sight.– *The Review and Herald, July 3, 1894.* (CS 340.2)

As a Gift, Not as a Right

Peter said, "Behold, we have forsaken all, and followed Thee; what shall we have therefore? This question on the part of Peter showed that he thought that a certain amount of work on the part of the apostles would be deserving of a certain amount of reward. Among the disciples there was a spirit of complacency, of self-exaltation, and they made comparisons among themselves. If any one of them signally failed, others felt themselves superior. Jesus saw a spirit coming in that must be checked. He could read the hearts of men, and He saw their tendencies to selfishness in the question, "What shall we have?" He must correct this evil before it assumed gigantic proportions. (CS 340.3)

The disciples were in danger of losing sight of the true principles of the gospel. By the use of this parable [of the laborers who were called] He teaches them that the reward is not of works, lest any man should boast, but it is all of grace. The laborer called into the vineyard at the beginning of the day had his reward in the grace that was given him. But the one to whom the last call came, had the same grace as had the first. The work was all of grace, and no one was to glory over another. There was to be no grudging one against another. No one was privileged above another, nor could any one claim the reward as his right. Peter expressed the feelings of a hireling.– *The Review and Herald, July 10, 1894.* (CS 341.1)

Chapter 66
Treasure in Heaven

Christ entreats, "Lay up for yourselves treasures in heaven." This work of transferring your possessions to the world above, is worthy of all your best energies. It is of the highest importance, and involves your eternal interests. That which you bestow in the cause of God is not lost. All that is given for the salvation of souls and the glory of God, is invested in the most successful enterprise in this life and in the life to come. Your talents of gold and silver, if given to the exchangers, are gaining continually in value, which will be registered to your account in the kingdom of heaven. You are to be the recipients of the eternal wealth that has increased in the hands of the exchangers. In giving to the work of God, you are laying up for yourselves treasures in heaven. All that you lay up above is secure from disaster and loss, and is increasing to an eternal, an enduring substance. (CS 342.1)

Profit for Time and Eternity

It should be your determined purpose to bring every power of your being into the service of Christ. Why, His service is profitable for the life that now is, and for that which is to come.... (CS 342.2)

"The light of the body is the eye: if therefore thine eye be single, thy whole body shall be full of light." If the eye is single, if it is directed heavenward, the light of heaven will fill the soul, and earthly things will appear insignificant and uninviting. The purpose of the heart will be changed, and the admonition of Jesus will be heeded. You will lay up your treasure in heaven. Your thoughts will be fixed upon the great rewards of eternity. All your plans will be made in reference to the future, immortal life. You will be drawn toward your treasure. You will not study your worldly interest; but in all your pursuits the silent inquiry will be, "Lord, what wilt Thou have me to do?" Bible religion will be woven into your daily life. (CS 342.3)

The true Christian does not allow any earthly consideration to come in between his soul and God. The commandment of God wields an authoritative influence over his affections and actions. If everyone seeking the kingdom of God and His righteousness would be always ready to work the works of Christ, how much easier would become the path to heaven.... (CS 343.1)

If the eye is single to the glory of God, the treasure will be laid up above, safe from all corruption or loss; and "where your treasure is, there will your heart be also." Jesus will be the pattern that you will seek to imitate. The law of the Lord will be your delight, and at the day of final reckoning you will hear the glad words, "Well done, thou good and faithful servant: thou hast been faithful over a few things, I will make thee ruler over many things: enter thou into the joy of thy Lord."– *The Review and Herald, January 24, 1888*. (CS 343.2)

Strengthening the Bonds of Unity

The Lord has made us His almoners. He places in our hands His gifts, in order that we shall divide with those who are needy, and it is this practical giving that will be to us a sure panacea for all selfishness. By thus expressing love to those who need help, you will cause the hearts of the needy to give thanksgiving unto God because He has bestowed the grace of benevolence upon the brethren, and has caused them to relieve the necessities of the needy. (CS 343.3)

It is through the exercise of this practical love that the churches draw nearer together in Christian unity. Through the love of the brethren, love to God is increased, because He has not forgotten those who were in distress, and thus thank offerings ascend to God for His care. "For the ministration of this service not only supplieth the want of the saints, but is abundant also by many thanksgivings unto God." The faith of the brethren is increased in God, and they are led to commit their souls and bodies unto God as to a faithful Creator. "Whiles by the experiment of this ministration they glorify God for your professed subjection unto the gospel of Christ, and for your liberal distribution unto them, and unto all men."– *The Review and Herald, August 21, 1894.* (**CS 344.1**)

Engraven on Christ's Hands

Christ will keep the names of all who count no sacrifice too costly to be offered to Him upon the altar of faith and love. He sacrificed all for fallen humanity. The names of the obedient, self-sacrificing, and faithful will be engraven upon the palms of His hands; they will not be spewed from His mouth, but be taken in His lips, and He will specially plead in their behalf before the Father. When the selfish and proud are forgotten, they will be remembered; their names will be immortalized. In order to be happy ourselves, we must live to make others happy. It is well for us to yield our possessions, our talents, and our affections in grateful devotion to Christ, and in that way find happiness here and immortal glory hereafter.– *Testimonies for the Church 3:250, 251.* (**CS 344.2**)

Chapter 67
Temporal Blessings to the Benevolent

When human sympathy is blended with love and benevolence, and sanctified by the Spirit of Jesus, it is an element which can be productive of great good. Those who cultivate benevolence are not only doing a good work for others, and blessing those who receive the good action, but they are benefiting themselves by opening their hearts to the benign influence of true benevolence. (CS 345.1)

Every ray of light shed upon others will be reflected upon our own hearts. Every kind and sympathizing word spoken to the sorrowful, every act to relieve the oppressed, and every gift to supply the necessities of our fellow beings, given or done with an eye to God's glory, will result in blessings to the giver. Those who are thus working are obeying a law of Heaven, and will receive the approval of God. The pleasure of doing good to others imparts a glow to the feelings which flashes through the nerves, quickens the circulation of the blood, and induces mental and physical health.– *Testimonies for the Church 4:56.* (CS 345.2)

A Healing Blessing

The sympathy which exists between the mind and the body is very great. When one is affected, the other responds. The condition of the mind has much to do with the health of the physical system. If the mind is free and happy, under a consciousness of right doing and a sense of satisfaction in causing happiness to others, it will create a cheerfulness that will react upon the whole system, causing a freer circulation of the blood and a toning up of the entire body. The blessing of God is a healer; and those who are abundant in benefiting others will realize that wondrous blessing in their hearts and lives.– *Testimonies for the Church 4:60, 61.* (CS 345.3)

The Work of Benevolence Twice Blessed

Divine wisdom has appointed, in the plan of salvation, the law of action and reaction, making the work of benevolence, in all its branches, twice blessed. God could have accomplished His object in saving sinners without the help of man, but He knew that man could not be happy without acting a part in the great work of redemption. That man might not lose the blessed results of benevolence, our Redeemer formed the plan of enlisting him as His coworker.– *The Review and Herald, March 23, 1897.* (CS 346.1)

The Power of Earth Broken

Christ came to give to men the wealth of eternity, and this wealth, through connection with Him, we are to receive and impart. Not to ministers only, but to every believer, Christ says, The world is enshrouded in darkness. Let your light so shine before men, that they may see your good works, and glorify your Father which is in heaven. Everyone who truly loves God will be a light in the world. (CS 346.2)

He who is a citizen of the heavenly kingdom will be constantly looking at things not seen. The power of earth over the mind and character is broken. He has the abiding presence of the heavenly Guest, in accordance with the promise, "I will love him, and will manifest Myself to him." He walks with God as did Enoch, in constant communion.– *The Review and Herald, November 10, 1910.* (CS 346.3)

The Earthly Life Enriched

No scheme of business or plan of life can be sound or complete that embraces only the brief years of this present life, and makes no provision for the unending future. Let the youth be taught to take eternity into their reckoning. Let them be taught to choose the principles and seek the possessions that are enduring–to lay up for themselves that "treasure in the heavens that faileth not, where no thief approacheth, neither moth corrupteth;" to make to themselves friends "by means of the mammon of unrighteousness," that when it shall fail, these may receive them "into the eternal tabernacles." *Luke 12:33; 16:9,* R.V. (**CS 346.4**)

All who do this are making the best possible preparation for life in this world. No man can lay up treasure in heaven without finding his life on earth thereby enriched and ennobled. (**CS 347.1**)

"Godliness is profitable unto all things, having promise of the life that now is, and of that which is to come." *1 Timothy 4:8. – Education, 145.* (**CS 347.2**)

The Heart of the Giver Expanded

The offerings of the poor, given through self-denial to aid in extending the precious light of saving truth, will not only be a sweet-smelling savor to God, and wholly acceptable to Him as a consecrated gift, but the very act of giving expands the heart of the giver, and unites him more fully to the Redeemer of the world.– *The Review and Herald, October 31, 1878.* (**CS 347.3**)

God's Standing Promise

Whenever God's people, in any period of the world, have cheerfully and willingly carried out His plan in systematic benevolence and in gifts and offerings, they have realized the standing promise that prosperity should attend all their labors just in proportion as they obeyed His requirements. When they acknowledged the claims of God, and complied with His requirements, honoring Him with their substance, their barns were filled with plenty.– *Testimonies for the Church 3:395.* (**CS 347.4**)

Chapter 68

Sharing in the Joys of the Redeemed

There is reward for the wholehearted, unselfish workers who enter this field, and also for those who contribute willingly for their support. Those engaged in active service in the field, and those who give of their means to sustain these workers, will share the reward of the faithful. (CS 348.1)

Every wise steward of the means entrusted to him, will enter into the joy of his Lord. What is this joy?–"Likewise, I say unto you, there is joy in the presence of the angels of God over one sinner that repenteth." There will be a blessed commendation, a holy benediction, on the faithful winners of souls. They will join the rejoicing ones in heaven, who shout the harvest home. (CS 348.2)

How great will be the joy when the redeemed of the Lord shall all meet,–gathered into the mansions prepared for them! O, what rejoicing for all who have been impartial, unselfish laborers together with God in carrying forward His work in the earth! What satisfaction will every reaper have, when the clear, musical voice of Jesus shall be heard, saying, "Come, ye blessed of My Father, inherit the kingdom prepared for you from the foundation of the world." "Enter thou into the joy of thy Lord." (CS 348.3)

The Redeemer is glorified because He has not died in vain. With glad, rejoicing hearts, those who have been colaborers with God see of the travail of their soul for perishing, dying sinners, and are satisfied. The anxious hours they have spent, the perplexing circumstances they have had to meet, the sorrow of heart because some refused to see and receive the things which make for their peace, are forgotten. The self-denial they have practiced in order to support the work, is remembered no more. As they look upon the souls they sought to win to

Jesus, and see them saved, eternally saved–monuments of God's mercy and of a Redeemer's love–there ring through the arches of heaven shouts of praise and thanksgiving.– *The Review and Herald, October 10, 1907.* (CS 348.4)

Realization Greater Than Expectation

Christ accepted humanity, and lived on this earth a pure, sanctified life. For this reason He has received the appointment of judge. He who occupies the position of judge is God manifest in the flesh. What a joy it will be to recognize in Him our Teacher and Redeemer, bearing still the marks of the crucifixion, from which shine beams of glory, giving additional value to the crowns which the redeemed receive from His hands, the very hands outstretched in blessing over His disciples as He ascended. The very voice which said, "Lo, I am with you alway, even unto the end of the world," bids His ransomed ones welcome to His presence. (CS 349.1)

The very One who gave His precious life for them, who by His grace moved their hearts to repentance, who awakened them to their need of repentance, receives them now into His joy. Oh, how they love Him! The realization of their hope is infinitely greater than their expectation. Their joy is complete, and they take their glittering crowns and cast them at their Redeemer's feet.– *The Review and Herald, June 18, 1901.* (CS 349.2)

The Promise Sure

Long have we waited for our Saviour's return. But none the less sure is the promise. Soon we shall be in our promised home. There Jesus will lead us beside the living stream flowing from the throne of God, and will explain to us the dark providences through which He led us in order to perfect our characters. There we shall see on every hand the beautiful trees of Paradise, in the midst of them the tree of life. There we shall behold with undimmed vision the beauties of Eden restored. There we shall cast at the feet of our Redeemer the crowns that He has placed on our heads, and, touching our golden harps, we shall offer praise and thanksgiving to Him that sitteth on the throne.– *The Review and Herald, September 3, 1903.* (CS 349.3)

Only a Little While Now

It will only be a little while before Jesus will come to save His children and to give them the finishing touch of immortality. "This corruptible shall have put on incorruption, and this mortal shall have put on immortality." The graves will be opened, and the dead will come forth victorious, crying, "O death, where is thy sting? O grave, where is thy victory?" Our loved ones who sleep in Jesus will come forth clothed with immortality. (CS 350.1)

And as the redeemed shall ascend to heaven, the gates of the city of God will swing back, and those who have kept the truth will enter in. A voice, richer than any music that ever fell on mortal ear, will be heard saying, "Come, ye blessed of My Father, inherit the kingdom prepared for you from the foundation of the world." Then the righteous will receive their reward. Their lives will run parallel with the life of Jehovah. They will cast their crowns at the Redeemer's feet, touch the golden harps, and fill all heaven with rich music.– *The Signs of the Times, April 15, 1889.* (CS 350.2)

For Further Study

The Benevolent Contribute to Their Own Happiness and Great Physical Blessings, *Testimonies for the Church 4:59-61*

Every Gift Results in Blessing to the Giver, *Testimonies for the Church 4:56*

A Safe and Secure Investment in Bags Without Holes, *Testimonies for the Church 4:78, 79*

Values Beyond Estimate, *Thoughts From the Mount of Blessing, 133-135*

We Should Feel Satisfied to Receive Heavenly Treasure in Proportion to Our Investment in Heavenly Stock, *Testimonies for the Church 4:119*

Spiritual Prosperity Is Closely Bound Up With Christian Liberality, *The Acts of the Apostles, 344, 345*

No Interest Will Accumulate in Bank of Heaven for Means Withheld, *Testimonies for the Church 9:131*

Earthly Treasure Will Soon Be Destroyed in the Great Conflagration; Only the Treasure Laid Up in Heaven Will Be Safe, *Testimonies for the Church 4:49*

Every Opportunity for Benevolence Seized Adds to Heavenly Treasure, *Testimonies for the Church 3:249, 250*

An Assurance of Divine Care in Famine Times, *Testimonies for the Church 1:173, 174*

Every Sacrifice Recompensed According to "the Exceeding Riches of His Grace" *The Desire of Ages, 249*

A Hundredfold Now, *Testimonies for the Church 5:428*

And the Joy of Seeing Souls Saved, *Testimonies for the Church 9:59*

Printed in Great Britain
by Amazon

26501163R00106